Shakespeare's Goddess

THE DIVINE FEMININE ON THE ENGLISH STAGE

j. SNODGRASS

Shakespeare's Goddess

THE DIVINE FEMININE ON THE ENGLISH STAGE

j. SNODGRASS

A City of Light imprint

New Idea Press
A City of Light imprint

City of Light Publishing
266 Elmwood Ave. Suite 407
Buffalo, New York 14222

info@CityofLightPublishing.com
www.CityofLightPublishing.com

Book design by Ana Cristina Ochoa

ISBN 978-1-952536-36-6 (paperback)
ISBN 978-1-952536-37-3 (ebook)

Printed in Canada
10 9 8 7 6 5 4 3 2 1

Library of Congress Cataloging-in-Publication Data
Names: Snodgrass, j., author.
Title: Shakespeare's goddess : the divine feminine on the English stage / J. Snodgrass.
Description: Buffalo, New York : New Idea Press, a City of Light imprint, 2024. | Includes bibliographical references and index. | Summary: "In what plays by Shakespeare do goddesses appear? Roman goddesses Diana, Juno, Ceres, Iris, and Hecate appear on stage, and Venus stars in his epic poem Venus and Adonis. The Egyptian queen Cleopatra was considered divine, and Shakespeare practically deified Queen Elizabeth. The Fairy Queen Titania embodies pagan English magic, and Shakespeare often casts Nature as a goddess, not as mere scenery. Why? What is this mysterious passion for the divine feminine? Explore Shakespeare's lifelong fascination with Greek, Roman, Egyptian, and English goddesses. Well researched and documented for scholars, yet playful enough for beginners."-- Provided by publisher.
Identifiers: LCCN 2023040658 (print) | LCCN 2023040659 (ebook) | ISBN 9781952536366 (trade paperback) | ISBN 9781952536373 (epub) | ISBN 9781952536373 (kindle edition) | ISBN 9781952536373 (mobi) | ISBN 9781952536373 (nook edition) | ISBN 9781952536373 (pdf)
Subjects: LCSH: Shakespeare, William, 1564-1616--Criticism and interpretation. | Women heroes in literature. | Goddesses in literature. | BISAC: LITERARY CRITICISM / Shakespeare | LITERARY CRITICISM / Feminist | LCGFT: Literary criticism.
Classification: LCC PR2991 .S66 2024 (print) | LCC PR2991 (ebook) | DDC 822.3/3-- dc23/eng/20230912
LC record available at https://lccn.loc.gov/2023040658
LC ebook record available at https://lccn.loc.gov/2023040659

"The earth that's nature's mother, is her tomb;
What is her burying grave, that is her womb:
And from her womb children of divers kind
We sucking on her natural bosom find.
Many for many virtues excellent,
None but for some, and yet all different."
— Shakespeare, *Romeo and Juliet* Act 2 Scene 3

"Hail, sovereign queen of secrets, who hast power
To call the fiercest tyrant from his rage
And weep unto a girl; that hast the might
Even with an eye-glance to choke [war's] drum
And turn th' alarm to whispers; that canst make
A cripple flourish with his crutch, and cure him
Before Apollo; that mayst force the king
To be his subject's vassal, and induce
Stale gravity to dance."
— Shakespeare, *Two Noble Kinsmen* Act 5 Scene 1

For Elizabeth

Dedicated to Terry Gilliam, Amy Lee, David Gahan, Andy Fletcher, Alan Wilder and the Man with the Wings, Martin L. Gore

And thank you to Marti Gorman, Matthew LaChiusa, Brooke Goergen, Sarah Emmerling, Cameron Kogut, Charles McGregor, Monish Bhattacharyya and Justin Karcher, Ellen Falank, Madison Sedlor, Emily Bystrak, Julie Grygier, Ashton DeCaro, Stefanie Warnick, Isabel Deschamps, Justin Chortie, Maryna Sofia, Bekki Sliwa, Kate LoConti Alcocer, the Unsinkable Michael Breen, Adam Batt, Grace Adams, Matt Boyle, Mike Fanelli, Neal Radice, Sandra Roberts, Bill Lovern, Jessica Dean, Cheyenne DeLuca, Julius Dickey, Alyssa Genovese, Nicole Gorny, Aiden Isbrandt and Edwin Lozada, and Courtney Grim.

Contents

Preface

Very early in the process of my research for *Supernatural Shakespeare: Magic and Ritual in Merry Old England,* it became clear that a single volume on all the witches, fairies, ghosts, gods, and goddesses would be massive and intimidating–for the writer, as well as for readers. So, I decided to split it into two volumes: one to examine English folklore and festivals, and another to explore the many references to Greek, Roman, and Egyptian deities.

While researching and writing this volume about Shakespeare's pagan deities, a fascinating pattern emerged. There are many references to Jupiter/Jove, Mercury, Hercules and other male gods of the Classical Pantheon, but these tend to be pretty simple, stock characters representing a fairly narrow spectrum of masculinity.

However, Shakespeare approaches goddesses with his full range of imagination and nuance. Venus can inspire lust and also defend a doctoral dissertation on the nature of desire. Diana is the virgin huntress, divine midwife, and murderous moon. And perhaps the most multifaceted goddess is Shakespeare's personified Nature, an ever-swarming swirl of fertility and fatality: birth, budding, burial, and rebirth. In a sense, all of Shakespeare's goddesses are avatars of this single divine feminine power.

In this book, situating personified Nature among the goddesses enabled a synthesis of ancient religious symbolism with modern works of ecocriticism and ecofeminism. As explained by Gordana Galić Kakkonen and Ana Penjak, "Ecofeminism underlines the relation of men to culture and that of women to nature. Culture has been perceived as surpassing 'untamed' nature while men are seen as dominant and of higher rank than 'untamed' women... Since women are related to nature in many different ways (reproductive status, discrimination, possession, violence)...women and nature have been oppressed at the same time in the same way."[1] Cultural attitudes toward "Nature" tend to mirror male attitudes toward females, whether as equal partners or as private productive property. And research in this area naturally opened up some fascinating avenues of exploring Shakespeare's quirky notions about gender, human and divine, and sometimes somewhere in between.

This approach also allows an exploration of William Shakespeare in relation to his favorite classical author, the Roman poet .. Throughout Shakespeare's career he continually turned to this writer for reference and inspiration. Because Shakespeare inherited Greek mythology through this Latin lens, the deities in this book will generally be referred to by their Roman names (for example, Aphrodite will be called Venus, Artemis will be called Diana). This is a bit bothersome because really these are Greek gods and goddesses, but this is what Shakespeare calls them.

Please be aware that Ovid (and sometimes Shakespeare paraphrasing Ovid) wrote about sexual violence in ways that can be disturbing. These references will be explored in this book where it is deemed necessary for our understanding of Shakespeare's education and inspiration. If these issues are mentioned in a brisk tone, the intention is to keep things moving, not to be flippant or dismissive about trauma.

Supernatural Shakespeare was organized using a concordance approach, choosing a topic, and compiling fragments from different plays, sometimes disregarding context and characters. In *Shakespeare's Goddess*, more attention is paid to how each phenomenon interacts with a story and its players. If the first volume was like a scavenger hunt, this one is more of a holistic gathering. It seemed a more appropriate approach to the topic. If sections of this book seem to wander, get chatty, flighty, please be patient. Each section will eventually get back on track.[2]

I want this book to be fun. I wouldn't have researched and written it if it weren't fun. William Shakespeare clearly loved a good giggle. Even his great tragedies have clowns running around, or Hamlet tossing a dead clown's skull. Shakespeare did write a few tragedies without fools and clowns–they're the tragedies we've never heard of, like the dreary *Timon of Athens* and *Coriolanus*. Even Shakespearean comedy is getting a little dry these days because we don't get all the jokes. And sadly, the only way to get the jokes is to dig through dry, often joyless commentary volumes. Punchlines are buried in tomb-like tomes. So, I've dug through thousands of pages looking for little comedy gems.

I don't have any scholarly pedigree or doctoral regalia, and I don't read Latin (thank you tabulators and translators of primary sources!) So what makes me the right person to write this book? Well, I've got a curiosity and energy for the project. And I don't take these topics too seriously. Personally, I think the Greeks and Romans and Shakespeare are all overrated, white men playing god, pretending to be impartial while propping up a preposterous hierarchical patriarchy. And it turns out hierarchical patriarchy is poisonous to this planet. So, I think these ancient emperors need an idiot kid pointing with a smirk at their naked bottoms. I volunteer to be that idiot.

One last thing before we jump in. In this book, a character or symbol can show up numerous times interpreted in numerous ways, signifying numerous different things. That is not a sign of editorial sloppiness or inconsistency (there will no doubt be other signs of that). Different essayists consulted have fit these phenomena into different interesting patterns. And it's part of the fun of Shakespeare that his phenomena are kaleidoscopic, or like prisms that turn different colors when held at different angles. With that said, welcome to the crazy rainbow of *Shakespeare's Goddess*.

Prologue

What's Past is Prologue

Once upon a time in some cold and cloudy place there magically appeared the Englishman, a fully formed stiff Brit, like Roger Moore in a powder-blue tuxedo. The White Man, burdened with the Protestant work ethic and the spirit of capitalism, was preprogrammed like a swarm of wasps to colonize and civilize the world.

Well, that's just a myth. Actually, the Englishman was a latecomer to the civilization party. The tower of Babel rose and fell time and again until the fertile crescent was a barren desert littered with ghost towns; the Harappan utopia blossomed and was buried in India; the matriarchy of Crete invented indoor plumbing and got crushed by a tidal wave; great Pyramids emerged on the Nile; cliff cities and irrigation systems were built and abandoned in New Mexico; David and Solomon made Jerusalem almost as magnificent as modern New Jersey, then Babylon trashed it; Athens raised its pillars and poets and philosophers, then lost all interest in itself and was sacked by Sparta, Macedonia, and Rome.

And while all of this was going on, the natives of Britain were swinging in the trees, naked bodies painted blue. Shepherds erected henges to throw drunken barbecues, goddesses were painted in caves, and some barbarians were honored with slumpy burial mounds. Then, about two thousand years ago, the Roman Empire showed up to drag Britain into civilization, savage aborigines kicking and screaming. And the legions were shocked to find that one of their fiercest adversaries was not a warlord king, but a warrior-queen, the legendary Boudica.

Indigenous English religion is pretty much lost in the mists of history. There seems to have been an ancient belief that spiritual totems should be carved of wood, and that something sacred should not be set in stone unless it was being abandoned or consecrated to the dead.[3] So we don't inherit much in the way of ritual objects or statues. Under Roman influence the natives produced some figurines from more durable materials and scrawled a few religious inscriptions, but not much. There also seems to have been a belief that sacred knowledge should be transmitted orally, never written down.

Popular in British iconography was a triple goddess, or a single goddess with three aspects representing different stages of life: the purity of youth, the creativity of maturity, and the wisdom of age. These align with the cyclical phases of the moon as governess of birth, reproduction, and death. Numerous stone carvings have been found, usually three women seated, cradling bowls of fruits, loaves, and/or flowers, the abundance of maternal nature. We also find some of the voluptuous so-called Venus figurines that were common throughout old Europe as devices to communicate with the powers controlling human fertility.

English representations of male divinity often had horns, variously of the bull, goat, or stag (Shakespeare may preserve an element of this with the legend of Herne the Hunter in *The Merry Wives of Windsor*, and Robin Goodfellow, the template for Puck, was also known to have goat horns). The horned man signifies the hunter's reciprocal relationship with the prey and appears in numerous mythologies as the goddess's consort who is periodically slain and resurrected.

Roman documents preserve the names of some indigenous deities but give us little information except for what Roman god they resembled. The hot spring at Bath was the domain of Sulis, whom the Romans likened to Minerva, although she may have more closely paralleled the virginal moon goddess Diana. Other springs were sacred to the healing goddess Coventina. Belatucadrus, "the bright beautiful one," was a warrior god with horns and a large phallus, and Cocidius was likened to the war god Mars and the wild-nature god Silvanus.

There seem to have been female war gods as well, such as Brigantia and Andate, whose name meant "victory," the favorite goddess of the warrior queen Boudica.[4] But these are just fragments, pieces of different jigsaw puzzles—each region seems to have had its own complete set of local deities and nature spirits. Assembling an indigenous English pantheon or systematic theology is pretty much impossible. However, even the scattered shards of surviving evidence are sufficient for a simple deduction: pagan Britain seems to have had a balance of male and female deities, and if it were slightly weighted to one side, it would tilt toward the divine feminine.

About three hundred years after Rome's invasion of Britain, the Emperor Constantine decided that unruly pagan deities were a bad influence on the taxpayers, and the Empire adopted a new mascot, someone who encouraged non-violence and promised heavenly rewards to those who "render unto Caesar" (a quote that was taken out of context—Rome had killed Jesus for mincing words on the topic of taxation). The old Vatican shrine to the mother goddess Cybele and her sacrificial son was re-christened Saint Peter's Basilica, and the blood of slaughtered bulls was replaced with watered wine from a lamb.[5]

Rome thrust its Christianity upon England and (drum-roll, please...) nothing happened. The idea of a trinitarian divinity was nothing new, although oddly, this time it was a fraternity rather than a sorority. Christianity also came with a vast pantheon of spirits who specialized in healing, herding, and harvesting, essentially the same spirits in an animist religion but now called "saints." And most importantly, Roman Christianity had Mary. Really, three Marys: Mary the virgin/mother, Mary the whore of Magdala, and the first Mary again as the widow watching the crucifixion.[6] Combined, this triple Mary comprised the familiar spectrum of the divine feminine. The natives revered the goddess as they always had, as their ancestors had done, *"A rose by any other name would smell as sweet."* Of course, this diva stole the show. They even called her Madonna!

Medieval Christianity was rocked to its foundations by the Protestant Reformation. In the early 1500s, some Northern Europeans began to wonder why a colonial peasant who'd been tortured to death by Rome kept telling colonial peasants to render unto Rome. And as the Bible began to circulate in languages other than Latin, careful readers began to note that Christianity had adopted many *un*-Biblical traditions, pagan elements like Christmas trees and Easter rabbits and Jack-o-Lanterns and laughing children. Fundamentalists sought to wipe out all that stuff: no more merry colors and jolly jigs, no more charitable donations for lavish Vatican Bacchanalia, and no more semi-demi-goddess. The Puritans pledged to put Mary "in her place."

Of course, this was not easy. The English have always loved their mothers, goddesses, and queens. Ted Hughes wrote that, at the time of Shakespeare's birth, "two-thirds of the country (including his mother and most probably his father too) had been worshippers of the cult of the sacrificed god and the Great Goddess, taking the myth absolutely seriously, and where numbers of them, even in the 1590s (including one of his own distant relatives), were evidently ready to be half-hanged, castrated, disemboweled, quartered, and to have their heads stuck on prominent spikes, all for taking this myth–of the sacrificed god and the Great Goddess–too seriously."[7]

Would this be the end of the divine feminine in England?

Fair Vestal Throned by the West
(A MIDSUMMER NIGHT'S DREAM | HENRY VIII)

In *A Midsummer Night's Dream*, the fairy king Oberon recalls:

> *"My gentle Puck, come hither. Thou rememb'rest*
> *Since once I sat upon a promontory,*
> *And heard a mermaid on a dolphin's back*
> *Uttering such dulcet and harmonious breath*
> *That the rude sea grew civil at her song,*
> *And certain stars shot madly from their spheres*
> *To hear the sea-maid's music...*
> *That very time I saw, but thou couldst not,*
> *Flying between the cold moon and the earth*
> *Cupid, all arm'd; a certain aim he took*
> *At a fair vestal, thronèd by the west,*
> *And loos'd his love-shaft smartly from his bow,*
> *As it should pierce a hundred thousand hearts;*
> *But I might see young Cupid's fiery shaft*
> *Quench'd in the chaste beams of the wat'ry moon;*
> *And the imperial vot'ress passed on,*
> *In maiden meditation, fancy-free."* (MND II.i)

The fairy king's report sounds fantastical, but he's actually referring to an historical event, the pageant at a lawn party thrown for Queen Elizabeth. "At the entertainment at Elvetham in 1591, Elizabeth was throned by the west side of a garden lake to listen to music from the water; the fairy queen came with a round of dancers and spoke of herself as wife to Auberon."[8] Having apparently spied on this event, Shakespeare's Oberon saw something no one else did: the Greek godling Cupid firing an arrow. It made sense for Cupid to show up, since the Elvetham party was engineered as a blind date, an elaborate scheme to set Elizabeth up with some nobleman. But the watchful moon foiled the plot and the archer's arrow hit a bystanding pansy.

But why would Shakespeare refer to this exclusive garden party in the play? Very few in the original audience would know of it, and only the nerdiest of modern scholars have heard of it. This is the kind of triviality that nerdy scholars pick on *nerdier* scholars about. Writing *A Midsummer Night's Dream*, Shakespeare had to explicitly locate the *"fair vestal"* virgin Queen offstage to protect her from the implication that she was represented *onstage* by the fairy queen Titania, who would soon be shown snuggling with a donkey-monster. More importantly, Shakespeare had to protect *himself* from any suspicion that he'd satirically presented the Queen engaging in sexual bestiality. Or worse, of cuddling a common handyman.[9] In 1597, the Puritan John Stubbes published a pamphlet prying into the Queen's personal life, and as punishment, they hacked off his writing hand "(As his right hand was publicly removed, Stubbes is reported to have lifted his hat with his left and shouted 'God Save the Queen!')"[10] So we can only imagine what a playwright might have faced for presenting the Queen getting cozy with an ass-man.

William Shakespeare dodged that cleaver and also paid the Queen a compliment: she was so chaste that Cupid had to make a custom arrow with enough aphrodisiac to turn the whole world upside down. That's what the flower's name "Love-in-Idleness" meant, not laziness but total madness. Harold Bloom wrote, "It is as though Elizabeth's choice of chastity opens up a cosmos of erotic possibilities for others, but at a high cost of accident and arbitrariness replacing her reasoned choice."[11]

That word, "choice," is at the center of our most heated modern political debates. And it was also at the center of the biggest political debate in Elizabethan England: should the queen be allowed to choose *not* to marry and spawn a successor? Throughout her forty-five-year reign, the English people went to bed every night wondering if the queen might choke on a mutton bone and unexpectedly die, leaving the nation without a rightful heir. Shakespeare himself got famous writing plays about contested royal successions and civil wars. That's why he wrote seven plays called "Henry"! The prospect of a monarch dying childless could tear apart all of England, grinding the whole stiff-Brit experiment into a bloody, soupy, apocalyptic chaos.

Queen Elizabeth herself was adamantly independent. In her mid-twenties she stood firm before Parliament, declaring "I have already joined myself in marriage to a husband, namely the kingdom of England. Better beggar woman and single than Queen and married." And in her mid-forties, she remained resolute: "If I were a milkmaid with a pail on my arm, whereby my private person might be little [noticed], I would not forsake that poor and single state to match with the greatest monarch." Whether she was physically a *virgin* all this time is another subject. She does seem to have been somewhat foot-loose and *"fancy-free,"* but marriage and maternity held no appeal.[12]

A Midsummer Night's Dream takes place in ancient Athens, 1,500 years before the birth of Jesus. So, when Oberon refers to Elizabeth as a vestal virgin and votary, he doesn't mean a Christian nun but a priestess of the lunar goddess Diana. Was Shakespeare implying that England's queen was a pagan? That gets a bit complex.

Because Elizabeth had come to power amid the civil strife of the Protestant Reformation, one of her first decrees was that the theater must avoid "matters of religion." In shutting the door on the Father, Son, and Holy Ghost, she opened the windows to Classical gods who came swarming onto the English stage. Whether intentionally or inadvertently, Queen Elizabeth became a protective patron saint of paganism in the arts. It can't have escaped her notice that the Christian Trinity is an old boys' club, no girls allowed, and that Classical mythology made space for the divine feminine. One could go so far as to say that, after centuries of medieval Christian mystery plays and devotional art, Ovid's *Metamorphoses* became the Elizabethan artists' scripture.

Shakespeare very seldom refers to the Christian Trinity or Biblical stories. His characters use the Roman god Jupiter's nickname "Jove," occasionally to mean the God of the Bible, but usually it refers to the pagan thunderlord. And Shakespeare's works show a fascinating balance of male and female deities, with a great interest in the mysterious ways of the divine feminine.

How might Elizabeth have felt about being symbolically placed within a pagan pantheon? Well first off, if the word "pagan" fills our minds with witches on broomsticks, naked torch-dancers, and fertility figurines, that's not what we're talking about. Nobody was comparing Elizabeth to the voluptuous, lusty Venus. Shakespeare refers to Elizabeth as a devotee of the virgin huntress and moon-goddess, Diana. And the queen herself was known to encourage this association: "The pearls Elizabeth wears in royal portraits replicate the moon's luminous surface, and in the 'Rainbow' portrait [the] crescent moon is depicted above her headdress."[13]

A textual example of Elizabeth as Diana (moon-like, eternally virginal, and shut-up-about-her-personal-life-choices) survives in a ballad by an admirer:

"Prais'd be Diana's fair and harmless light;
Prais'd be the dews, wherewith she moists the ground;
Prais'd be her beams, the glory of the night;
Prais'd be her power, by which all powers abound!
Prais'd be her nymphs, with whom she decks the woods;
Prais'd be her knights, in whom true honor lives;
Prais'd be that force by which she moves the floods!
Let that Diana shine, which all these gives!
In heaven, queen she is among the spheres;
She mistress-like, makes all things to be pure;
Eternity in her oft-change she bears;
She, Beauty is; by her, the fair endure.
Time wears her not; she doth his chariot guide;
Mortality below her orb is plac'd;
By her the virtues of the stars down slide;
In her is Virtue's perfect image cast!
A knowledge pure it is her worth to know:
With Circes let them dwell that think not so!"[14]
("Circes" meaning untrustworthy witches)

In masques and pageants, Elizabeth was celebrated for her autonomy, including a show where Diana herself congratulated her favorite devotee (the thinly veiled "Zabeta"), singing "I joy with you, and leave it to your choice what kind of life you best shall like to hold. And in meanwhile I cannot but rejoice to see you thus bedecked with glistering gold."[15] Virginia Mason Vaughan writes that, like Elizabeth, "the moon is self-contained and unobtainable. It rules over others and can never itself be ruled. The moon is magic; it can entrance, but it can also bewitch. The moon is constant, but it undergoes change."[16]

The identification with the virgin huntress Diana also came with a veiled threat. In a well-known story from Ovid's *Metamorphoses* a young hunter once stumbled into a grove where the goddess was bathing, and for the crime of seeing her naked she transformed him into a stag to be torn apart by his own hounds. Similarly, anyone who bumbled into Elizabeth's private affairs quickly found himself in deep trouble. The Diana iconography was a political statement, warning that forbidden knowledge of semi-divine royalty would transform any voyeur, gossip, or tattletale into a frightened fugitive, a hunted deer. We take a closer look at the story of Diana and Actaeon later.

Elizabeth was also often compared to the virgin goddess of justice, Astraea, who ascended from the earth in disgust as humanity fell from grace, ending the paradisal "Golden Age" in the first chapter of Ovid's *Metamorphoses*. Some Elizabethan poets celebrated her reign as Astraea's return, heralding a new "Golden Age" in England: a return to peace, prosperity, and propriety. This identification continued throughout her reign and even after it. Shakespeare's biography of Elizabeth's father, *Henry VIII* climaxes with a prophecy of how the newborn princess will bring peace and plenty to England.

> "*This royal infant – heaven still move about her!*
> *Though in her cradle, yet now promises*
> *Upon this land a thousand blessings,*
> *Which time shall bring to ripeness.*
> [And] *all the virtues that attend the good,*
> *Shall still be doubled on her. Truth shall nurse her,*
> *Holy and heavenly thoughts still counsel her;*
> *She shall be lov'd and fear'd. Her own shall bless her:*

Her foes shake like a field of beaten corn,
And hang their heads with sorrow. Good grows with her;
In her days every man shall eat in safety
Under his own vine what he plants, and sing
The merry songs of peace to all his neighbours...
She shall be, to the happiness of England,
An agèd princess; many days shall see her,
And yet no day without a deed to crown it.
Would I had known no more! But she must die –
She must, the saints must have her – yet a virgin;
A most unspotted lily shall she pass
To th' ground, and all the world shall mourn her." (H8 V.v[17])

This birth song is actually an epitaph, written about ten years after the Queen's death. William Shakespeare likely knew her in person, but not *personally*; this loving tribute is distant and lacks the warmth of friendship. The author's familiarity with Elizabeth is obviously open to all kinds of conjecture, but it's clear he admired and perhaps even idolized her.

And You, (Other) Brutus?

"We prayed to ladies in the Queen's time," a London lawyer wrote in his diary after her death, "this superstition shall be abolished we hope in our king's reign."[18] When Elizabeth's cousin James assumed the throne of England, he did not seek identification with ancient gods. But he encouraged and cultivated his association with two ancient Romans: Caesar Augustus and Brutus. Not the famous Brutus who stabbed Caesar, but Brutus the legendary namesake of Britain.

In Virgil's *Aeneid*, a displaced refugee from fallen Troy ventured off to become the founder of Rome. A British monk in the twelfth century wrote a sort of English *Aeneid*, in which Aeneas's grandson Brutus established another Trojan refugee camp called Britain.[19] Or more precisely, three camps: Brutus, like King Lear, divided Britain into three kingdoms, and as James of Scotland assumed the English throne, a poet joyfully wrote "England, Wales, & Scotland, by the first Brute severed and divided, is in our second Brute reunited."[20]

The mythical linkage of Brutus with Aeneas was a brilliant piece of political propaganda, announcing England as the heir and successor of ancient Rome. And James as the new Brutus positioned himself to restore the mythic primal unity that Brutus had shortsightedly sundered. Meanwhile, England's rising dominance of the seas led to identification with Rome's imperial period. Like Rome, England was a major economic power and peacekeeper (to the extent that the British navy "pacified" anyone who interfered with England's commercial interests). King James also liked to be known as a second Caesar Augustus, who famously solidified the Roman Empire.

James's propaganda, comparing him to ancient Roman nation-builders, all sounds very shiny but it never really caught on with the populace. He was loud and rude (and spoke with a Scottish accent that grated on English ears), a witch-hunt wacko who demanded to be taken seriously as a scholar and got the tabloid treatment over his bisexuality. His personal motto, *Beati Pacifici*, "Bringer of Peace," was overshadowed by another Latin epigram: *Rex fuit Elizabeth, nunc est regina Iacobus*, "Elizabeth was king, now James is queen."

There's plenty of room for debate about Shakespeare's attitude toward James. The king became patron of the theater company, which was renamed the King's Men, but it would be hard to make a case that Shakespeare admired or personally liked him. However, Shakespeare throughout his career showed great enthusiasm about England as the successor of Greece, Troy, and Rome. And he lived in a time when the English language was flexing its muscles to challenge Roman Latin as the language of poetry and philosophy. From the distance of history, it's clear that Shakespeare's scripts and King James's Bible translation project both played major roles in English overcoming Latin as the language of Western discourse.

Thirteen of Shakespeare's major works are set in the Classical world: five of his comedies (*The Comedy of Errors, A Midsummer Night's Dream, Pericles, Prince of Tyre, The Winter's Tale* and *The Two Noble Kinsmen)*; six of his tragedies (*Titus Andronicus, Julius Caesar, Troilus and Cressida, Antony and Cleopatra, Coriolanus,* and *Timon of Athens*); and both of his narrative poems (*Venus and Adonis* and *The Rape of Lucrece*).[21] Jonathan Bate writes: "That constitutes one-third of his corpus, a body of work ranging from erotic and narrative poetry to tragedy to comedy to ancient history to satire to romance, covering a time-span from the Trojan War to fifth-century

Athens to the early years of Rome to the assassination of Julius Caesar to the Roman Empire, with excursions into mythical narratives, Hellenistic seafaring romance, and more."[22] For Shakespeare, ancient Greece, Troy, and Rome were not just a "once upon a time," but the prehistory of England.

PUBLY

Ovidy Nasonis.

Metamorphosis.

ofte

Transformatie.

Tot Rotterdam.
By P. van Waesberge.
A°. MVI.XXXVII.

Shakespeare and the Metamorphoses

Wanton Pictures
THE TAMING OF THE SHREW

reek and Roman mythology were very popular in Shakespeare's time. Those who could afford schooling were well versed in Latin Classics and some delved further, into Greek. The highly educated and erudite Ben Jonson famously said Shakespeare knew "small Latin and less Greek," but the obvious use of Latin source texts in his writing demonstrates that Jonson's idea of "small Latin" would be very impressive by modern educational standards. Classical mythology was not only high art but also multimedia pop culture: statues and paintings for the elite, penny-pictures and printed ballads for the commoners, and of course, the theater, where cocktails of art and pop could be viewed by peasants and heard by patrons. A great part of William Shakespeare's authorial charm, then as now, was his ability to blend high and low art for mass appeal.

One of his first comedies, *The Taming of the Shrew*, begins with a metatheatrical "Induction," which situates the audience (groundlings and gentry) in relation to the action that plays out on the stage. Sadly, this scene is generally cut from productions, although really it should be staged before every Shakespearean comedy as an "audience orientation" program. And for the purposes of this book, it also functions as an introduction to how classical mythology was appropriated as Elizabethan pop culture.

A nobleman and his hunting buddies stumble over a slumped form outside a country tavern. *"What's here? One dead, or drunk? See, doth he breathe?"* (TS Induction i) The smell of his breath makes it evident that the warmth of ale in his veins is all that keeps him from freezing to death.

> *"LORD. O monstrous beast! how like a swine he lies!...*
> *Sirs, I will practise on this drunken man.*
> *What think you, if he were convey'd to bed,*
> *Wrapp'd in sweet clothes, rings put upon his fingers,*
> *A most delicious banquet by his bed,*
> *And brave attendants near him when he wakes,*
> *Would not the beggar then forget himself?*
> *SECOND HUNTSMAN. ...It would seem strange unto him when he wak'd.*
> *LORD. Even as a flattering dream or worthless fancy.*
> *Then take him up, and manage well the jest.*
> *Carry him gently to my fairest chamber,*
> *And hang it round with all my wanton pictures...*
> *And with a low submissive reverence*
> *Say 'What is it your honour will command?'"* (TS Induction i)

They decide to prank this drunken bumpkin into thinking he's a nobleman with amnesia. Or in mythic/poetic terms, they're going to transform this half-dead pig into a lofty lord. The drunkard awakens surrounded by servants, ready with their version of Disney's "Be Our Guest": he's swamped with fine food and clothes, one of the servant boys even dresses up to play the part of his wife (*"Thou hast a lady far more beautiful / Than any woman in this waning age,"* a smirky joke about women played by boys on stage). And he gets to see the lord's pornographic stash of *"wanton pictures."*

But these don't get pulled out from under the mattress. Noblemen in Shakespeare's time collected mythological erotica, commissioning lurid snapshots (paintings and statues) of Greek gods and mortals caught with their pants down. Giant murals depicted sexual fantasies of seduction, rape, infantilism, voyeurism, and bestiality, mostly drawn from Ovid's *Metamorphoses*. This book, composed about 2,000 years ago, was a Roman mashup of old Greek myths, with particular attention to the most tabloid-worthy episodes.

The *Metamorphoses* is sometimes called the "Renaissance Painter's Bible." In the Medieval period, art had generally been commissioned by the Church and/or State, depicting the Christian canon of stories and characters, plus portraits of royalty. But the Renaissance made millionaires of merchants and middlemen, while re-integrating Classical literature into the mainstream, and all of a sudden, nerdy accountants could afford to commission vast pornographic panoramas of sexual deviance.

> *"SECOND SERVANT. Dost thou love pictures? We will fetch thee straight*
> *Adonis painted by a running brook,*
> *And Cytherea all in sedges hid,*
> *Which seem to move and wanton with her breath*
> *Even as the waving sedges play with wind.*
> *LORD. We'll show thee Io as she was a maid*
> *And how she was beguilèd and surpris'd,*
> *As lively painted as the deed was done.*
> *THIRD SERVANT. Or Daphne roaming through a thorny wood,*
> *Scratching her legs, that one shall swear she bleeds*
> *And at that sight shall sad Apollo weep,*
> *So workmanly the blood and tears are drawn."* (TS Induction ii)

All three of these images come from Ovid's *Metamorphoses*, and they are "wanton" in the sense of gods making sexual advances upon humans. None of the stories ends well. Adonis in this scene is just about to be gored by a wild boar as his stalker Venus (Cytherea) looks on. This would be the subject of Shakespeare's epic poem *Venus and Adonis*.[23] But here the scene is mixed with another Ovidian narrative: when Actaeon spied Diana bathing in a forest spring.

That Io was *"beguiled and surpris'd"* is a jovial way of saying the young maid was ambushed and assaulted by Jupiter himself (his jealous wife Juno later punished the victim by transforming her into a cow). The report of Daphne running is also oddly distorted: *"sad Apollo"* was chasing her in a rape attempt, and what made him *"weep"* was that she transformed into a tree before he could get his hands on her.[24] All three are images of predation, gods hunting humans like humans hunt wild game. The natural instincts of a hunted animal are fight and flight, but in the headlights of supernatural sexual predation, something else can happen: an unnatural transformation, a metamorphosis.

Some in Shakespeare's audience owned paintings like this, others did not, so the poet deftly transforms syllables in our ears to images in our minds, inviting the groundlings to catch a voyeuristic peep into the world of ancient myth and the realm of noble decadence. And the flashes of imagery are not posed portraits, they're candid action shots—the sedges seem to sway, the blood and tears are streaming, *"As lively painted as the deed was done."* These are flashing glances of titillation and terror, captured in still images, gods on display for human consumption.[25]

Not only do these images show Venus, Jupiter, and Apollo attempting to do *"the deed"* with humans, transgressing the boundary between gods and mortals, but these mortals are about to cross species boundaries: Adonis will become a flower, Daphne will transform into a tree, and Io will be turned into a heifer. And all of this is being displayed to transform the unwitting drunk, a *"beast...like a swine"* into a nobleman.

If we take another step back to view this scene in the context of Elizabethan theater, we can see that this "Induction" into the play is also transforming the audience, groundlings and patrons alike, into omniscient gods who can whisk off to Italy and watch unseen as mortals do their birdlike mating rituals. And although the audience might smirk at Sly being hoodwinked by a boy in a dress, a few minutes later they'll have to believe this same boy is the beautiful Bianca or the whole show falls apart.

Having initiated the drunkard as the audience, the nobles will now present him with an entertainment: the story of two bachelors seeking wives in Padua. *The Taming of the Shrew* will be a play-within-a-play, so the swine-turned-nobleman can watch a Medusa-like shrew mouse transform into a bride, and then into a hunter's falcon.

Shakespere's Book

In *Titus Andronicus*, one of Shakespeare's earliest plays, a general asks a boy what book he's been reading: *"Grandsire, 'tis Ovid's Metamorphoses."* (TA IV.i) In *The Taming of the Shrew*, a young lady asks her tutor what he's reading: *"I read that I profess, the Art to Love,"* (TS IV.ii) Ovid's *Ars Amatoria.* In *A Midsummer Night's Dream,* a bunch of greasy mechanics carry script adaptations of Pyramus and Thisbe, a chapter of Ovid's *Metamorphoses,* and then in *Cymbeline,* Imogen falls asleep with a copy of the *Metamorphoses* open on her bedside table. At the end of *The Tempest,* Prospero quotes a speech from the *Metamorphoses* and then drops his magical book into the sea. We never find out what the title of the book is, but by this point we could take an educated guess.

Shakespeare's literate characters tend to be fairly well versed in the Classics. They quote various authors and occasionally appear onstage with some volume or another. But the only prop books that are explicitly identified by title or author are the works of Ovid.[26] The copies of Ovid's books strewn about the Shakespearean stage are not just props, however. In some ways, they are portals into the poet's own subconscious or soul. Shakespeare's writings contain references to a wide range of Roman authors, but 90 percent of his mythical allusions spring from Ovid's *Metamorphoses.*[27]

Ovid lived about two thousand years ago. His lifetime overlapped with those of Jesus of Nazareth, the Roman Emperor Caesar Augustus, and the historian Virgil. Virgil's grand masterpiece, the Aeneid, was pure political propaganda, penned to establish the manifest destiny of Rome, praise the living god Augustus, and promote manly valor. Ovid did pretty much the opposite, exploring the anarchic chaos of unbridled male lust and female longing. He was particularly famous for the *Metamorphoses,* an epic poem remixing the Greatest Hits of Greek Mythology as a steamy supernatural soap opera with a particular attention to the sexy episodes. We might call these the Roman locker room versions of Greek myths.

In the *Metamorphoses,* the lofty gods lose their dignity and lust topples them from their pedestals to circus animal sideshow antics. It would be comical except that it's often violent, filled with sexual victimization. And it's usually the innocent who suffer terror and trauma (why do bad things happen to good people? Because the universe is a sex-crazed sociopath). As Lisa Starks-Estes wrote, Ovid "was at the same time revered and notorious, stylistically beautiful, and graphically violent, sophisticated and yet shot through with the raw energy of uncontrolled desire."[28] He became quite notorious in his time. Publius Ovidius Naso was one of those celebrities known by one name, like Madonna, Prince, or Voltaire. "Ovid" means something like the id of the egg.

At about the age of fifty, Ovid was banished by personal order of Caesar Augustus. The poet obliquely likens his fall to the story of Actaeon accidentally seeing the virgin goddess Diana naked and getting torn apart for it. This has inspired speculation that perhaps he was enamored of Augustus's granddaughter Julia, and exile to the Black Sea was an ancient restraining order.

In Shakespeare's *As You Like It*, the banished clown Touchstone refers to Ovid's exile while courting a lovely goatherd: *"I am here with thee and thy goats, as the most capricious poet, honest Ovid, was among the Goths... When a man's verses cannot be understood, nor a man's good wit seconded with the forward child understanding, it strikes a man more dead than a great reckoning in a little room"* (AYL III.iii). Touchstone says that banishment over a misunderstanding is a fate worse than death. Being a clown, he also throws in the pun "capricious," which means goat-like.[29] By resurrecting Ovid as Touchstone, Shakespeare gives him a happy ending; he's exiled but then marries a native of the forest.

Ovid died in exile, but he gained immortality through his work. The *Metamorphoses* ends with the poet himself saying:

"The Roman Empire by the right of conquest shall extend,
So far shall all folk read this work. And time without all end
(If Poets as by prophecy about the truth may aim)
My life shall everlastingly be lengthened still by fame."
(Book XV, Golding translation, updated)

As far as the Roman Empire could spread, spatially, Ovid would spread that far. And as long as the Roman Empire should last, temporally, he would survive. Actually, Ovid did even better; his works are known beyond the farthest reaches of Roman imperial conquest and survived long after the Empire's fall.

If there could be anything more bizarre and surreal than Ovid's *Metamorphoses*, it would be the adoption of this sleazy text in Medieval Christianity. For centuries, the greatest minds in Christendom struggled with great intellectual acrobatics and contortions to moralize Ovid, to metamorphosize the *Metamorphoses* into a complex allegory for Christian ethics and the Church's ardent love for souls gone astray. One could as easily say that the priests and monks simply enjoyed it, and their obsessing over this naughty-Bible just goes to show the repressed predatory sexuality of the clergy. Christianity spent centuries clicking it around like a Rubik's Cube, trying to separate the colors to make some moral lesson (although a Rubik's Cube is an ironic metaphor, since Ovid was all about swirling colors together in a psychedelic spiraling gyre, not segregating them into separate sides of a box).

Ovid was, as the old expression goes, "a riddle, wrapped in a mystery, inside an enigma." Especially in Christianity, with its doctrinal insistence that the soul-self is eternal, and God created everything in a certain fixed form. And of course, in the Bible, God doesn't impregnate virgins (...alright, bad example) and godlings don't chase earth-girls around (...another bad example) and donkeys don't talk (...oops, yet another bad example)[30].

After centuries stashed under priests' pillows and monks' mattresses (not literally, but remember Latin literacy was pretty much confined to clerics) Ovid's *Metamorphoses* emerged in a slew of English translations, just in time to be mass produced by the printing press. Most editions were squeamishly abridged and crowded with Christian commentary. But at last, Arthur Golding produced an English translation of the full book, releasing Ovid from the murky morass of medieval moralization.[31] "In Ovid's poem, Shakespeare and his contemporaries stumbled on the unconscious mind of the Roman world, on which their society had founded its own dreams of civilization; and thus they came face to face with uncanny versions of themselves."[32]

Whoever the author "Shakespeare" was, and however he encountered Ovid, he was clearly struck by the freedom and fluidity with which Ovid blended nature, gender, humanity, and divinity. Shakespeare was stiff, squeamish, idiosyncratic, constrained by personal neuroses and insecurities, and Ovid (as devious author and revered icon) endorsed and validated a liberty that Shakespeare clearly found intoxicating and addictive.

The *Metamorphoses* abounded with the wacky antics of "playful, polymorphous, polyamorous pagan gods."[33] Sensational stories of these supernatural sociopaths were a natural springboard for Shakespeare's nuanced exploration of character, liberating the poet from strict Christian archetypes of saint and sinner. Ovid's *Heroides*, a collection of fictional letters from Classical heroines, provided Shakespeare with "examples of female characters who are witty as well as amorous, not merely moody but also full of vitality, linguistically adept and good at arguing."[34] Medieval literary heroines had been rigid and frigid, but Ovid inspired Shakespeare to explore multifaceted female characters.

Shakespeare devoured Ovid. In *Love's Labour's Lost*, a Latin teacher assesses a clumsy sonnet full of worn-out cliches. He sneers, *"for the elegancy, facility, and golden cadence of poesy, caret* [it is insufficient]. *Ovidius Naso was the man. And why, indeed, 'Naso' but for smelling out the odoriferous flowers of fancy, the jerks of invention? Imitari* [imitation] *is nothing: so doth the hound his master, the ape his keeper, the tired horse his rider"* (LLL IV.ii). The pedant is saying it's not enough to regurgitate solid chunks of Ovid, rather his work must be fully digested and dissolved so that a poet can transform it into something new.

This became one of the central projects of Shakespeare's career. His early works are filled with explicit Ovidian references, like *Titus Andronicus* and his epic poem *Venus and Adonis,* an adaptation of a story from the *Metamorphoses.* But with *A Midsummer Night's Dream* he achieves liftoff, creating something entirely Ovidian but without the need for a launch pad, and he brings the plane to a smooth landing, an ending that "affirms love and life in an everyday world—a picture that is found nowhere in Ovid."[35] Shakespeare manages to channel the poet's super-charged erotic energy toward marital legitimacy. And he celebrates his graduation from strict imitation by lambasting a ridiculously literal stage adaptation of Ovid's "Pyramus and Thisbe."

In the last book of the *Metamorphoses,* the philosopher Pythagoras gives a speech about reincarnation (metempsychosis, the transmigration of souls), how he had lived lives before and would live again after his death. And in 1598, Francis Meres wrote, "As the soul of Euphorbus was thought to live in Pythagoras: so the sweet witty soul of Ovid lives in mellifluous [melodious] and honey-tongued Shakespeare."

Brush Up Thine Ovid
THE TAMING OF THE SHREW | TITUS ANDRONICUS | A MIDSUMMER NIGHT'S DREAM

In the musical *Kiss Me, Kate,* two thugs sing a Cole Porter song called "Brush Up Your Shakespeare," about how a young man's best way into a woman's heart (and other parts) is to quote the bard of Stratford-upon-

Avon. The song contains a mix of Shakespearean titles, sometimes mangled to match with puns and rhymes ranging from clever to cringeworthy. In Porter's defense, none are as bad as Shakespeare's old standby, "Love/ move," which apparently rhymed at the time but sets our teeth on edge today. As the song goes on it becomes increasingly dark and creepy, but the core statement still rings true: having a Shakespeare quote ready can be pretty romantic. If nothing else, it demonstrates some education, and statistics show that higher education can lengthen a marriage.

But what about Shakespeare's characters? We could say, in a sense, that they all knew their Shakespeare; his suitors overflow with quotations to impress fair maidens. Ironically, his heroines are often unimpressed by a young fop's ability to ramble off great Shakespearean pickup lines. Rosalind in *As You Like It* and Rosaline in *Love's Labour's Lost* throw handmade Shakespearean poetry back in their wooers' faces, and an unseen Rosaline even rejects the great Romeo himself! Every Rosalind has her thorn. There's a pun to cringe at.

Shakespeare would likely have said "Brush up thine Ovid," his favorite author. And indeed, Shakespeare's educated characters tend to know their Ovid pretty well, particularly his female characters. From Ovid's *Ars Amatoria*, his heroines learn about erotic love, from *Heroides* they learn about loss and longing, and from *Metamorphoses* they learn about the lurking danger of male lust. Ovid himself had been an early proponent of female education: "A learned woman [should] know how to hold the quill in her right hand and the lyre in her left."[36]

In *The Taming of the Shrew*, young Lucentio journeys to Padua for his classical education. As they enter the town, his manservant cautions him not to stifle himself in joyless philosophy: *"Let's be no stoics nor no stocks, I pray; / Or so devote to Aristotle's checks / As Ovid be an outcast quite abjur'd."* (TS I.i, "abjured" meaning rejected). But Tranio could have saved his breath. They've barely crossed the city gate before the young student spies the fair Bianca, and all stoicism melts away:

> "O, yes, I saw sweet beauty in her face,
> Such as the daughter of Agènor had,
> That made great Jove to humble him to her hand,
> When with his knees he kiss'd the Cretan strand."
> (TS I.i, "strand" meaning shore)

Aristotelian moderation is out the window and Lucentio leaps into the second book of Ovid's *Metamorphoses,* where "Jove," the Roman Jupiter whom the Greeks called Zeus, first beheld the lovely Phoenician princess Europa. So, the mighty king of Olympus went slumming. The god disguised himself as a beast, and perhaps it was with this image in mind that the nobleman Lucentio devised his own plan to pursue Bianca in the disguise of a lowly tutor. We in the audience might see it another way: physical attraction has transformed this head-in-the-clouds philosopher into a head-over-heels animal. Bianca will certainly see through him. She wants something in between a god and a bull, she wants a man. And over the course of the play, while we're distracted by Petruchio's attempts at "taming" Kate, Bianca will tame Lucentio.

The schoolboy who's skipping his lessons decides to pass himself off as a teacher. For a textbook he chooses Ovid's *Heroides,* a collection of fictionalized letters, and clumsily inserts his secret messages into a Latin lesson: "Hic ibat, *as I told you before,* Simois, *I am Lucentio,* hic est, *son unto Vincentio of Pisa,* Sigeia tellus, *disguised thus to get your love,* Hic steterat, *and that Lucentio that comes a-wooing,* Priami, *is my man Tranio,* regia, *bearing my port,* celsa senis, *that we might beguile the old pantaloon."* (TS III.i, the interspersed Latin is "Here flowed the river Simois; here is the Sigeian land; here stood the lofty palace of old Priam," from Ovid's *Heroides,* 1.33-34)

In a sense he's chosen the passage wisely. The Trojan king Priam unwittingly accepted a wooden horse into the walled city, not knowing it was full of soldiers. And Bianca's father Baptista has unwittingly accepted a tutor into his house, not knowing it was a young suitor in disguise–Lucentio is the Trojan Horse. But in another sense, he's chosen the passage poorly; this is Ovid's fictionalized letter from Penelope, who is surrounded by suitors she doesn't want.

Whether or not this text is appropriate, he bumbles through Ovid's verse like a bull in a china shop, shattering the first line into fragments. Bianca repeats the line back to him, but politely repairs the Latin syntax: *"Now let me see if I can construe it:* Hic ibat Simois, *I know you not;* hic est Sigeia tellus, *I trust you not;* Hic steterat Priami, *take heed he hear us not;* regia, *presume not;* celsa senis, *despair not."* (TS III.i) Meanwhile, she inserts her reasonable responses to his cavalier charade: she doesn't know or trust him. He shouldn't presume that she's as love-struck as he is, but that doesn't necessarily mean he should give up. Her response contains the kind of prudent suspicion that could have saved Europa from getting carried away.

The next time we see them together it's clear that she has warmed to him. He's still disguised as a teacher and they must still speak in code, but he's ramped up from Ovid's lovelorn *Heroides* to his *Ars Amatoria*, the Art of Love, the Sun Tzu of seduction:

> "*LUCENTIO. Now, mistress, profit you in what you read?*
> *BIANCA. What, master, read you? first resolve me that.*
> *LUCENTIO. I read that I profess, the Art to Love.*
> *BIANCA. And may you prove, sir, master of your art!*" (TS IV.ii)

The groundlings in Shakespeare's audience would have easily picked up the message: she hopes he can practice what he preaches. But those with a Classical Education would have had an additional smirk, knowing that Ovid's *Ars Amatoria* concludes by instructing readers on the importance of the simultaneous orgasm.[37] It's unclear whether Lucentio has reached the end of the book, but Bianca likely has. This is a good example of a running joke in Shakespeare's comedies, where characters can be playfully competitive over who has the deeper knowledge of Ovid.

R. W. Maslen notes that, "Tudor translations of Ovid are invariably accompanied by the sixteenth century equivalent of government health warnings, like that of Arthur Golding in the preface to his translation."[38] Golding worried that, "Some naughty person seeing vice showed lively in this hue.../ [might] take occasion by and by like vices to ensue."[39] He feared that this energetic anthology of erotic atrocity tales might be mistaken for a glorification of violence, and this fear comes nightmarishly to life in the most lamentable Roman tragedy of *Titus Andronicus*, a grueling carnival of cruelty, dismemberment, and blood by the bucketful (and that's "carnival" in the *old* sense of "flesh devoured"). *Titus Andronicus* is a family feud in which both sides use the *Metamorphoses* as an instruction manual for violence and vengeance.[40]

Tamora, queen of the defeated Goths, has been dragged to Rome in chains, and immediately one of her children is sacrificed by order of general Titus to satisfy the bloodthirsty ghosts of two sons slain during the campaign. The vendetta between Tamora and Titus escalates to a rampage of revenge until just about everyone is dead, some of them having been raped, mutilated, and eaten.

The kidnapped queen instructs her two sons to assault Titus's daughter Lavinia in the forest, and they silence their victim by cutting out her tongue, as Ovid's Tereus did to his victim Philomel. Then, recalling how Philomel identified her rapist by weaving a tapestry, they hack off Lavinia's hands as well. However, what they don't count on is that Lavinia is literate too. She uses the stumps of her wrists to flip through a copy of the *Metamorphoses*, indicating the Philomel story to her father, and then like Io (who was ravished by Zeus and transformed into a cow), she fills in the names by writing in the dirt. Titus then refers to his own knowledge of Ovid for a proper response: Philomel's sister Procne punished her rapacious husband by decapitating their child. Getting ahold of Tamora's sons, Titus intones:

> *"TITUS. Hark, villains! I will grind your bones to dust,*
> *And with your blood and it I'll make a paste...*
> *And make two pasties of your shameful heads;*
> *And bid that strumpet, your unhallowed dam,*
> *Like to the earth, swallow her own increase...*
> *For worse than Philomel you us'd my daughter,*
> *And worse than Progne I will be reveng'd."*
> (TA V.ii, "dam" meaning mother)

Like a gleeful Sweeney Todd, he makes meat-pies of Tamora's sons, then reveals the secret ingredients while her mouth is full: *"Why, there they are, both baked in this pie, / Whereof their mother daintily hath fed."* (TA V.iii) If we're not sufficiently grossed out, "dainties" was Elizabethan slang for testicles.[41] Leonard Barkan wrote: "This is mythology viewed in the competitive mode. And the author is the most avid competitor. What is horrible in Ovid's Tereus story Shakespeare makes twice as horrible in *Titus Andronicus*. Not one rapist but two, not one murdered child but five, not one or two mutilated organs but six, not a one-course meal but two."[42]

Shakespeare could also be lighthearted with Ovid. In *A Midsummer Night's Dream*, newlyweds seek entertainment between the reception and bedtime (the Elizabethan equivalent of waiting forty minutes after lunch before jumping in the pool). Numerous theater troupes have prepared

Ovidian stage adaptations, including the death of Orpheus and a battle with centaurs, and a bunch of bumpkins have prepared *"A tedious brief scene of young Pyramus and his love Thisbe; very tragical mirth."* They've written and rehearsed this adaptation, but don't seem to have fully read their sources. Their misunderstandings of the Classical material turn their tragedy to a comic travesty.

> *"PYRAMUS. I see a voice; now will I to the chink,*
> *To spy an I can hear my Thisbe's face. Thisbe!*
> *THISBE. My love! thou art my love, I think.*
> *PYRAMUS. Think what thou wilt, I am thy lover's grace;*
> *And like Limander am I trusty still.*
> *THISBE. And I like Helen, till the Fates me kill.*
> *PYRAMUS. Not Shafalus to Procrus was so true.*
> *THISBE. As Shafalus to Procrus, I to you."* (MND V.i)

Leander drowned while swimming to his forbidden love Hero (Thisbe slips, calling Hero "Helen," reminding us of Greek history's most infamous adulteress), Cephalus and Procris suspected each other of cheating, and just when the confusion was finally cleared up, he killed her in a hunting accident.[43] Taken together, this mix-up mash-up of old love stories creates a clash of comedy. It's like a wedding band playing a medley of "Leader of the Pack," "Tell Laura I Love Her" and "Bat Out of Hell."[44]

To paraphrase the schoolmaster Holofornes, imitating Ovid is not enough. The characters in these early plays are very literal in their use of Ovid, and during this period Shakespeare also wrote an adaptation of the Venus story from the *Metamorphoses*, which we'll closely examine later. But it seems no coincidence that Shakespeare parodies the aping of Ovid in *A Midsummer Night's Dream*, just at the point in his development when he has deeply internalized his favorite author, to the point where he can generate his own Ovidian creations. Or more precisely, Shakespeare will be able to put a distinctly Ovidian twist on his adaptations of popular novels and plots. And he'll do this so masterfully that the boundary will dissolve between "Ovidian" and "Shakespearean."

PART I

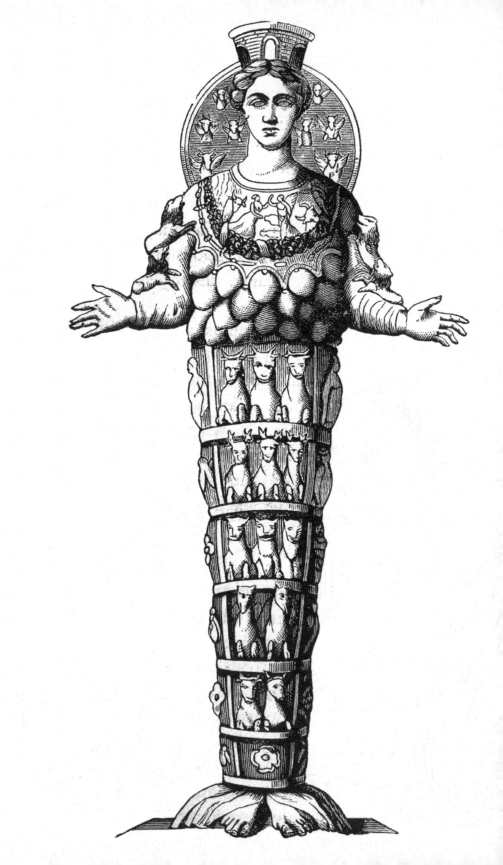

Diana of Ephesus

Lost in the Matrix
COMEDY OF ERRORS

A disoriented fool unwittingly bumbles into a twisting, shapeshifting otherworld. He is swept up, fed, and pampered by an overwhelming woman, and can't escape a nagging fear that this strange place can transform a man into an ass. This is the premise of *The Comedy of Errors*, one of young Shakespeare's first forays into the tangled web of the divine feminine. The play does not technically have deities on the stage, although it will end with something quite like a *Deus ex Machina*. But for our study, this early play will serve as an orientation (or *dis*-orientation) into the full spectrum of Shakespeare's goddess archetypes and how they intersect with one another.

The setting is Ephesus, a city that had grown around a religious pilgrimage site, the *Artemision*, Temple of Artemis, one of the seven wonders of the ancient world. The centerpiece of this shrine was described by Sir James Frazer as "the many-breasted idol of the Ephesian Artemis, with all its crowded emblems of exuberant fecundity."[45] The sculpture has at least sixteen bosoms (or some commentators suggest they may be bull testicles, another symbol of rampant fertility). Artemis was known to the Romans as Diana, and yet this abundant maternal fertility goddess was clearly distinct from the eternal-virgin tomboy huntress Diana of Roman mythology. The Diana of Ephesus had more in common with the local

Turkish fertility goddess Cybele. It seems likely that when Rome invaded, the indigenous Ephesians continued worshiping their divine mother under a Roman name.[46]

Ephesus was well known to Shakespeare's audience from the Biblical *Acts of the Apostles*.[47] When Paul journeyed there and condemned their "curious arts," the statue-makers gathered saying, "not only this our craft is in danger to be set at nought; but also that the temple of the great goddess Diana should be despised, and her magnificence should be destroyed, whom all Asia and the world worshippeth. And when they heard these sayings, they were full of wrath, and cried out, saying, Great is Diana of the Ephesians. And the whole city was filled with confusion." (Acts 19, KJV) In The Comedy of Errors, "Ephesus" is only a thin disguise for Shakespeare's London, and yet giving it this infamous name warned his audience from the start that they'd stumbled into an exotic world of witchery, trickery, and enchantment—a place where women have strange powers, and tourists should beware.

> *"They say this town is full of cozenage* [swindles]*;*
> *As, nimble jugglers that deceive the eye,*
> *Dark-working sorcerers that change the mind,*
> *Soul-killing witches that deform the body,*
> *Disguisèd cheaters, prating mountebanks,*
> *And many such-like liberties of sin."* (COE I.ii)

The tourists in question are Antipholus and his manservant Dromio, but here things get confusing because they each have an identical twin who lives there, also named Antipholus and Dromio. Antipholus of Ephesus is well connected in town—he has a wife and a running flirtation with an interested potential mistress, he has friends, and all of this despite being a real jerk. But then his identical twin trips into this web of relationships, and we spend two hours waiting for him to say "This is not my beautiful house! This is not my beautiful wife!"

Plus, Antipholus keeps losing Dromio, whom he refers to as *"the almanach of my true date,"* in modern terms, his driver's license, passport, and external memory thumb-drive (Dromio is not quite a cell phone; he can't access the internet, and also, he's kind of a dolt). Comedy ensues as the two Dromios keep getting switched at random.[48]

Trinity

COMEDY OF ERRORS

The tourists Antipholus and Dromio have supposedly come to Ephesus seeking their identical twins (to complete their identities), but upon arriving they immediately forget that they have lookalikes with the same names living there. This, of course, produces a comedy of confusion as various women push and pull at them: a maiden, an ogre, a wife, a wench, and finally, a semi-divine mother. The newcomers are mystified by these relationships, and only at the end do they realize that the complete selfhood they sought requires an integration of male and female energies. And their journey to this realization is a carnivalesque hall of mirrors showing many shapes and sizes of human and divine femininity.

Representing wild, hungry Nature is a kitchen wench who lurks deep in the bowels of the earth. Appropriate, since a kitchen is where life is transformed: a live pig becomes a ham, enters the hot womb of an oven, and emerges steaming, reborn as human sustenance.[49] Dromio gets sucked down into the dank, smarmy womb/tomb underworld and emerges traumatized, fearing that he's lost his human shape:

> *"I am an ass, I am a woman's man, and besides myself... She would have me as a beast: not that, I being a beast, she would have me; but that she, being a very beastly creature, lays claim to me... She's the kitchen-wench, and all grease; and I know not what use to put her to but to make a lamp of her and run from her by her own light... No longer from head to foot than from hip to hip: she is spherical, like a globe; I could find out countries in her."* (COE III.ii)

He then goes on to describe her topography in geographical terms: she has bogs like Ireland, France is her forehead being invaded by her hairline, and he was too terrified to explore her Netherlands. *"This drudge or diviner laid claim to me* [and] *I, amaz'd, ran from her as a witch. And, I think, if my breast had not been made of faith, and my heart of steel, she had transform'd me to a curtal dog, and made me turn i' th' wheel."*[50] (COE III.ii) Apparently his counterpart, the local Dromio, is quite pleased with all this, but the visiting manservant fled like Indiana Jones with a giant stone Venus-of-Willendorf rolling after him. However, this is no monster, just a fertile maid with a healthy build (a physique we never see on the Shakespearean stage). But Dromio is horrified by her hearty sexual appetite, fearing that, like the witch-goddess Circe, she will transform him into a beast.

While Dromio barely escaped the subterranean steatopygous Venus, Antipholus has had an ethereal experience of divine femininity on the second floor. His brother's wife Adriana has left the dinner table exasperated, and her chatty little sister Luciana stays behind to talk sense into him. She delivers a long sermon about the marital bond, then prattles that it's all right for a husband to marry for money and cheat on his wife as long as he still gives her some attention. Luciana is Shakespeare's joke about the bridesmaid who's full of marital advice, and she tends to babble off in silly directions.

Fortunately for her, this Antipholus (her unknown future husband) doesn't seem to hear any of it. He's off in the clouds: *"Are you a god? Would you create me new? / Transform me, then, and to your pow'r I'll yield."* Luciana, whose name means "radiant," is transfigured by Antipholus's gaze into a glowing goddess, at once virginal and maternal.[51] His vision of her encompasses the cosmos, from the heavens to the lands to the depths of the sea:

> *"Less in your knowledge and your grace you show not*
> *Than our earth's wonder—more than earth, divine.*
> *Teach me, dear creature, how to think and speak;*
> *Lay open to my earthy-gross conceit,*
> *Smoth'red in errors, feeble, shallow, weak,*
> *The folded meaning of your words' deceit...*
> *O, train me not, sweet mermaid, with thy note,*
> *To drown me in thy sister's flood of tears.*
> *Sing, siren, for thyself, and I will dote;*
> *Spread o'er the silver waves thy golden hairs."*[52] (COE III.ii)

While Dromio thinks he's seen a cave troll, Antipholus heard the song of a mermaid. They're lodging at an inn called The Centaur and visiting a house called the Phoenix—quite a menagerie of mythical beasts. But it makes sense in this city of fluid identity and bewildering enchantment.

Between these subterranean and ethereal realms are the play's two down-to-earth women: Adriana and an unnamed "Courtesan," Antipholus's frigid wife and frisky mistress. There is some wiggle-room on the question of whether he's been having an affair or just flirts with the idea, but that's beside the point. Locked out of his house, he decides that the necklace he's commissioned for Adriana will instead be given to the local Madam in exchange for her "ring" (whatever *that* means).

Just as the males of the play are split in two by the device of twinning, these two females can also be seen as a single split psyche (perhaps it's because of this that the "Courtesan" remains anonymous). One is *a wench of excellent discourse, pretty and witty* while the other is *starve[d] for a merry look* and wonders *Are my discourses dull? Barren my wit?* Adriana may have some anxiety about infertility—they've been married a while with no offspring—and definitely suspects infidelity. Bound as one flesh in marriage, she feels, *My blood is mingled with the crime of lust; / For if we two be one, and thou play false, / [I'm] strumpeted by thy contagiòn.* (COE II.ii)[53]

Shakespeare will repair this situation with a poetic device: the chain, magically imbued with the Courtesan's eroticism, will be redirected to Adriana, thereby combining the two women into one who can be, as an old country song says, "A saint on a Sunday morning, a devil on a Saturday night."[54] Presumably, this will freshen the stagnant marriage and fix the fertility issues. The combination of saint and strumpet will produce a full Venus archetype.

I should say here that I'm not standing up for this duct tape relationship fix, just guessing at the symbolic intentions of a poet who ditched his wife for two decades and left her his second-best bed in his will (at least he doesn't seem to have bequeathed his collection of STDs, since she outlived him by seven years).

Madonna ex Machina
COMEDY OF ERRORS

Shakespeare adapted *Comedy of Errors* from Plautus's *Menaechmi*, an ancient Roman romp about identical twins.[55] And the play adheres to Classical comedic conventions: unity of place and time, no loose ends (Shakespeare called several plays *The Tragedy of Such-and-Such*, but this is the only comedy with *Comedy* in the title).[56] Shakespeare also added the twist of making the servants identical twins as well, and doubling the names, multiplying the comic possibilities. But ultimately, the interwoven plot strands become so hopelessly tangled that Shakespeare will have to depart from Plautus again, digging further back into theatrical history. The only way to sort this out will be a *Deus ex Machina*, an old Greek theatrical device for resolving debates on the stage, a platform-and-pulley system floats in a "God from the Machine" to deliver a verdict.

When the characters have gathered at the end and told their stories, the Duke, as authority figure, can offer no better solution than *"I think you all have drunk of Circe's cup."* He deduces that they've been bewitched by a sorceress, Circe, who transformed Ulysses's crewmates into swine in the *Odyssey*. This makes a certain sense, bringing us back to Ephesus's reputation as a coven of *"Soul-killing witches that deform the body,"* and Dromio's fear that the kitchen *"witch"* would turn him into a dog or an ass.

The pilgrim Antipholus has wandered lost in the labyrinth of Ephesus and finally stumbles into the center: a womblike abbey. And although the locals and the police and the Duke himself demand the fugitive, the Abbess emerges with a declaration of sanctuary. She interviews Adriana about the marriage and judges that the jealous wife has been *"not rough enough."* A sound thrashing should cure his wanderlust, but the incessant nagging will only wear away at his sanity.

By this point, every female in the play has been called a "witch," and yet it turns out that Circe is not the ultimate authority figure in Ephesus, the Abbess is. None of the citizens, including the police and the Duke, is allowed to contradict her. But from what higher power is this godlike authority derived? Although she's called the "Abbess," implying a Christian nun, she never once mentions the Father, Son, Holy Ghost, or the Virgin Mary. The closest she comes is saying she'll rehabilitate Antipholus *"With wholesome syrups, drugs, and holy prayers, / To make of him a formal man again."* But these prayers could be directed any which way, and the drugs make her sound more like a witch-doctor than a nun. The Abbess stands in for Diana of Ephesus.

Then it's revealed that the Mother Superior is the long-lost biological mom of the Antipholus twins, separated in a shipwreck long ago, and she describes their reunion as a lengthy labor:

> *"Thirty-three years have I but gone in travail*
> *Of you, my sons; and till this present hour*
> *My heavy burden ne'er deliverèd."* (COE V.i)

If this isn't magic enough, she also saves the life of a death-sentenced wanderer who turns out to be her long-lost husband. Shakespeare leaves her religious affiliation open to interpretation for now, but returns to Ephesus about fifteen years later, at the end of his career. *Pericles, Prince of Tyre* repeats the family parted by a tempest shipwreck, streamlined this time with a single daughter instead of two sets of twins. And once again the tangle must be sorted out in Ephesus. But this time the wandering father is summoned there by an appearance of the *real* goddess Diana. Once again, the high priestess of Ephesus turns out to be the long-lost wife, but Shakespeare had reached the point in his career when he could bring the goddess out of the Christian closet, making explicit what was only implied in *The Comedy of Errors:* Great is the Diana of Ephesus.

Categorization and its Discontents
COMEDY OF ERRORS

In terms of Shakespeare's feminine and goddess archetypes, we have the full set here in *The Comedy of Errors*. Luciana stands in for the virginal Diana (not a precise match; she is very puritanical in her thoughts about gender dynamics[57]). Adriana and the Courtesan ultimately combine to become a composite Venus of sexually mature womanhood. The Abbess Emilia is a widow with healing powers, the maternal Diana whose virginity has been magically restored by years in the convent. And the kitchen wench is raw Nature, an avalanching *"mountain of mad flesh"* with an unapologetic mix of good, bad, and ugly. In a sense, the city of Ephesus itself is Circe, the crafty witch whose dark magic must be dispelled by the enlightened Mother Superior.

The city of Ephesus appears to be a blind maze in which men lose themselves, but reaching the center we finally view it from a divine perspective: an intricate matrix where they find themselves, not as isolated individuals but in relation to female partners and at last their own mother. In the story, male law personified by the Duke can't sort out identity crises; his only tools are inquisition and execution. The death-sentenced father and lost twins (by this point all fugitives) are restored by the combined power of a virgin, wife, and mother.

Commentators have seen for centuries that most of Shakespeare's female characters can be categorized in some trinitarian scheme of maiden/wife/widow or maiden/mother/crone or virgin/whore/witch. This tends to link up well with studies of fairy tales, pagan goddesses, and the moon with its cycles of waxing/fullness/waning, followed by death and rebirth. It makes for a fun scholarly game, a Shakespearean scavenger hunt, checking off these three boxes to make a trinity set in scripts like *The Comedy of Errors, All's Well That Ends Well, The Winter's Tale*, etc. We'll play a few rounds of that game in this book. But we also need to be aware that these archetypes are from a *male* perspective.

In her powerful book, *The Shakespearean Wild*, Jeanne Addison Roberts wrote, "In the male imagination, the female Wild seems to be peopled with these three main types, and the inability to reconcile them causes paralysis, reluctance, and delay. Clearly each of the categories is defined in terms of sexual relationship to males. The virgin is young, innocent of sex, but with sexual potential; the whore/wife is sexually active and therefore dangerous; the crone, although allied with possible motherhood, has become an infertile reminder of death... The commonplace triangulation—one might even say triage—of women is reductionist, but it is also enlightening."[58]

Playing the lady-triangle game can teach us a good deal about Shakespeare and his views on women and feminine power. For example, female power in Shakespeare's plays tends to be cooperative. Ophelia by herself is dead in the water, but a collaborative maiden, wife, and mother engineer a brilliant rehabilitation in *All's Well That Ends Well*. Cleopatra pretty much manages to combine all three archetypes into one person but cannot escape the grave, whereas the trinitarian team in *The Winter's Tale* successfully staves off an eternal ice age.[59] Shakespeare's tragic heroes tend to stand and fall alone, but his heroines often triumph in trinities. When women at three stages of life combine their energies of vitality, fortitude, and wisdom, they attain a super-human power.

The trinitarian system has some value, providing we acknowledge from the start that it's not a *universal* truth. Roberts again cautions us, "Neoclassical, romantic, and Victorian critics regularly celebrated Shakespeare's astonishing representations of 'universal human' values, and it has only very gradually become apparent that those 'universal' values were axiomatically male values."[60] Not just male, but an exceptionally neurotic man in a long-ago land barely emerged from Medievalism.

Even the most adventurous theorists don't speculate that Shakespeare was female. He was horrified of women (and also worshipped them). And of course, in the modern age, women can achieve status and identity in ways that have nothing to do with men: many opt out of motherhood, some aren't attracted to males, and menopause can open whole new vistas of adventure and opportunity. We should furthermore approach these classifications with caution because historically, patriarchal cultures have had a great distrust for women who reject or subvert these so-called traditional roles.

Diana

A Whiter Shade of Pale
A MIDSUMMER NIGHT'S DREAM

A Midsummer Night's Dream takes place in ancient Greece. Actually, this is a bit confusing because, as soon as the young lovers venture out of town, they're in an Elizabethan English forest. But the bookend scenes of the play take place in Athens overseen by Duke Theseus, the mythical hero famous for fighting the Minotaur and infamous for his ill-fated romances. He's prepping for one of his numerous disastrous marriages, this time to Hippolyta, Queen of the Amazons who he conquered in a bloody battle of the sexes (*"Hippolyta, I woo'd thee with my sword, / And won thy love doing thee injuries."* MND I.i). Then a nobleman drags his daughter into the room, furious that she insists on choosing her own husband, and demands that Theseus uphold the Athenian law: Hermia must marry her father's chosen suitor or be put to death.

Theseus feels the heat of his captive fiancée's glare and nimbly improvises a third option: the girl can become a nun. Then he idiotically blurts out that she'll have three days to decide, and he'll expect her answer on his wedding day. This guarantees that, whatever Hermia chooses, Theseus's bride will get to watch a young girl crying her eyes out just before the ceremony—and maybe getting hanged as well.

Theseus does have some sympathy for Hermia's plight, we can hear it in his speech, far more flowery than Hamlet's curt *"Get thee to a nunnery."* Theseus becomes rather poetic:

"THESEUS. Either to die the death, or to abjure [to abandon]
For ever the society of men.
Therefore, fair Hermia, question your desires,
Know of your youth, examine well your blood,
Whether, if you yield not to your father's choice,
You can endure the livery of a nun,
For aye to be in shady cloister mew'd,
To live a barren sister all your life,
Chanting faint hymns to the cold fruitless moon.
Thrice-blessèd they that master so their blood
To undergo such maiden pilgrimage;
But earthlier happy is the rose distill'd
Than that which withering on the virgin thorn
Grows, lives, and dies, in single blessedness." (MND I.i)

Hermia's problems stem from *"the society of men."* She lives in a world where she's owned by her father. Under Athenian law (written by dead men, represented by Duke Theseus.[61]) he can barter her off to any man of his choosing. So, Theseus offers her the option of forsaking men altogether by going to live in a society of women. And since he has just crushed the Amazon society of women, he suggests that Hermia join a convent.

But this concept of the nunnery is complicated by the fact that baby Jesus hadn't even been born yet; Christianity wouldn't exist for another fifteen hundred years. And in Shakespeare's time, the English convents had all been closed.[62] When Theseus speaks of nuns, he's talking about the virginal priestesses at some early version of Diana's Temple in Ephesus. *"Chanting faint hymns to the cold fruitless moon"* is meant literally: worshiping the moon aspect of the goddess variously known as Artemis, Phoebe, Diana, Cynthia, and Hecate. *"Thrice blessed"* refers to the goddess's trinitarian aspects of youth, maturity, and age, linked to the phases of the lunar cycle. The moon's timelessness, young and old at once, is the answer to a riddle in *Love's Labour's Lost*: *"What was a month old at Cain's birth that's not five weeks old as yet? ...Dictynna [Diana] A title to Phoebe, to Luna, to the moon."*[63] (LLL IV.ii)

At the same time that Shakespeare was writing *A Midsummer Night's Dream*, he was drafting *Romeo and Juliet*, which also contains a reference to virginal moon-priestesses. When Romeo gives his speech about light breaking through the window and Juliet being the sun, he continues: *"Arise fair sun and kill the envious moon... / Be not her maid since she is envious; / Her vestal livery is but sick and green, / And none but fools do wear it; cast it off."* (R&J II.ii, "vestal livery" meaning a nun's robe) He's praying that this girl he met is not some aspiring vestal virgin.

Theseus calls the moon *"fruitless"* in the sense that Diana was eternally chaste, and yet the moon was believed to be profoundly influential in fertility. Human pregnancy, for example, is tied to lunar cycles of menstruation, and Roman women would pray to the moon goddess because labor is easier under a full moon. If this sounds like superstition, just ask a modern midwife or obstetrician. The moon holds sway over ocean tides and can have curious effects on human thought and emotion—it's from the Latin "luna" that we get the word "lunatic" for abnormal psychological states. Priestesses chanting hymns to the moon were not just spouting lovelorn poetry at a lonely light in the sky, but playing an essential role in steadying universal cycles.

The Fairy Queen Titania explains the disastrous consequences of fairies neglecting their circle dances for the moon:

> *"No night is now with hymn or carol blest;*
> *Therefore the moon, the governess of floods,*
> *Pale in her anger, washes all the air,*
> *That rheumatic diseases do abound.*
> *And thorough this distemperature we see*
> *The seasons alter: hoary-headed frosts*
> *Fall in the fresh lap of the crimson rose;*
> *And on old Hiem's chin and icy crown*
> *An odorous chaplet of sweet summer buds*
> *Is, as in mockery, set. The spring, the summer,*
> *The childing autumn, angry winter, change*
> *Their wonted liveries; and the mazed world,*
> *By their increase, now knows not which is which."* (MND II.i,
> "Hiem" meant personified Winter[64])

Titania is saying that the seasons have swapped their costumes till no one can tell what time of year it is. Without fairy dances and virginal hymns to steady lunar cycles, the whole cosmic clockwork has been a train-wreck with dangerous consequences for humans, crops, and livestock.

Shakespeare was commenting on current events: Europe in the 1590s suffered a series of wet springs and cold summers, causing crop failure. Modern climatologists refer to this period as a "Little Ice Age," which the Elizabethans found inexplicable. "Earth scientists today discuss the relative importance of factors such as deforestation, automobile and industrial exhausts, and bovine flatulence in determining the nature, pace, and effects of global warming."[65] (Yes, you read that correctly: heifer-farts are no laughing matter). In Shakespeare's time, bad weather was often blamed on witchcraft, resulting in superstitious attempts to resolve climate cooling with witch-burnings. But Shakespeare here playfully proposes that the wacky weather, English even by English standards, may have resulted from a fairy domestic dispute disrupting ritual reverence of the moon.

Forest Moon
A MIDSUMMER NIGHT'S DREAM

The moon plays a special role in *A Midsummer Night's Dream* (it will even appear as an actor on the stage). The opening lines of the play, our first impressions of Theseus and Hippolyta, will be their different perspectives while looking at this same celestial body.

> *"THESEUS. Another moon; but, O, methinks, how slow*
> *This old moon wanes! She lingers my desires,*
> *Like to a step-dame or a dowager,*
> *Long withering out a young man's revenue.*
> *HIPPOLYTA. Four days will quickly steep themselves in night;*
> *Four nights will quickly dream away the time;*
> *And then the moon, like to a silver bow*
> *New-bent in heaven, shall behold the night*
> *Of our solemnities."* (MND I.i)

To Theseus, the moon is like a rich old spinster aunt whose fortune will pass to a young man in her will (if she doesn't spend it all before she dies). He's chosen the new moon for his wedding, since he doesn't want the sinister waning moon to cast any ill omens on this marriage. Good call, Theseus, but it won't work. You will eventually murder Hippolyta, and the son you have together, Hippolytus, will cause your next wife Phaedra to hang herself, and then he'll be torn apart by horses, and later you'll be shoved off a cliff. But in theory, yes, it's better to marry under a new moon.

While Theseus sees the moon as an old crone delaying his marital gratification, the Amazon Hippolyta envisions the coming new moon in the shape of a *"silver bow,"* appropriate since Diana was an archer, and the Amazons were fearsome warriors. And yet she describes the bow not as a weapon but as an ornament, symbolic of a cease-fire.[66] In *A Midsummer Night's Dream,* the captive Amazon queen is relatively quiet and the Amazon attack on Athens is dismissed in a couple of lines. But later, in *The Two Noble Kinsmen,* we'll hear that the invasion had nearly been successful. A widowed queen will say to Hippolyta:

> *"Most dreaded Amazonian, that hast slain*
> *The scythe-tusked boar; that with thy arm, as strong*
> *As it is white, wast near to make the male*
> *To thy sex captive, but that this thy lord,*
> [Subdued] *thy force and thy affection."* (TNK I.i)

Hippolyta will marry Theseus for peace, but she's not broken. Theseus will have to learn to make space for her perspective before there will be any wedding night *"solemnities."*[67]

The news of Theseus and Hippolyta's wedding reaches their exes— the fairy queen Titania who had a thing with Theseus, and Oberon who had a dalliance with *"the bouncing Amazon."*[68] The fairy king mutters a cold greeting, *"Ill met by moonlight, proud Titania,"* and she explains that their fairy quarrel is exacerbating the wackiness of the weather. But she proposes that they fix the situation: *"If you will patiently dance in our round, / And see our moonlight revels, go with us."* (MND II.i) The spiral dance, or *"roundel,"* was a pagan ritual to steady the cycles of nature and the cosmos, a dance to remind the moon of its rhythm.

But Oberon sulks; he's got another idea. He tells his henchman, Puck, that he once saw Cupid *"flying between the cold moon and the earth,"* taking aim at *"a fair vestal"* (virgin, Queen Elizabeth), but the arrow missed its mark and the fiery shaft was *"quench'd in the chaste beams of the wat'ry moon."* (MND II.i) The virgin goddess Diana doused the flame of Cupid's arrow, and yet it still has magic, so Puck finds the shafted pansy and brings back its love juices. Titania, drugged with this aphrodisiac, falls for the first creature she sees, a jackass named Bottom who, by the power of a plot device, also has the head of an ass.[69] Once she's got him, she commands her servants *"to fan the moonbeams from his sleeping eyes"* because she fears the virgin goddess will infect his brain with purity: *"The moon, methinks, looks with a watery eye / And when she weeps, weeps every little flower; / Lamenting some enforcèd chastity."* (MND III.i)

The name Titania means "the female Titan," and "Titania" was a title Ovid once used for Diana. In Shakespeare's time, the name Diana was sometimes applied to the Queen of Fairies, as King James wrote in his witch-hunting manual *Daemonologie*: "the fourth kind of spirits, which by the Gentiles [ancient pagans] was called Diana and her wandering court, and amongst us is called Fairy." But Shakespeare is careful to distinguish the fairy queen Titania from the moon-goddess Diana: his Diana is always virginal, whereas Titania is sexually active.

Oberon and Titania will ultimately be reconciled. She will give him the changeling child and he will join in her circle dance, resolving their marital dispute and restoring the regular cycle of seasons:

> *"Then, my Queen, in silence sad,*
> *Trip we after night's shade.*
> *We the globe can compass soon,*
> *Swifter than the wand'ring moon."* (MND IV.i)

Lovers and Lunatics
A MIDSUMMER NIGHT'S DREAM

Hermia's romance, forbidden by the light of day, has been carried out at night. Her father accuses Lysander: *"Thou hast by moonlight at her window sung."* Hermia rejects Diana and the nunnery, swearing by *"cupid's strongest bow"* and *"Venus' doves"* that she will elope in defiance of the patriarchy (her father, and Athenian law personified by Theseus). But Lysander, who has wooed her by moonlight, now proposes that Diana can aid in their escape:

> *"LYSANDER. To-morrow night, when Phoebe doth behold*
> *Her silver visage in the wat'ry glass,*
> *Decking with liquid pearl the bladed grass,*
> *A time that lovers' flights doth still conceal,*
> *Through Athens' gates have we devis'd to steal."*
> (MND I.i, "Phoebe" is a Greek name for Diana)

Lysander's idea of star-crossed lovers running off by moonlight likely comes from a story he dimly recalls from Ovid's *Metamorphoses*: Pyramus and Thisbe. He doesn't seem to remember the ending, where their attempt to elope led to their gruesome double death. But Lysander and Hermia are not particularly bright; they make their top-secret escape plan and then babble it to the first person they see. This is their lovelorn friend Helena, hopelessly devoted to her ex, Demetrius, Hermia's unwanted fiancé. As Lysander said, Helena *"dotes,"* depends religiously *"devoutly dotes, dotes in idolatry / Upon this spotted and inconstant man,"* comparing Demetrius to the cloudy and ever-changing moon. Helena will use the inside information as bait to lure Demetrius into the wood. Hermia and Lysander will steal away that night, stalked by Demetrius who is doggedly pursued by Helena.

The four young Athenians will spend the next couple of days chasing each other through the forest, and each time they go to sleep they'll wake up reshuffled by Puck and the magic flower. The flower's name, *"love-in-idleness"* did not mean "idle" in the modern sense of "inactive"–very much the opposite. "Idleness" at the time meant delirium, "being out of one's senses."[70] Both suitors will change like the moon, shifting their competitive affections to Helena and insisting that their love for Hermia was just a phase (yes, pun intended).[71]

In Nietzsche's famous Apollonian/Dionysian dichotomy, Shakespeare's Athens is "Apollonian," overseen by Apollo, god of sunlight and order. Thus, by Nietzsche's logic, the forest should be "Dionysian," ruled by Dionysus, god of intoxication and dark appetite. But Shakespeare hadn't read Nietzsche, his forest is something else. We could call it *Dian*-ysian," overseen by the prim and proper moon, Phoebus, Apollo's twin sister Phoebe/Diana. Even the forest gods are under her spell: Oberon is something like the maiden-snatching Pluto and Puck resembles the priapic satyr Pan, but under Diana's stern gaze there will be no Ovidian jungle lust.[72] If this were the *Metamorphoses*, Oberon would have hunted Hermia, and Helena would have transformed into a tree to escape the lusty clutches of Puck. Instead of impish sexual predators, these male fairies become fixated on assisting these nymphs to attain lawful matrimony and legitimate offspring. It seems the moon has cooled them with "*some enforcèd chastity.*"

Using an aphrodisiac from Venus's son Cupid, Oberon and Puck play a shell game, shuffling the lovers' affections. But the roundel of romantic musical-chairs must come to an end, and Oberon will undo the magic of Venus with another flower containing the tears of Diana: "*Dian's bud o'er Cupid's flower / Hath such force and blessed power.*" (MND IV.i, in a comical twist, Demetrius does *not* get de-flowered, he remains drugged in love with Helena.) The moon goddess solidifies the results and then Theseus ratifies them the following morning. No doubt the Minotaur-slayer is aware that the moon's silver bow will be pointed at him that night if Hippolyta has to watch him hang poor Hermia.

Moonshine
A Midsummer Night's Dream

Shakespeare has shown us the moon, but only indirectly. Symbols scribbled on a page, transformed by tongues into syllables of speech have entered our ears and painted an image in the eyes of our minds. In some ways he's made the moon more real than real. Through the kaleidoscope of poetry it's a withered crone; no, it's a gleaming virgin, it's the goddess's watery eye; no, it's her silver bow, it's fruitless; no, it's fertile. Remote yet omnipresent like an Orwellian Big Sister, Diana hovers in constant surveillance. And all of this regardless of any prop or piece of scenery, the greatest set designers of the sixteenth century or the twenty-first century could not produce a stage moon so alive, fluid, and luminescent. Even in an outdoor performance, the moon itself would pale in comparison.

So, when Shakespeare pats himself on the back, we've got to hand it to him, he's earned it.

He calls our attention to his masterful poetic illusion by showing us its opposite: a bunch of bumbling builders attempting to get the moon into their play. An amateur community troupe has decided to audition for Athenian Idol so they can quit their day jobs and go pro. They're doing an adaptation of a tale from Ovid's *Metamorphoses*, which they've entitled *"A Tedious Brief Scene of Young Pyramus and His Love Thisbe; Very Tragical Mirth."* This is a story about star-crossed lovers whose parents forbade their marriage. They tried to elope by moonlight, but misunderstandings resulted in their suicides. We could call it a Babylonian *Romeo and Juliet*, except that really *Romeo and Juliet* is a reboot of Pyramus and Thisbe.[73]

Gathering for their first rehearsal in the forest, the mechanics immediately get hung up on a technical difficulty: *"To bring the moonlight into a chamber; for, you know, Pyramus and Thisbe meet by moonlight.... Doth the moon shine that night we play our play?... A calendar, a calendar! Look in the almanack; find out moonshine... Yes, it doth shine that night... Why, then may you leave a casement of the great chamber window, where we play, open; and the moon may shine in at the casement.... Ay; or else one must come in with a bush of thorns and a lantern, and say he comes to disfigure or to present the person of Moonshine."* (MND III.i) Without this divine diva their production is doomed. In classic Elizabethan fashion, the lunar prima donna will eventually be played by a male understudy.

> *"MOON. This lanthorn doth the hornèd moon present;*
> *Myself the Man I' th' Moon do seem to be.*
> *THESEUS. This is the greatest error of all the rest; the man should be*
> *put into the lantern. How is it else the man i th' moon?*
> *DEMETRIUS. He dares not come there for the candle; for, you see, it*
> *is already in snuff.*
> *HIPPOLYTA. I am aweary of this moon. Would he would change!*
> *THESEUS. It appears, by his small light of discretion, that he is in*
> *the wane...*
> *LYSANDER. Proceed, Moon.*
> *MOON. All that I have to say is to tell you that the lanthorn is the*
> *moon; I, the Man i' th' Moon; this thorn-bush, my thorn-bush; and*
> *this dog, my dog...*[74]
> *HIPPOLYTA. Well shone, Moon. Truly, the moon shines with a good*
> *grace."* (MND V.i)

Here we find that the amateurs don't know how to be actors, but the nobles *really* don't know how to be an audience. Helena and Hermia are politely silent, but the others won't shut up. Maybe the grooms are jittery because of their own performance anxiety. If Helena, Hermia, and Hippolyta were to heckle their new husbands an hour later, the morning would no doubt bring the gloomy peace of a triple suicide. But in terms of this particular scene, there's also a kind of catharsis. These characters have all been moonstruck in their various ways and now they get to laugh at it (while Shakespeare protects Diana with a human shield: their cruel mockery strikes a *man* playing the *man* in the moon, not a goddess).

Theseus and Hippolyta, former enemies in combat, join forces ganging up on this poor performer. And in this friendly moment, Hippolyta finally concurs with Theseus' earlier statement about the moon delaying gratification: *"I am aweary of this moon."* Now that she has seen Theseus grant Hermia's choice in marriage, the Amazon seems to feel warmer toward him. In the opening scene she referred to their approaching wedding night as *"solemnities,"* but now she sees some *"good grace"* in the coming night.

The show is not quite over yet, however. The *"Tedious Brief Scene"* must go on. Although this amateur amusement is *"said to be 'some ten words long,'* [it] *actually lasts about twenty minutes, yet fills up the three hours from suppertime to midnight."*[75] Bottom bumbles onto the stage as Pyramus, and blurts a mouthful of Quince's bad poetry:

> *"PYRAMUS. Sweet Moon, I thank thee for thy sunny beams;*
> *I thank thee, Moon, for shining now so bright;*
> *For, by thy gracious golden, glittering gleams,*
> *I trust to take of truest Thisbe sight..."* (MND V.i)

Discovering Thisbe's bloody robe, he draws his sword and bitterly calls, *"Moon, take thy flight"* and the moon-man walks off, *"Now die, die, die, die, die,"* as he stabs himself. Then Thisbe discovers his stiff cadaver and valiantly falls on his sword. Pyramus is justified in his anger at the moon: under Diana's chaste gaze they both die virgins. But the show ends on a festive note with the bloody dead lovers leaping up to do a festive jig (oddly enough, *Romeo and Juliet* originally ended this way as well, with the tragic cadavers doing a lively dance during curtain calls). *A Midsummer Night's Dream* concludes, the four couples go off to do their coupling, and the play ends as it began, with talk of the moon:

> *"PUCK. Now the hungry lion roars,*
> *And the wolf behowls the moon...*
> *And we fairies, that do run*
> *By the triple Hecate's team*[76]
> *From the presence of the sun,*
> *Following darkness like a dream...*
> *I am sent with broom before,*
> *To sweep the dust behind the door."* (MND V.ii)

Hecate is the moon goddess's menacing death-aspect. But Puck speaks here of *"triple Hecate"* as the totality of the trinitarian moon goddess who appears by three names in the script: Diana, Phoebe, and Hecate.

This play has featured the moon in all three phases: the virginal huntress with her silver bow, the *"governess of floods"* (ocean tides and menstruation), and the old spinster.[77] Oddly enough, if we've paid close attention, we see that the moon was waning when the play began, then the almanac tells us *"it doth shine that night"* for the wedding, then a new crescent emerges—so somehow there's a miraculous full moon when there should be none at all.

The deified moon is central in *A Midsummer Night's Dream*. Shakespeare will also refer to it in other plays. Orlando in *As You Like It* will sing to her while littering the forest with love notes to Rosalind:

> *"Hang there, my verse, in witness of my love;*
> *And thou, thrice-crownèd Queen of Night, survey*
> *With thy chaste eye, from thy pale sphere above,*
> *Thy huntress' name that my full life doth sway."* (AYL III.ii)

She is also the *"sovereign mistress of true melancholy,"* (A&C IV.ix) and Coriolanus will refer to his wife's spinster friend as *"The moon of Rome, chaste as the icicle / That's curdied by the frost from purest snow / And hangs on Dian's temple."* (COR V.iii) Falstaff will mention her when encouraging his drinking buddy Hal to not change into the grim Henry V: *"Let us be Diana's foresters, gentlemen of the shade, minions of the Moon; and let men say we be men of good government, being governed, as the sea is, by our noble and chaste mistress."* (1H IV I.ii) Othello will refer darkly to the moon causing lunacy: *"It is the very error of the moon. / She comes more nearer to the earth than she was wont / And makes men mad."* (Othello I.ii)

In Shakespeare's plays, Hecate, goddess of the dark side of the moon, is associated with witchcraft and murder, a theatrical assassin in *Hamlet* uses a poison *"with Hecate's ban thrice blasted, thrice infected,"* (HAM III.ii, "blasted" being the opposite of blessed), King Lear curses Cordelia by *"the mysteries of Hecate and the night,"* (KL I.i) and, as Macbeth lurches to kill the sleeping king, he muses, *"Witchcraft celebrates / Pale Hecate's offerings."* (MAC II.i) Hecate herself appears as a fourth witch in *Macbeth*, the Weird Sisters' supervisor. We'll look at Hecate when we explore Shakespeare's witches.

The Huntress

In *A Midsummer Night's Dream*, we only see Diana indirectly, the moon reflected in the eyes of the various characters. She is presented as the cold anti-aphrodisiac, the watery eye, even an Orwellian Big Sister, the ever-vigilant enforcer of chastity. Like an eclipse, we don't get to look straight at her, because a direct glimpse of the divine huntress is deadly.

In Elizabethan England, arguably the most popular classical myth was not about Zeus or Hercules or even Aphrodite, but about the virgin huntress goddess Artemis (whom the Romans called Diana) transforming a peeping-tom named Actaeon into a stag to be hunted by his own dogs. The most famous version of this myth is in the third book of Ovid's *Metamorphoses*.

The story takes place in a deep forest grove where a trickling fountain feeds a pool. "Here, when a-wearied with exciting sport, the Sylvan [forest] goddess loved to come and bathe her virgin beauty in the crystal pool. After Diana entered with her nymphs, she gave her javelin, quiver, and her bow to one accustomed to the care of arms; she gave her mantle to another nymph who stood nearby her as she took it off; two others loosed the sandals from her feet; [a nymph] gathered up the goddess' scattered tresses in a knot;—her own were loosely wantoned on the breeze. Then in their ample urns dipt up the wave and poured it forth."

But on this particular day, a young prince named Actaeon, who had been hunting with his squires and hounds, went strolling alone in the forest. "While they bathed Diana in their streams, Actaeon, wandering through the unknown woods, entered the precincts of that sacred grove; with steps uncertain wandered he as fate directed, for his sport must wait till morn. Soon as he entered where the clear springs welled or trickled from the grotto's walls, the nymphs, now ready for the bath, beheld the man, smote on their breasts, and made the woods resound, suddenly shrieking. Quickly gathered they to shield Diana with their naked forms, but she stood head and shoulders taller than her guards. As clouds bright-tinted by the slanting sun, or purple-dyed Aurora, so appeared Diana's countenance when she was seen.

"Oh, how she wished her arrows were at hand! But only having water, this she took and dashed it on his manly countenance, and sprinkled with the avenging stream his hair, and said these words, presage of future woe; 'Go tell it, if your tongue can tell the tale, your bold eyes saw me stripped of all my robes.' No more she threatened, but she fixed the horns of a great stag firm on his sprinkled brows; she lengthened out his neck; she made his ears sharp at the top; she changed his hands and feet; made long legs of his arms, and covered him with dappled hair—his courage turned to fear." Actaeon ran in terror, and his thirty-three hunting dogs tore him to pieces while he tried in vain to use his human voice. "They gathered round him, and they fixed their snouts deep in his flesh: tore him to pieces, he whose features only as a stag appeared. 'Tis said Diana's fury raged with none abatement till the torn flesh ceased to live."[78]

This story stands out in the context of Ovid's *Metamorphoses*, much of which involves supernatural sexual predation: Olympian gods assaulting mortal women, often in forests.[79] And the titular transformations in the *Metamorphoses* (assault victims turned into animals, vegetables, or minerals) are a means of silencing survivors. The gods would use metamorphosis as the "mute" button on a universal remote control.

But this story of sex and violence is different. Actaeon doesn't seem to mean any harm, he's in the wrong place at the wrong time. But he has nonetheless caught this forbidden glimpse of the goddess's nakedness, penetrated the secret pool in the shrubbery, there's no way to say it that doesn't sound dirty. In viewing her nudity, Actaeon accidentally gains a flash of godlike omniscience, and reduces her to an object. But Diana refuses to be objectified (she's furious that his mental snapshot will become a trophy, something he can tell his friends about) so she reduces him to an animal that can never tell the tale. Now it's *his* turn to be objectified and consumed: he's eaten by dogs, and perhaps by his hunting buddies too. Actaeon the hunter was a predator, then the divine huntress turns him into prey. Not just that, she gives him the full blender-treatment on all three settings: he's muted, mutated, and mutilated. Adding to the humiliation, he's got to run with that ridiculous stag-tail sticking up, displaying his buck nakedness.

Stag-humor aside, we should also take a moment to recall that in Elizabethan England, bloody dismemberment by animals was not just some poetic abstraction or Looney Toons slapstick comedy. This was a time when nobles still hunted with hounds who'd tear foxes and stags apart. Bear-baiting was also a major form of popular entertainment; spectators would cheer as numerous pit bulls ripped into a live bear tied to a stake. The Actaeon story evoked vivid images of blood-spattered animal savagery. And for those who couldn't afford elite hunting trips or the animal arena, there were public executions (by order of the Diana-like virgin Queen) that frequently involved human dismemberment. This could include a traitor's four limbs being tied to horses running in opposite directions, and the neighborhood stray dogs would show up to clean the mess. The stag prince's fairy tale tapped into something primal in an English psyche that was simultaneously enraptured and repulsed by bestial violence.

Elizabethan Emblems of Diana
WORKS BY WHITNEY, MARLOWE, AND JONSON

The story of Diana the virgin goddess really struck a chord in an England ruled by a virgin queen, and Elizabeth promoted this identification by encouraging the inclusion of Diana iconography in her portraits. Like Elizabeth, Diana's mythic chastity was not passive, not a sign that she wasn't desirable. Her virginity was a choice, and she was fiercely protective of it. Diana was really tough—the character of Wonder Woman was named after her. Even Batman respected the danger of this goddess (here I mean the Elizabethan English mythographer, Stephen Batman).

In 1577, "Batman describe[d] Actaeon as 'a man seeking more for vain pleasure and jollity than Virtue,' who was 'for his unmannerly viewing transformed into a Hart and so devoured by his own dogs.'"[80] Actually, that does sound like something Batman might say (and Matt Wagner's 2004 graphic novel *Trinity* contains a scene in which Batman unwittingly stumbles like Actaeon into a forest grove where Diana is bathing. She socks him in the face and he almost gets torn apart by angry Amazons[81]).

Another good example of Actaeon as a cautionary tale can be found in Geoffrey Whitney's 1585 *Choice of Emblems*, an anthology of woodcut images and poems. On page 15 there is a picture of the stag-headed Actaeon being ripped apart by his dogs while the huntress Diana looks on, and this poem:

> "Actàeon here, unhappy man behold,
> When in the well he saw Diana bright,
> With greedy looks, he waxèd over bold,
> That to a stag he was transformèd right,
> Whereat amazed, he thought to run away,
> But straight his hounds did rend him, for their prey.
> By which is meant, that those who do pursue
> Their fancies fond, and things unlawful crave,
> Like brutal beasts appear unto the view,
> And shall at length, Actàeon's [wages] have:
> And as his hounds for their affections base
> Shall them devour, and all their deeds deface."

A few years later, Christopher Marlowe would refer to Actaeon in his 1588 play, *Doctor Faustus*. The sorcerer promised a king that he could conjure a phantasmic pageant about Alexander the Great (like the goddess masque Prospero would later conjure in Shakespeare's *The Tempest*). A heckler from the audience challenged that, if Faustus could accomplish this, "I'll be Actaeon and turn myself into a stag." Faustus replies, "And I'll play Diana, and send you the horns presently," which he does. Stag-horns spring from the man's forehead and the crowd hounds him with laughter. In this context, the man is punished for an attempt to peer behind the curtain of stage magic.

Marlowe would also use the Actaeon story in his play Edward II (circa 1592), to hint about the king's homosexuality:

> "Sometime a lovely boy in Dian's shape,
> With hair that gilds the water as it glides,
> Crownets of pearl about his naked arms,
> And in his sportful hands an olive-tree,
> To hide those parts which men delight to see,
> Shall bathe him in a spring; and there, hard by,
> One like Actæon, peeping through the grove,
> Shall by the angry goddess be transform'd,
> And running in the likeness of an hart,
> By yelping hounds pull'd down, shall seem to die:
> Such things as these best please his majesty."

The more uptight playwright Ben Jonson preferred the stately Virgil to Ovid, considering the *Metamorphoses* to be childish tripe for the commoners. But in 1599, a scandal broke out when the Earl of Essex brashly "burst into the Queen's chamber in his riding-habit (Actaeon's dress) while she had 'her hair about her face.'"[82] He was banished to his country house, accused of an attempted coup, and the queen of all but hearts called the verdict: off with his head. In the midst of this turmoil, Ben Jonson wrote a monologue in his 1600 *Cynthia's Revels*, in which Diana (standing in for the virgin queen Elizabeth) gives her justification:

> "For so Actàeon, by presuming far,
> Did, to our grief, incur a fatal doom...
> But are we therefore judgèd too extreme?

Seems it no crime to enter sacred bowers,
And hallowed places, with impure aspect,
Most lewdly to pollute? Seems it no crime
To brave a deity? Let mortals learn
To make religion of offending heaven.
And not at all to censure powers divine.
To men this argument should stand for firm,
A goddess did it, therefore it was good:
We are not cruèl, nor delight in blood."

There are many other examples of how this myth was interpreted and reinterpreted during the Elizabethan age. To this we can add that the Actaeon scene was also popular in illustrations, paintings, and sculptures. When Shakespeare's Rosalind says, *"I will weep for nothing, like Diana in the fountain,"* (AYL IV.i) she may be referring to the famous fountain at Nonsuch Palace. In *Cymbeline*, the fireplace mantle in a princess's bedroom features an engraving of *"chaste Dian bathing."* (CYM II.iv) Actaeon caught only a momentary glimpse, but the nobles of England could commission massive murals, statues, and fountains depicting the bathing goddess to really get an eye-full at their leisure—and live to tell the tale.

Beyond the Pale
TITUS ANDRONICUS

At the beginning of his career, at about the same time that he wrote *The Comedy of Errors*, Shakespeare also wrote his bloody shock-fest *Titus Andronicus*. Here he focuses on the gruesome elements of the Diana/Actaeon myth, twisting and painfully contorting the story. The Roman General Titus returns from a military campaign against the Goths with prisoners including their queen, Tamora, and her three sons, one of which he immediately sacrifices in vengeance for his own sons slain in battle. Titus sneers at Tamora's pleas for mercy, and thus begins a widening gyre of revenge and atrocity.

Rome's newly crowned Emperor Saturninus is smitten with the goth queen *"that, like the stately Phoebe 'mongst her nymphs, / Dost overshine the gallant'st dames of Rome."* (TA I.i, "Phoebe" meaning Diana) They wed at once and she becomes empress. But his identification of his new bride with Diana is imprecise. She already has sons, and also a lover, Aaron the Moor. The very next day, Titus's daughter Lavinia and her fiancé Bassianus are out walking in the woods and catch the new Empress and her lover making the beast with two backs.

> *"BASSIANUS. Who have we here? Rome's royal Emperess,*
> *Unfurnish'd of her well-beseeming troop?*
> *Or is it Dian, habited like her,*
> *Who hath abandonèd her holy groves*
> *To see the general hunting in this forest?*
> *TAMORA. ...Had I the pow'r that some say Dian had,*
> *Thy temples should be planted presently*
> *With horns, as was Actàeon's; and the hounds*
> *Should drive upon thy new-transformèd limbs,*
> *Unmannerly intruder as thou art!*
> *LAVINIA. Under your patience, gentle Emperess,*
> *'Tis thought you have a goodly gift in horning...*
> *Jove shield your husband from his hounds to-day!*
> *'Tis pity they should take him for a stag."* (TA II.iii)

In this playful banter, they take turns twisting the Actaeon myth like a Rubik's Cube. Bassianus contrasts the adulteress with Diana's chastity, Tamora wishes she had the power to make antlers sprout from Bassianus's forehead and dogs tear him to pieces. Titus's daughter Lavinia wittily responds that the empress's infidelity is turning her husband to a cuckold, "horny" in the sense of sexually unfulfilled, with the implication that he'll be hounded by his servants when word gets out.

Tamora is not amused. She sics her two sons on them. For the crime of having seen her nakedness, Bassianus is murdered and Lavinia is assaulted, her hands are hacked off and her tongue is cut out. Then one of the attackers taunts her by paraphrasing Diana's words to Actaeon: *"So now go tell, an if thy tongue can speak."* (TA II.iv)[83] Lavinia will have her revenge, assisting in a macabre plot that culminates in Tamora eating her slaughtered sons' testicles, but that relates to a different Ovidian myth. We'll return to Tamora, Lavinia, and Titus later.

With *Titus Andronicus* out of the way, Shakespeare has a lot more fun with the Actaeon story. When Petruchio first meets Kate in *The Taming of the Shrew*, he jokes about being a mortal in the presence of a goddess:

> *"Did ever Dian so become a grove*
> *As Kate this chamber with her princely gait?*
> *O! be thou Dian, and let her be Kate,*
> *And then let Kate be chaste, and Dian sportful!"* (TS II.i)

This is a bit confusing. I think he's saying he wishes Kate were naked like Diana but as wild as a shrew-mouse. On the opposite end of the spectrum from the brash Petruchio, the bashful Orsino in *Twelfth Night* uses the image of Actaeon as hart to describe his deer-in-headlights infatuation with the lady Olivia: *"That instant was I turned into a hart, / And my desires, like fell and cruèl hounds, / E'er since pursue me."* (I.i) Then he's distracted by a fresh-faced young man, *"Diana's lip is not more smooth and rubious,"* who turns out to be a maiden in disguise.[84] In *A Midsummer Night's Dream*, the bumbling Bottom will stumble into Titania's bower. Shakespeare carefully distinguishes Titania from Diana, but like Actaeon, Bottom will be unable to tell the tale: *"The eye of man hath not heard, the ear of man hath not seen, man's hand is not able to taste, his tongue to conceive, nor his heart to report, what my dream was."* (MND IV.i)

Dogs were considered Diana's disciples, since they howl at the moon. Ovid gives an exhaustive list of the pack who tore Actaeon apart, especially the first two who caught him, "a hounde of Crete, the other was of Spart." (Book 3, Golding translation) This seems to be on Shakespeare's mind when Hippolyta recalls a hunting trip *"when in a wood of Crete they bay'd the bear with hounds of Sparta,"* and Theseus responds, *"My hounds are bred out of the Spartan kind."* (MND I.i) These dogs don't bite the hand that feeds, but later Shakespeare will refer to Iago as a *"Spartan dog"* for betraying his commander Othello, and the assassins in *Julius Caesar* will be likened to *"hounds"* tearing a human *"hart"* apart.[85]

Virgin Huntress
LOVE'S LABOUR'S LOST |
ALL'S WELL THAT ENDS WELL

In *Love's Labour's Lost*, a French princess is dispatched by her father on a diplomatic mission to Navarre in Spain. Or so she was told. During the tedious negotiations, it gradually becomes apparent that her father has fallen behind in some mortgage payments, and the princess realizes that she has been sent in lieu of the money. Her father imagines a royal marriage pact will cancel the debt. The king of Navarre is not in on this (he and his three buddies are launching a ridiculous attempt to live as scholastic hermits) but he lodges the princess and her three friends in his private gaming reserve.

Soon all ivory tower illusions are abandoned and the king and his huntsmen begin playfully raiding the ladies' forest sanctum. They're fairly harmless, it's all sleepaway-camp hijinks. Elizabethan fops are the clowns of the animal kingdom. But they can still get a little creepy, especially when they imagine themselves as Cupid's army, advancing with phallic battle flagpoles: *"Saint Cupid, then! and, soldiers, to the field! / Advance your standards, and upon them, lords."*

So, the heroines take up arms, literally, practicing archery.[86] And as the princess muses on killing stags for sport, the topic subtly shifts to targeting men:

> *"Then, forester, my friend, where is the bush*
> *That we must stand and play the murderer in?*
> *...But come, the bow. Now mercy goes to kill,*
> *And shooting well is then accounted ill;*
> *Thus will I save my credit in the shoot:*
> *Not wounding, pity would not let me do't;*
> *If wounding, then it was to show my skill,*
> *That more for praise than purpose meant to kill...*
> *Only for praise; and praise we may afford*
> *To any lady that subdues a lord."* (LLL IV.i)

Her butler Boyet responds, *"My lady goes to kill horns; but, if thou marry, / Hang me by the neck, if horns that year miscarry."* (LLL IV.i) He bets his life that if the princess weds the king, she'll make a trophy of him and dominate him sexually. The princess's sadistic friend Rosaline delights in the idea of turning a young bachelor into a stag: *"That same Berowne I'll torture ere I go... How I would make him fawn, and beg, and seek."* (LLL V.ii) The sadist has met her match in the masochistic Berowne, who beckons, *"Here stand I, lady – dart thy skill at me... Cut me to pieces with thy keen conceit."* (LLL V.ii) The four wooers continue bumbling like Actaeon into the ladies' forest sanctuary and, in the end, the virgin huntress and her nymphs banish them to a year in exile. This is Shakespeare's only comedy that does not end in wedding and bedding, hence the title, *Love's Labour* [is] *Lost.*

Speaking of "Lost," Shakespeare also wrote a play called *"Love's Labour's Won."* We know this from two registries of play productions, but no script by this title has yet been found. Perhaps there was a direct sequel in which the four couples reunited a year later, but it's hard to imagine there would have been enough story left to make an entire play. It's possible that *"Love's Labour's Won"* was an alternate title for a comedy later published under the name of *Much Ado About Nothing* or *The Taming of the Shrew,* or revised and re-released as *All's Well That Ends Well.*

All's Well That Ends Well centers on a virgin huntress named Helena who sets an elaborate series of traps to ensnare an arrogant nobleman named Bertram. As scheming strategists go, Helena rivals Edmund and Richard III, and in fierce determination she could take on Lady Macbeth. But her heart is in the right place. She really likes this guy and goes on a mythic fairy tale hero-quest to prove she's worthy of him (really, to prove this to herself). She wins him right off the bat, betting her life that she can cure a king's illness. In reward, the king grants her a choice of husbands: Bertram is trapped.

Bertram fears his bride's powerful eroticism and flees their wedding night. His insecure masculinity longs for the hunt, both in warfare (*"War's no strife /* [compared] *to the dark house and the detested wife"*) and the sexual predation of vulnerable maidens, what some might call "chasing young tail." Deployed in a foreign land, he becomes fixated on a young virgin named Diana, determined to win her maidenhead as a trophy. The identification of this virgin with Diana is introduced with Bertram's misunderstanding of her name: he calls her "Fontibell," meaning beauty in the fountain:

> *"BERTRAM. They told me that your name was Fontibell.*
> *DIANA. No, my good lord, Diana.*
> *BERTRAM. Titled goddess;*
> *And worth it, with addition! But, fair soul,*
> *In your fine frame hath love no quality?*
> *If the quick fire of youth light not your mind,*
> *You are no maiden, but a monument."* (AWTEW IV.ii)

His provocative jab that she is like a statue may remind us of Rosalind in *As You Like It*, telling her wooer *"I will weep for nothing, like Diana in the fountain."*

But the predatory Bertram is pursued by Helena, who stalks and hunts him, and finally catches him by *becoming* the virginal Diana in a darkened sanctum. Bertram has been stalking a young maiden named Diana who agrees to lure him into a trap. Helena takes her place, and the blinded Bertram unknowingly impregnates his own abandoned bride. Bertram-as-Actaeon penetrates Helena-as-Diana's grove, the hunter becomes the prey, and he is captured. When Bertram finally admits defeat, accepting Helena as his wife, her last line in the play is a threat to hunt *and kill* him if he ever chases young women again: *"If it appear not plain, and prove untrue, / Deadly divorce step between me and you!"*[87]

Helena's dogged pursuit of Bertram may call to mind that other spurned Helena in *A Midsummer Night's Dream*, stalking Demetrius through the forest, wishing she could be his *"spaniel"* (perhaps another subtle reference to the dogs chasing Actaeon). But Shakespeare endows the Helena of *All's Well That Ends Well* with the cold, calculated cunning he usually reserves for archvillains. Too bad he made Bertram such a toad—it's nice to see Helena capture her prey, but it's hard to say the story *Ends Well*.

Buck, Buck, Buck
The Merry Wives of Windsor

Because the Actaeon legend involved a woman causing horns to sprout from a man's head, it also became linked with the concept of the horned cuckold, the gullible husband of an adulteress. Shakespeare's *The*

Merry Wives of Windsor is about two vivacious housewives whose mirth is misunderstood by men who see playfulness as a sign of promiscuity.

One of the husbands, Mr. Ford, is warned to *"Prevent, or go thou, like Sir Actaeon he, with Ringwood at thy heels. O, odious is the name! ... The horn, I say."* (MWW II.i) Ford fears that, like Actaeon pursued by dogs, he will be hounded by his neighbors. Already jealous and suspicious by nature, he goes absolutely cuckoo about cuckoldry. When confronted about this madness, he argues that his friend Mr. Page is not suspicious enough, comparing him to *"a secure and wilful Actaeon; and to these violent proceedings all my neighbours shall cry aim."* (MWW III.ii) The script is full of *"buck"* puns. When Mrs. Ford mentions *"bucking"* (bleaching) the laundry, her husband sputters about becoming a deer: *"Buck? I would I could wash myself of the buck! Buck, buck, buck! ay, buck! I warrant you, buck; and of the season too, it shall appear."* (MWW III.iii)

Mr. Ford's paranoia is not entirely unfounded. The lusty knight Falstaff has come to town, a poacher and trophy-hunting sexual predator determined to get rich as a jiggling, juggling gigolo. And when he learns of these two titular Merry Wives, he decides that he will pursue both of them. As Mrs. Ford and Mrs. Page plot to humiliate him for his lascivious advances, one of them recalls an old legend:

> *"MRS. FORD. There is an old tale goes that Herne the Hunter,*
> *Sometime a keeper here in Windsor Forest,*
> *Doth all the winter-time, at still midnight,*
> *Walk round about an oak, with great ragg'd horns;*
> *And there he blasts the tree, and takes the cattle,*
> *And makes milch-kine yield blood, and shakes a chain*
> *In a most hideous and dreadful manner.*
> *You have heard of such a spirit, and well you know*
> *The superstitious idle-headed eld*
> *Receiv'd, and did deliver to our age,*
> *This tale of Herne the Hunter for a truth.*
> *MRS. PAGE. Why yet there want not many that do fear*
> *In deep of night to walk by this Herne's oak.*
> *But what of this?*
> *MRS. FORD. Marry, this is our device –*
> *That Falstaff at that oak shall meet with us,*

Disguis'd, like Herne, with huge horns on his head."
(MWW IV.iv, "milch-kine" meaning dairy cows)

Ancient legends of an antlered man chained to a tree (captive consort to a huntress-goddess) had local variations in numerous Northern European cultures. Sir James Frazer compares various parallel versions of it in *The Golden Bough,* in which he writes that the myth of Actaeon is one variant of this archetypal narrative. The primary example Frazer uses is Virbius, another name of Theseus and Hippolyta's son Hippolytus, torn apart by mares and resurrected by Diana, who keeps him as her captive consort tethered to an oak. Anyone who manages to kill him gets to take his place.

England's local version of this seems to have been connected with the horned trickster Robin Goodfellow, also known as Robin Hud or Robin Hood ("Hud" meaning a log from a sacred oak tree[88]). In early folk legends, his beloved Marian was not a damsel in distress, but a huntress. A ballad from the early 1600s describes her as being like the goddess Diana:

> "His lovèd Marian,
> Was ever constant known, which wheresoe'er she came,
> Was sovereign of the woods, chief lady of the game:
> Her clothes tucked to the knee, and dainty braided hair,
> With bow and quiver armed, she wandered here and there
> Amongst the forest wild; Diana never knew
> Such pleasure, nor such harts as Mariana slew."[89]

In *The Merry Wives of Windsor,* Shakespeare uses two Robin characters: the deer-hunter Falstaff, who compares himself to Robin Hood (and has a squire named Robin), and a cameo by Robin Goodfellow, also known as Puck. For the horned hunter by the oak, Shakespeare uses the name "Herne," from the Old English "Cern" meaning horn (and core name of the European pagan deity Cernunnos).

Falstaff leaps at the merry wives' role-play proposition and arrives at Herne's Oak by moonlight wearing antlers. In an early version reprinted in the First Quarto, Falstaff wears a full stag mask: *"Enter sir John with a Bucks head upon him,"* and Sir Hugh comments, *"See I have spied one by good luck / his bodie man, his head a buck."* (MWW V.v)[90] The two wives he's been stalking appear there in the wood and excite him with talk of a threesome. He gleefully exclaims *"Divide me like a brib'd buck, each a haunch; I will keep my sides to myself, my shoulders for the fellow of this walk, and my horns I bequeath your husbands."* (MWW V.v)

Wearing antlers, Falstaff thinks he can become simultaneously bestial and celestial: he refers to Jupiter taking the form of a bull to seduce Europa. And in this forest grove he believes he can behold the nakedness of two chaste wives, be the meat in a double Diana sandwich, achieve Actaeon's forbidden glimpse, and live to tell the tale. Then he's suddenly surrounded by dancing fairies (village children in disguise) who torture him like Actaeon's hounds.

> *"FAIRY QUEEN. Fairies, black, grey, green, and white,*
> *You moonshine revellers, and shades of night...*
> *And 'Honi soit qui mal y pense' write...* [Latin: "evil be to him who thinks evil"]
> *EVANS. But, stay. I smell a man of middle earth...*
> *PUCK. Vile worm, thou wast o'erlook'd even in thy birth...*
> *FAIRY QUEEN. Corrupt, corrupt, and tainted in desire!*
> *About him, fairies; sing a scornful rhyme;*
> *And, as you trip, still pinch him to your time.*
> *[FAIRIES SING] Fie on sinful fantasy! Fie on lust and luxury!*
> *Lust is but a bloody fire, kindled with unchaste desire...*
> *Pinch him and burn him and turn him about,*
> *Till candles and star-light and moonshine be out."* (MWW V.v)

There's a fascinating parallel with *A Midsummer Night's Dream* here, as if we're encountering Helena and Hermia at a later stage in life, when once again they must resolve their problems with a moonlit trip to the forest. Titania and Puck even show up to help out. Mrs. Page and Mrs. Ford punish Falstaff for his presumptuous lust, proving that *"wives may be merry and yet honest, too."* (MWW IV.ii)

Shakespeare's use of the Actaeon myth here links back to the identification of Queen Elizabeth with the virgin goddess Diana. Apparently, the Queen had requested that he write a play in honor of the Order of Garter Knights, a fraternity of royal retainers sworn to uphold the chastity and majesty of the queen and defend her reputation from any slander. Their emblem and Latin motto, *Honi soit qui mal y pense*, "evil be to him who thinks evil," derive from an old story in which an English queen's garter fell during a royal procession and King Edward III picked it up, shooting nasty glances around and cursing anyone who'd peeked at it.[91] Thus, a queen's garter became symbolic of her virtue, somewhat like a king's crown symbolizing his wisdom. Furthermore, Elizabeth specified that the play must contain Falstaff, whom Shakespeare had already once called *"so fat a deer,"* (1H4 V.iv) so giving him Actaeon's antlers was a natural choice.

Diana Takes the Stage
PERICLES, PRINCE OF TYRE

The moon goddess Diana is benevolent in *A Midsummer Night's Dream*, but in *Pericles, Prince of Tyre*, we find that she can also be vindictive. The script of *Pericles, Prince of Tyre* was apparently begun by a pamphleteer (a blogger, in modern terms) called George Wilkins. A romantic prince in search of love evades a deadly Sphinx-like riddle, then enters a joust to win the hand of a virtuous princess. When the Princess Thaisa accepts Pericles's proposal, her father lies to her other suitors, saying she's become a temporary nun:

> "One twelve moons more she'll wear Diana's livery;
> This by the eye of Cynthia hath she vow'd,
> And on her virgin honour will not break it."
> (PER II.v, likely written by George Wilkins)

This blasphemous untruth, using Diana's name in vain (actually *two* names, since she's also called Cynthia) curses the marriage. Their honeymoon voyage is struck by storm, lunar tides turn against them, and it seems that all is lost.

But in the midst of this literary shipwreck, something of a miracle occurs. Shakespeare takes the wheel of writing this script. It seems George Wilkins, a lowlife innkeeper, pimp, and all around "unsavory fellow"[92] was also an aspiring playwright who churned out the first two acts of *Pericles, Prince of Tyre*. Then his friend Shakespeare penned the second half, rechristening the characters with a storm at sea (like the storms in *The Comedy of Errors* and *The Tempest*). Unfortunately, this is not the sprightly Shakespeare of *A Midsummer Night's Dream* and *Macbeth*, it's the older embittered Shakespeare of *Timon* and *Cymbeline*, but still it's Shakespeare.

How Shakespeare came to be associated with a brothel keeper is anybody's guess, but we know from official court documents of the 1612 case of "Bellott vs. Mountjoy" (And yes, Mary Mountjoy does seem to have been a legal name, not a professional alias) that both Shakespeare and Wilkins testified in a lawsuit concerning a wig maker's dubious dowry. Anyhow, moving on.

Pericles's bride Thaisa seems to die in childbirth aboard the storm-tossed boat, and she's thrown overboard in a sealed casket. Awakening later in a druggist's shop, her first thought is of the goddess: *"O dear Diana, where am I? Where's my* [husband]*? What world is this?"* (PER III.ii) She seems to realize that Diana has condemned the relationship, and decides to do penance:

> *"THAISA. But since King Pericles,*
> *My wedded lord, I ne'er shall see again,*
> *A vestal livery will I take me to,*
> *And never more have joy.*
> *CERIMON. Madam, if this you purpose as ye speak,*
> *Diana's temple is not distant far,*
> *Where you may abide till your date expire."* (PER III.iv)

Meanwhile, the heartbroken Pericles leaves their newborn daughter Marina to be raised by friends of his. Unfortunately, they have a daughter of their own, outshined by Marina in musicianship, embroidery, and beauty, so the foster mother turns into a wicked stepmother right out of Snow White, charging an assassin to murder the girl while she's out picking flowers. But before he can do this she's kidnapped by pirates, whisked away on their ship, and sold into a distant whorehouse.

During her brothel job orientation lecture (apparently written by Shakespeare himself, although again his familiarity with bawdy-houses is inexplicable), Marina mutters a prayer to the goddess: *"If fires be hot, knives sharp, or waters deep, / Untied I still my virgin knot will keep. / Diana, aid my purpose!"* (PER IV.ii) And indeed, Diana blesses the maiden with the magical power to sermonize customers until they shrivel with guilt. She earns her keep by tutoring local debutantes in the arts of lute playing, sewing, and making men feel bad about themselves.[93]

An aging Pericles is brought ashore, sickly and sunken. Someone gets the idea that this local celebrity, a multi-talented virginal virtuoso renaissance woman can cheer him up in one way or another, and at last the father and daughter are reunited. Then Diana herself comes to Pericles in a vision:

> *"DIANA. My temple stands in Ephesus: hie thee thither,*
> *And do upon mine altar sacrifice.*
> *There, when my maiden priests are met together,*
> *Before the people all,*
> *Reveal how thou at sea didst lose thy wife:*
> *To mourn thy crosses, with thy daughter's, call*
> *And give them repetition to the life.*
> *Perform my bidding, or thou livest in woe:*
> *Do it, and happy; by my silver bow!*
> *Awake and tell thy dream."* (PER V.i)

With the *Pericles, Prince of Tyre* finale, Shakespeare returns to Ephesus, about fifteen years after writing *The Comedy of Errors*. Once again, the couple separated in a storm is reunited, the priestess turning out to be the long-lost wife and mother. But this time, Shakespeare can make explicit what he could only imply at the start of his career: Ephesus is the city of Diana. The goddess has separated the family for fourteen years, but also protected them. Thaisa is still chaste, Pericles has been faithful, and Marina is still miraculously virginal despite the human trafficking of pirates and pimps. Thaisa is released from her vestal vow, remarrying Pericles, and he offers sacrifice to the goddess, *"Pure Dian, bless thee for thy vision! I / Will offer night-oblations to thee."*[94] (PER V.iii)

The Classical Diana is a complex figure, likely a composite of multiple goddesses from various ancient eras and regions. As the huntress Artemis and moon-goddess Phoebe she is older than Classical Greece and its Olympian pantheon (in Greek mythology she is among the Titans, from the generation before Zeus and his mythic siblings). As a moon goddess she has multiple manifestations, or phases, representing youth, maturity, and wisdom. And in the city of Ephesus, Diana seems to have been combined with the Turkish mother goddess, Cybele. Shakespeare highlights different aspects of Diana in different plays, but presents her as a single dynamic deity. She is clearly his favorite goddess, and when we gather all of these kaleidoscopic glances, we encounter one of his most fascinating characterizations.

Shakespeare's devotion to Diana also shines an interesting light on some of his daring heroines. The author loved writing maidens who could be fierce and independent, sometimes aggressive virgin huntresses like the Helenas in *A Midsummer Night's Dream* and *All's Well That Ends Well*, and Rosalind in *As You Like it*. He frequently thought of the Actæon myth when writing stories of women, defending their privacy by punishing intruders. And in his multigenerational epics, he conjured Diana as the virgin mother archetype to sort out tangled problems in *The Comedy of Errors* and *Pericles, Prince of Tyre*.

Venus

One Hit Wonder
VENUS AND ADONIS

Shakespeare did not publish the scripts of his plays.

Theater enthusiasts in his time could buy deluxe editions of Ben Jonson's scripts with behind-the-scenes essays and commentaries by the author, roughly the equivalent of bonus features on a DVD. But Shakespeare didn't authorize any releases. Perhaps it's for the best—when Elizabethan playwrights published their dramas, they would often edit out comic subplots to make their tragedies more formally correct, and it's sad to imagine Shakespeare's great tragedies without the peasants and fools saying idiotic things on the sidelines. Part of what makes Shakespeare so much fun is that no matter where or when his stories are set, British bumpkins keep popping up with a sort of Mystery Science Theater 3000 commentary.

Some of Shakespeare's plays circulated in bootleg form, however. An actor's script might be smuggled to a printer, or in some cases, people seem to have transcribed scripts during shows. There were numerous variant transcripts of *Hamlet* in circulation, and editors have spent centuries debating and hybridizing them. They explain this in the notes we don't read in the backs of scholarly editions, the pages that look like a coded rocket launch manual. But when Shakespeare died in 1616, he had not personally authorized the publication of a single script, and the bootlegs in circulation were nowhere near a full set. Jonathan Bate notes, "Had it not been for the diligence of his fellow-actors in seeing into print the First Folio of his collected comedies, tragedies, and histories in 1623, *Julius Caesar, Twelfth Night, Measure for Measure, Macbeth, Antony and Cleopatra, The Tempest,* and a dozen more would have been lost."[95]

Production lists contain references to Shakespeare's *Love's Labour's Won*, which may have been later published under another name, perhaps *Much Ado About Nothing* or *All's Well That Ends Well*. He likely wrote a play called *Dido and Aeneas,* but it may not have been staged—a monologue that Hamlet requests from the players is all we have of that.[96] And he may have collaborated with Fletcher on *Cardenio,* based on a subplot from Cervantes' *Don Quixote,* but the text is lost.[97] Why Shakespeare didn't publish his scripts is a mystery for the ages, although I like to think that it's because he believed a play should be heard and not read.

Shakespeare did publish during his lifetime, however. His 1593 epic poem *Venus and Adonis* was a smash hit. Reprinted eight times within a decade, it was one of the bestsellers of the era. During this first half of his career, if you asked people on the streets of London who "Shakespeare" was, they would have likely responded that he was the guy who'd penned that wanton pamphlet about Venus. It was written in a year when theaters were shuttered due to the plague, when he seems to have considered abandoning the common stage for the respectable mantle of the poet.

He'd already established himself with the *Henry VI* trilogy, *Richard III, Two Gentlemen* and perhaps an early version of *Hamlet* that got laughed off the stage, but Shakespeare refers to *Venus and Adonis* as *"the first heir of my invention."* And he publicly snubs theatergoers in its fancy Latin epigram, a quote from Ovid's *Amores,* loosely translated as: "Let the vulgar crowd admire worthless things. May the poet god Apollo lead me to the Muses' springs." After its success, he followed it up with another epic poem, *The Rape of Lucrece,* a companion piece, not so much a sibling as a placenta. Then the theaters re-opened and Shakespeare returned to scriptwriting. It seems he leveraged the income and celebrity of the two publications to become co-owner of the company for which he'd written and acted.

The basic plot of *Venus and Adonis* comes from book ten of Ovid's *Metamorphoses,* where the love goddess seduces a young man who then dies in a hunting accident. Shakespeare adds drama by having Adonis refuse Venus's advances, giving the young man characteristics of Ovid's Narcissus, who could only love himself, and Hermaphroditus, whose youthful insecurities caused him to reject the sexually aggressive nymph, Salmacis.

Shakespeare also enhances the character of Venus, giving her the poetic prowess of his sonnets. His strong and sympathetic portrait of Venus is particularly interesting because Shakespeare was such a devotee of Venus's nemesis, the virginal Diana. He would spend the next twenty years searching for Diana, from *The Comedy of Errors* to *Pericles, Prince of Tyre* (when he finally finds her and brings her onto the stage). And throughout this quest, Venus as the anti-Diana will be increasingly marginalized and demonized in his plays, until she is finally banished once and for all at the end of *The Tempest*. But here at the start of his career, he brings the love goddess to vibrant life with boundless energy, breadth of creativity, and depth of character.

Fawning
VENUS AND ADONIS

To say that Venus, whom the Greeks called Aphrodite, is a "love goddess" is not quite accurate. Juno was the goddess of marital devotion and Diana was arguably the goddess of let's-be-friends flirtation. Venus was the goddess of sexual desire, rampant and anarchic lust. While Diana's temple was run by nuns chanting to the cold moon, the priestesses of Venus's shrines combined the sacred and profane, conducting illicit rituals—the temple was a brothel. When Venus sets her sights on Adonis, she doesn't want him to croon hymns and sacrifice small animals, she wants to be worshiped in-the-flesh with sacramental sex. Unfortunately for her, Shakespeare puts her in the ring with a young Puritan (Adonis is not necessarily Christian, but his insistence on channeling his sexual energy into the hunt aligns him with the virgin huntress Diana). Shakespeare's *Venus and Adonis* is built on a great irony: *"She's love, she loves, and yet she is not loved."* (V&A ln 610)

Venus is not only the personification of human sexuality, she is also a force of nature, arousing the generative fertility of the earth. In one her speeches she becomes the land itself, a pre-agricultural paradise like the Golden Age described in Ovid's *Metamorphoses*, a time before people killed each other with swords and ravaged the land with plowshares: "The fertile earth as yet was free, untouched by spade or plough, / And yet it yielded of itself of everything enough." (Book 1, Golding translation updated) The polymorphously perverse goddess echoes this in describing her own body as a topographic map of erogenous zones, curvaceous peaks and valleys, cascading with abundance. Enclosing him in her strong, pale arms she whispers:

> *"'Fondling,' she saith, 'since I have hemm'd thee here*
> *Within the circuit of this ivory pale,*
> *I'll be a park, and thou shalt be my deer;*
> *Feed where thou wilt, on mountain or in dale:*
> *Graze on my lips, and if those hills be dry,*
> *Stray lower, where the pleasant fountains lie.*
> *Within this limit is relief enough,*
> *Sweet bottom grass and high delightful plain,*
> *Round rising hillocks, brakes obscure and rough,*
> *To shelter thee from tempest and from rain:*
> *Then be my deer, since I am such a park,*
> *No dog shall rouse thee, though a thousand bark.'"*
> (V&A ln 229-240)

If we can get our minds out of the gutter, we'll see allusions to the story of Diana transforming a hunter into a deer to be torn apart by his dogs.[98] Venus beckons Adonis into a lush grove with *"pleasant fountains"* in which he can graze like a stag without fear of hounds. There's an irony here: Actaeon was killed by his gathered hounds, and Adonis's hunting dogs will scatter, leaving him to be killed by a wild boar. So much for "man's best friend."

Venus describes her body as a fertile garden of delight, but also a *"park"* which, in Shakespeare's time, meant a private royal hunting preserve. In the *Metamorphoses*, Venus follows Adonis as a groupie, dressing like Diana: "Bare kneed with garment tuckèd up according to the wont [style] / Of Phoebe, and she cheered the hounds with hallowing like a hunt, / Pursuing game." (Book 10, Golding Translation updated) Shakespeare leaves these details out because his Venus is boldly bare. Actaeon died for a forbidden glimpse, but Adonis is not allowed to look away.[99] Venus fawns over Adonis with a medley of metaphors. Adonis as a deer can freely feed on her, but she will also be stalking him; both will play hunter and prey, mutually consuming and being consumed.

Venus's down-to-earth metaphor is also played out in action as the goddess keeps literally falling down to earth, often to comic effect. Knowing Adonis to be a Puritan, she presumes that he must prefer the missionary position, so finds every opportunity to present herself flat on her back.[100] And she's continually shocked that this should fail to get a rise out of him: *"Who sees his true-love in her naked bed, / Teaching the sheets a whiter hue than white, / But, when his glutton eye so full hath fed, / His other agents* [don't] *aim at like delight?"* (V&A ln 397-400) At one point she even plays possum, pretending to be dead, and lures him into administering medieval CPR:

> *"For on the grass she lies as she were slain,*
> *Till his breath breatheth life in her again.*
> *He wrings her nose, he strikes her on the cheeks,*
> *He bends her fingers, holds her pulses hard,*
> *He chafes her lips; a thousand ways he seeks*
> *To mend the hurt that his unkindness marr'd:*
> *He kisses her; and she, by her good will,*
> *Will never rise, so he will kiss her still."* (V&A ln 473-480)

It's a moment of slapstick comedy, but with a creepy undertone. The only time we see Adonis take an interest in her is when he thinks she's unconscious. And once the sleeping beauty rises, he shrinks away again in fear. So, she switches tactics. Venus will try almost every trick in the book, but even at her most aggressive she must feign passivity. Unlike the male Olympian gods, she cannot force this mortal, but must coerce his consent.

> *"She sinketh down, still hanging by his neck,*
> *He on her belly falls, she on her back.*
> *Now is she in the very lists of love,*
> *Her champion mounted for the hot encounter:*
> *All is imaginary she doth prove,*
> *He will not manage her, although he mount her;*
> *That worse than Tantalus' is her annoy,*
> *To clip Elysium and to lack her joy."* (V&A ln 593-600)

Tantalus was cursed by the gods to spend eternity confined and hungry with fruits dangling just out of reach, hence the modern word "tantalize." Venus, despite presenting herself as low-hanging-fruit for Adonis, finds that even when she gets him on top of her, he's still out of reach. As her arousal builds to fever pitch, Venus, who described herself as a peaceful park, becomes volcanic with tremors: *"My boding heart pants, beats, and takes no rest, / But like an earthquake, shakes thee on my breast."* (V&A ln 647-648)

Love's Insecurities
VENUS AND ADONIS

Venus is larger than life, both emotionally and physically. She is all peaks and valleys. She is dramatic, beckoning Adonis toward an immersive theatrical (and sexual) experience, and often becomes melodramatic, even campy. If this were on the stage, Venus could not be played by a little boy. The role would be better suited to a full-on brawny and boisterous drag queen. Or perhaps Bette Middler, stalking young Macaulay Culkin.

"Venus's [verbal] self-portraiture is of an irresistible, insatiable sexual being in a permanent state of arousal," Pauline Kiernan wrote, and "our overpowering sense of Venus's physical body is one of heavy weight and enormous volume."[101] She is a muscular giantess who can physically lift this teenager and haul his thousand-pound horse.

> *"Being so enrag'd, desire doth lend her force*
> *Courageously to pluck him from his horse.*
> *Over one arm the lusty courser's rein,*
> *Under her other was the tender boy."*
> (V&A ln 29-32, "enrag'd" meaning inflamed or engorged, not angry)

We later discover she's insecure about her weight. Adonis finds her overbearing, and she starts babbling about how she's so light that she doesn't even make an impression on the ground:

> *"Bid me discourse, I will enchant thine ear,*
> *Or like a fairy, trip upon the green,*

Or like a nymph, with long dishevell'd hair,
Dance on the sands, and yet no footing seen.
Love is a spirit all compact of fire,
Not gross to sink, but light, and will aspire.
Witness this primrose bank whereon I lie:
These forceless flowers like sturdy trees support me;
Two strengthless doves will draw me through the sky,
From morn till night, even where I list to sport me.
Is love so light, sweet boy, and may it be
That thou shouldst think it heavy unto thee?" (V&A ln 145-156)

In Shakespeare's plays, the ideal woman is built like a prepubescent boy. Yes, his heroines had to be played by boys, but the texts themselves favor scrawny girls. Shakespeare's suitors are generally looking for a nymphet in her mid-teens. They prefer blondes, someone *"fair"* but not overly fertile—they never mention child-birthing hips and impressive breasts. They want a girl who's abundantly endowed with a dowery and inheritance; they're always eyeing her father's assets.

In this poem, Shakespeare equips Venus with the full deluxe model package, statuesque and voluptuous, and Adonis *"with her plenty press'd"* is just horrified. He's like Dromio running from the kitchen wench, whom he calls a *"mountain of mad flesh."* (COE IV.iv) Toward the end of the poem, when Venus is heartbroken, the narrator at last sympathetically agrees that she's not too heavy: *"The grass stoops not, she treads on it so light."* (V&A ln 1028)

And then there's the age difference—she's thousands of years older than him. Some commentators see in *Venus and Adonis* "a jibe at that old comic standby, the voraciousness of a mature woman."[102] But is she really some cougar who thinks seducing this boy-toy will restore her youth? No, she's the immortal Venus. Her youth is annually renewed:

"Were I hard-favour'd, foul, or wrinkled old,
Ill-nurtur'd, crooked, churlish, harsh in voice,
O'erworn, despisèd, rheumatic, and cold,
Thick-sighted, barren, lean, and lacking juice,
Then mightst thou pause, for then I were not for thee;
But having no defects, why dost abhor me?

Thou canst not see one wrinkle in my brow,
Mine eyes are grey and bright, and quick in turning;
My beauty as the spring doth yearly grow,
My flesh is soft and plump, my marrow burning." (V&A ln 133-142)

In case we need a second opinion, the Sun god is just at that moment shifting the shade so he can get a better view, wishing he could put Adonis in the solar chariot and take his place beside Venus.[103]

Venus, like the earth, is rejuvenated each spring–our frisky month of April is named after Aphrodite. So physically she's as fresh and new as Adonis, and yet there's a more significant age difference between them: she comes from another era. Catherina Belsey writes, "In a true golden age pleasure is indeed lawful and according to the will of nature, but in a fallen age nature works contrarily, encouraging pleasure on the one hand while denying it on the other. Venus might be regarded less as a goddess than as a creature from a perfect world who has strayed into a lesser one and has to adjust to different principles."[104] Venus comes from the primal age of pleasure and mutual satisfaction, Shakespeare's Adonis is an uptight Elizabethan Puritan (and ironically *he's* the one we would call "old fashioned.") They happen to meet in the middle, a Roman poet's fantasy realm. Ultimately, they're just too different.

The hot pursuit of this young guy is not a symptom of Venus's midlife crisis. Although neither brings it up, it's true that she's married and has a son about his age, named Cupid. But she's a Classical Goddess, and what we call "scandal" the Greeks called scripture. Venus's midlife crisis occurs at the end of the poem—when Adonis dies, she goes through stages of embitterment, but finally emerges with a new acceptance of maturity.

Erotic Rhetoric
VENUS AND ADONIS

But let's not just gawk and gape at Venus's body; she also has an incredibly fertile mind. Venus is a genius of erotic oration, an acrobatic rhetorical contortionist. Of the poem's 1,200 lines, she speaks nearly 550, and Shakespeare gives her the reins of his full range of love and logic, seduction, philosophy, biology, and legalism.[105]

The first twist, of course, is that she's a female courting a male. Shakespeare milks this for gender-bending comedy: She *"like a bold-fac'd suitor 'gins to woo him"* and he demurely declines, blushing with *"maiden burning of his cheeks."* (V&A ln 6, 50) Like the Sonneteer obsessing over the genetic destiny of a beautiful boy, she entreats Adonis to join in Nature's spiral dance of reproduction:

> *"Seeds spring from seeds, and beauty breedeth beauty;*
> *Thou wast begot; to get it is thy duty.*
> *Upon the earth's increase why shouldst thou feed,*
> *Unless the earth with thy increase be fed?*
> *By law of nature thou art bound to breed,*
> *That thine may live when thou thyself art dead;*
> *And so in spite of death thou dost survive,*
> *In that thy likeness still is left alive."* (V&A ln 167-174)

Venus gives a logical lecture on how it would be a crime against nature for Adonis not to beget offspring. Since Adonis was a seed nurtured by Nature, he must repay this debt by planting seeds of his own or he's just a parasite. She mingles this with the theme of Shakespeare's first seventeen Sonnets, imploring the beautiful young man to produce a copy of himself by sowing his oats.[106]

Then she brings his mother into it, saying that if she'd rebelled against nature in this way, Adonis would not have been born: *"O had thy mother borne so hard a mind, / She had not brought forth thee, but died unkind."* (V&N ln 203-204) It would a good point, but she's leaving out the distasteful detail that Myrrha seduced her own father and Adonis was conceived of incest.[107]

Venus is also well versed in classical literature. Apparently, she got ahold of an advance copy of Plato's *Symposium* thousands of years before it was written.[108] Plato had proposed a hierarchy of the senses, from the lowliest to the loftiest: taste, smell, touch, sound, and sight. Venus flips this upside down. Having praised Adonis's beauty, she tosses it aside to explore his sound, touch, and smell, culminating in his taste:

"Had I no eyes but ears, my ears would love
That inward beauty and invisible;
Or were I deaf, thy outward parts would move
Each part in me that were but sensible:
Though neither eyes nor ears, to hear nor see,
Yet should I be in love by touching thee.

Say that the sense of feeling were bereft me,
And that I could not see, nor hear, nor touch,
And nothing but the very smell were left me,
Yet would my love to thee be still as much;
For from the stillitory of thy face excelling
Comes breath perfum'd, that breedeth love by smelling.

But oh what banquet wert thou to the taste,
Being nurse and feeder of the other four;
Would they not wish the feast might ever last,
And bid suspicion double-lock the door,
Lest Jealousy, that sour unwelcome guest,
Should by his stealing in disturb the feast?" (V&A ln 433-450)

This has long been noted as a very nerdy dirty joke, an erotic parody of Platonic instruction. Pauline Kiernan comments, "The amatory predator even manages to reduce the banquet of the senses to a lecher's litany...by reversing the order found in Plato's seminal text."[109]

But like the best of dirty jokes, this speech also operates on a deeper level. Plato's hierarchy of the senses is counterintuitive and artificial—that's why people listened to him, because Plato said things you wouldn't naturally come up with on your own. To say that sight is more important than smell separates humans from other land animals, who operate primarily by scent.[110] As Camille Paglia wrote, "The Apollonian eye is the brain's great victory over the bloody open mouth of mother nature."[111] The exaltation of sight above scent and taste is also a very male thing, and a great deal of feminist scholarship has been dedicated to exploring the male gaze which objectifies and consumes.[112] Shakespeare refers over and over again to a male propensity to choose a mate by sight, his most famous example being Friar Lawrence teasing young Romeo that *"young men's love then lies / Not truly in their hearts, but in their eyes."* (R&J II.iii)

Venus's subversion of this patriarchal hierarchy brings us closer to nature, where the scent of a potential mate encodes a complex medical history, detailing complementary immunities and genetic compatibility. "Why did she choose *him?*" It's got something to do with his smell. Shakespeare generally avoids scent. His female characters have no sense of smell (put a mask on the man, or a woman in male clothes, and Shakespeare's heroines can't tell the difference). But apparently, he's aware of the importance of scent. If Venus lost all her other senses, she would know Adonis by his distinctive musk. So, the joke works on two levels: from a patriarchal Platonic perspective, Venus is ruled by her "lower" senses. But really the joke's on us—her sensuality is natural and our squeamish hierarchy is artificial.

Venus assails Adonis with poetry and rhetoric, playing the male wooer. She tries everything except standing beneath his window with a boombox blasting Heart's "What About Love?" But he won't budge. As a sonneteer wrote, "The tender nibbler would not touch the bait."[113] "And in case the reader should forget how these things are traditionally done, the poem gives us horses that behave in a much more predictable manner."[114] For sixty-five lines, the narrator wanders off to follow an equine encounter, a romantic comedy subplot roughly equivalent to country bumpkins on the outskirts of a great tragedy.

Shakespeare describes Adonis's stallion as a masterpiece of nature, as if *"a painter would surpass the life / In limning out a well-proportioned steed."* (V&A ln 289-290) And apparently, he's hung like a horse, too *"Look what a horse should have he did not lack."* When this stud spots a fertile mare, he's all business, *"He sees his love, and nothing else he sees... He looks upon his love and neighs unto her, / She answers him as if she knew his mind."* (V&A ln 287, 307-308) He needs no sugared sonnets, they're off to the races, doing the Discovery Channel thing. We don't find out if the horse comes back. Perhaps it's the lack of this magnificent stallion that gets Adonis killed in the hunt. Jan Kott wryly observed, "In *Richard III* the entire kingdom turned out to be worth less than a horse."[115]

Dark Sarcasm in the Classroom
(*VENUS AND ADONIS*)

Venus is well versed in wordplay-as-foreplay. Her irrepressible wit is fluid, lurid, and florid; she's a flowing fountain of Shakespearean love poetry. But the grim Puritan Adonis shrugs it all off, critiquing her rhetorical skills like a cold schoolmaster. In the following speech, he grades her *"theme"* and *"treatise,"* what we today would call an academic essay, and her *"device,"* meaning her oratory.

> *"'Nay then,' quoth Adon, 'you will fall again*
> *Into your idle over-handled theme;*
> *The kiss I gave you is bestow'd in vain,*
> *And all in vain you strive against the stream;*
> *For by this black-fac'd night, desire's foul nurse,*
> *Your treatise makes me like you worse and worse.*
> *If love have lent you twenty thousand tongues,*
> *And every tongue more moving than your own,*
> *Bewitching like the wanton mermaid's songs,*
> *Yet from mine ear the tempting tune is blown...*
> *No, lady, no; my heart longs not to groan,*
> *But soundly sleeps, while now it sleeps alone...*
> *I hate not love, but your device in love*
> *That lends embracements unto every stranger.*
> *You do it for increase: O strange excuse!*
> *When reason is the bawd to lust's abuse...*
> *Call it not, love, for love to heaven is fled,*
> *Since sweating lust on earth usurp'd his name...*
> *Which the hot tyrant stains and soon bereaves,*
> *As caterpillars do the tender leaves.'"*
>
> (V&A ln 769-798, Abridged, "bawd" meaning pimp)

Adonis assesses her entreaty as though it were a doctoral dissertation and gives it a resounding "F." His stern dismissal, *"Leaves Love upon her back deeply distressed."* Ironically, Shakespeare gives prim and prudent Adonis the dirtiest line in the poem, about the caterpillar leaving a white trail on a tender leaf. Eww.

Adonis's line *"Call it not love, for Love to heaven is fled, / Since sweating Lust on earth usurp'd his name"*[116] will be echoed by Hamlet, berating his mother for remarrying: *"You cannot call it love... O shame! where is thy blush?"* (HAM III.iv) In his relations with women, the melancholy Dane will bear a strong resemblance to Adonis. Hamlet will forsake women to hunt the boar who, in a Fight Club-style twist, is not Claudius but himself. In his famous *"To be or not to be"* speech, Hamlet is afraid to take his own life, so instead he creates another Hamlet (by murdering Laertes' father) to kill him, thus committing suicide indirectly. And both of the women he spurns will die.

Adonis also has his insecurities. As a young man he fears being smothered and infantilized. Some of Venus's affection for Adonis sounds like the fairy queen Titania cradling the ass-headed Bottom (whom Oberon sent to replace her foster child). Bottom is anything but self-conscious; the actor who wants to play a hero, a woman, and a lion at the same time is clearly comfortable with his masculine, feminine, and animal aspects. So, he's cool with it. But Adonis is very young, a man-boy who fears being entrapped in infantile eroticism. Venus essentially tries to send him to the petting zoo of hunting rabbits, but he insists he's manly enough to take on the scythe-tusked boar.[117]

Adonis's cool critique of Venus's babbling fountain of Shakespearean love poetry also gives the poet a playful chance to poke fun at his own flowery excesses. I mean, let's face it—Shakespeare is good but he's no Leonard Cohen.[118]

Venus and Mars
VENUS AND ADONIS

Venus's powers of seduction need no introduction, and yet she can't help but share a bit of her romantic résumé. She chooses her favorite story: how she conquered the war god Mars.

"I have been woo'd as I entreat thee now,
Even by the stern and direful god of war,
Whose sinewy neck in battle ne'er did bow,
Who conquers where he comes in every jar; ["jar" meaning battle]
Yet hath he been my captive and my slave,
And begg'd for that which thou unask'd shalt have.

Over my altars hath he hung his lance,
His batter'd shield, his uncontrollèd crest,
And for my sake hath learn'd to sport and dance,
To toy, to wanton, dally, smile, and jest;
Scorning his churlish drum and ensign red
Making my arms his field, his tent my bed.

Thus he that overrul'd I oversway'd,
Leading him prisoner in a red rose chain:
Strong-temper'd steel his stronger strength obey'd,
Yet was he servile to my coy disdain.
Oh be not proud, nor brag not of thy might,
For mast'ring her that foil'd the god of fight." (V&A ln 97-114)

Venus presents her mastery of Mars as a proud accomplishment. The dominatrix reduced the god of war to a whimpering love-slave, and his phallic lance became her prized trophy. It's a bit daunting. But she assures Adonis that winning her will make him more manly than the mighty Mars, and this time she wants to play the submissive role.

She's also a bit selective in her memory, leaving out the part where her husband, the weapon-smith Vulcan, learned of her affair with Mars and set a trap. During one of their sexual encounters, an unbreakable net slung them up and the cuckolded husband brought the whole Olympian pantheon to jeer at their embarrassment. Unfortunately, Vulcan's plan backfired, everybody burst out laughing. "The reaction of the gods was not one of sympathy for Vulcan, but rather envy for Mars."[119] Venus and Mars still bump together every spring, when the harsh month of March (Mars) submits to the coming of lovely April (Aphrodite/Venus).

The lusty Venus and the hunchback weaponsmith Vulcan are an odd pair. In *Troilus and Cressida*, Ulysses uses them as a classical example of a mismatched couple, *"as near as the extremest ends of parallels, as like as Vulcan and his wife,"* (T&C I.iii), whereas Venus and Mars are symbolic of superhuman passion, *"as red as Mars his heart inflam'd with Venus."* (T&C V.ii) In *Antony and Cleopatra*, a eunuch will compare the legendary lovers to Venus and Mars while lamenting his own sexlessness: *"I can do nothing...Yet have I fierce affections, and think what Venus did with Mars."* (A&C I.v) Like Venus and Mars, Antony and Cleopatra will find themselves in a tightening snare. Then, through death, they will escape into demi-deification.

Unseen Ensemble
VENUS AND ADONIS

The poem *Venus and Adonis* is tightly focused on its two titular characters, and Shakespeare keeps spicing up the scene with comic inversions. She is the ardent suitor and he the blushing, bashful maiden. The immortal is a giddy schoolgirl and the young boy acts like a crotchety old teacher. Venus is a towering giant who can lift Adonis off his horse but keeps falling to the ground and can't get him to mount her.

In addition to these, there is a subtler inversion that is easy to miss. Adonis is described in exalted religious terms, while Venus is humanized. She's breathless and fleshy, sweaty and pungent, *"her face doth reek and smoke, her blood doth boil."* It's a running gag throughout the poem, the comical irony that the mortal is sacred, and the goddess is profane.

But she is still the goddess in this story, so she can see into the spirit realm as Adonis and the narrator cannot. The narrator catches a quick glimpse of the Titan Sun, but Venus can see the whole paranormal panorama of the Olympian pantheon.[120] She talks with them, and we can eavesdrop, like overhearing one side of a telephone conversation. Through her interactions, we get an indirect glimpse into this other dimension where the larger cast of the story is assembled, including Diana, Jupiter, Death (Pluto), and personified Jealousy (possibly Mercury). The bold, even bullying tones she takes in berating her fellow Olympians give us a clearer sense of her power.

She also gets to exclude the gods most likely to hamper her efforts: her husband Vulcan, her ex-lover Mars (who she talks *about* but doesn't talk *to*), and her son Cupid. Why she doesn't enlist Cupid to drug Adonis is a question for the ages. Perhaps she needs the affirmation of winning this young guy fair-and-square, or maybe she respects Adonis too much to reduce him to a brainwashed love-machine. A third possibility: it would just be too awkward. Cupid's a permanent preteen; helping Mom seduce this dude could be developmentally disturbing.

Venus warns Adonis about personified Jealousy. She says "Jealousy" as though it's a proper name, but the characteristics she lists sound a lot like the messenger god Mercury.

> "For where love reigns, disturbing Jealousy
> Doth call himself affection's sentinel;
> Gives false alarms, suggesteth mutiny,
> And in a peaceful hour doth cry 'Kill, kill!'...
> This sour informer, this bate-breeding spy,
> This canker that eats up love's tender spring,
> This carry-tale, dissentious Jealousy,
> That sometime true news, sometime false doth bring."
> (V&A ln. 649-652, 655-658)

Shakespeare's characters often use Mercury as a symbol of quicksilver speed, but his messages cannot always be trusted. In *Twelfth Night*, the disguised Viola tampers with transmissions, and the clown Feste says, *"Now Mercury endue thee with leasing* [lying], *for thou speak'st well of fools!"* (TN I.v) Mercury will appear at the end of *Love's Labour's Lost* as Marcadé, whose message of doom breaks the spell and causes the lovers to part; he thwarts four weddings with a funeral ("Love" in the play's title refers to Cupid, whose labors are blocked by Mercury). He'll appear again in *Romeo and Juliet* as Mercutio, the bitter harbinger of doubt who must die so Romeo can plunge headlong into love. Maybe Romeo should have listened. And the mercurial Mercutio will arguably be reincarnated as Iago, the false messenger in *Othello*. We'll return to Mercury later, in the exploration of Autolycus in *The Winter's Tale*. If "Jealousy" here were indeed Mercury, it would add to the interesting twist that Mercury and Venus once had a child together, combining their Greek names Hermes and Aphrodite into Hermaphrodite, whose tragic death somewhat resembles Adonis's. Venus is harsh on Jealousy here, but later in a fit of embitterment, she'll enlist Jealousy as a permanent assassin of love.

In Venus's speech about her body as a pleasant forest glen, she contrasts herself with Diana, the virgin huntress who punished Actaeon for stumbling into a forbidden grove. Later, Venus invokes Diana as the moon bashfully hiding behind a cloud for fear that a glimpse of Adonis would shake her vows of chastity: *"So do thy lips / Make modest Dian cloudy and forlorn, / Lest she should steal a kiss and die forsworn."* (V&A ln 724-726) Obviously, voracious Venus and demure Diana are not friends, and in her catty way, Venus goes on bad-mouthing Diana as if the moon can't hear her. She accuses the virgin goddess of a jealous attempt at bribing nature to make mortals less beautiful than gods, and when this plan failed, of doing the wicked-stepmother thing by concocting poisonous STDs: *"The marrow-eating sickness, whose attaint / Disorder breeds by heating of the blood."* (V&A ln 739-742) That's a poetic way of saying "syphilis," a subject on which Shakespeare may have been an expert. John Roe comments, "There would be some irony, and no little guile, in the goddess of *venereal* pursuits blaming any consequent disease on the goddess of chastity."[121]

When Venus fears for Adonis's safety, she angrily calls the *"King of graves, and grave for kings, / Imperious supreme of all mortal things,"* Death with a capital D, whom the Greeks called Hades and the Romans knew as Dis or Pluto, lord of the underworld.

> *"'Hard-favour'd tyrant, ugly, meagre, lean,*
> *Hateful divorce of love,' thus chides she Death,*
> *'Grim-grinning ghost, earth's worm, what dost thou mean?*
> *To stifle beauty and to steal his breath...*
> *Dost thou drink tears, that thou provok'st such weeping?*
> *What may a heavy groan advantage thee?'"*
> (V&A ln 931-934, 949-950)

After insulting his looks, she threatens him: *"The destinies will curse thee for this stroke; / They bid thee crop a weed, thou pluck'st a flower."* (V&A ln 945-946) The flower here foreshadows Adonis's transformation but also hits Pluto below the belt, a reminder of how Proserpina was out picking flowers when he abducted and deflowered her. In other myths, Proserpina, the underworld queen, also becomes sexually obsessed with Adonis, but Shakespeare doesn't mention this bizarre love triangle.

Then, during a momentary glimmer of hope that Adonis lives, Venus has a chummy moment with her buddy Pluto, *"'No, no,' quoth she, 'sweet Death, I did but jest... / Then, gentle shadow, - truth I must confess - / I rail'd on thee, fearing my love's decess.'"* (V&A ln 997, 1001-1002) And she tries to distract Death from Adonis's nearby boar hunting, reminding Pluto of his many *"trophies, statues, tombs and stories / His victories, his triumphs and his glories."* (V&A ln 1013-1014)

What Says Jupiter?
VENUS AND ADONIS | CYMBELINE

Having bullied the lord of the underworld, Venus goes all the way to the top, summoning Jupiter himself, king of the gods. Perhaps he shows up, but we can't see him. Venus knows well that her exalted nephew has often degraded and humiliated himself pursuing mortal lovers (most of whom have been tragically destroyed as a result of his sexual predation), so she expects some sympathy here. And she uses a different approach: instead of insulting Jupiter as she has the others, she cajoles him like a kindly scatterbrained aunt.[122] Then, in her most theatrical stanza, Venus transitions from light, chirpy giggles to the low and heavy intonation of a threat:

> *"'O Jove!' quoth she, 'how much a fool was I,*
> *To be of such a weak and silly mind,*
> *To wail his death who lives, and must not die*
> *Till mutual overthrow of mortal kind;*
> *For he being dead, with him is beauty slain,*
> *And beauty dead, black Chaos comes again.'"* (V&A ln 1015-1020)

By *"Chaos"* she means the total ruin of the created world: earthquakes and floods on a Biblical, apocalyptic scale, dissolving the bountiful earth back to dark primordial ooze, the formless void.[123] She is engaging Jupiter in an atomic standoff with mutually assured destruction. Yes, it turns out she's bluffing, but nonetheless she's awfully bold, talking to the King of Olympus in this way.

Shakespeare sometimes uses the names "Jove" and "Jupiter" for the Christian God whose name was not allowed onstage, but usually in reference to the Classical deity. The principle difference is that Jupiter is a parasite. He was not the creator, but a king who took all he could get without destroying the host. And Jupiter was ruled by his own appetites. He was fed by agricultural sacrifice as a form of taxation, *"Laud we the gods; and let our crooked smokes climb to their nostrils from our bless'd altars,"* (CYM V:v) and saw the world as a gaming preserve for sexual predation.

Shakespeare's Jupiter is a mixed blessing, sometimes considered good (*"Shall I have justice? What says Jupiter?"* TA IV.iii), sometimes bad ("And if Jove stray, who dares say Jove doth ill?" PER I.i) and sometimes ugly (*"Jove shield thee well for this,"* says Bottom when Tom Snout makes an obscene hand-gesture[124]). Jupiter is known for justice and lust, which often makes him a liar at best and a bestial serial rapist at worst. *"At lovers' perjuries, they say Jove laughs,"* says Juliet, quoting Ovid's *Ars Amatoria.* Hearing sweet little lies of pillow-talk, Jove smirks in smug recognition. Shakespeare frequently refers to Jupiter's sexual conquests, especially the episode in which he took the form of a bull to kidnap the princess Europa (after whom he supposedly named an entire continent).

Jupiter himself will finally be dragged onto the Shakespearean stage in *Cymbeline.* Angry ghosts call him out for his *"adulteries, rates and revenges,"* and threaten to support the other gods in his overthrow if he fails to assist them: *"No more, thou thunder-master, show thy spite on mortal flies... Help! Or we poor ghosts will cry / To th' shining synod* [council] *of the rest against thy deity."* In a stage direction, *"Jupiter descends in thunder and lightning, sitting upon an eagle. He throws a thunderbolt. The Ghosts fall on their knees."* Then the great patron of patriarchalism tells them to shut up, and that he'll handle the situation in his own way, at his own time: *"Whom best I love I cross; to make my gift, / The more delay'd, delighted. Be content."* (CYM I.iv)[125]

Shakespeare's Jupiter represents great power and great responsibility... until he gets aroused, and then all bets are off. Venus knows that he has frequently gotten into trouble over desire for mortals, but also expects him to do what's best for creation overall. In her threat of chaos, the love goddess may even be reminding him of an earlier episode in which he handed over the grain goddess's daughter against her will, and Ceres blighted the land until Jupiter faced starvation and compromised.

Milk and Blood
VENUS AND ADONIS

In exploring the ensemble cast of *Venus and Adonis,* the boar who kills Adonis is obviously a major player. But this character can be read and interpreted in several different ways, from a mindless beast to a disguised divinity. It may be the underworld queen Persephone in animal form.[126] In early forms of the Adonis story, Aphrodite and Persephone split custody of the orphan: Aphrodite in the bright, warm months, Persephone in the dark, cold months, and she kills him during a custody dispute. But Ovid doesn't specify this and neither does Shakespeare. And really, if we were going to investigate the boar as a disguised deity, the list of suspects would be long since Venus has angered everyone: her husband Vulcan, her ex-lover Mars, her eternal rival Diana, her resentful nephews Jupiter, Pluto, or Mercury.

Venus describes the boar in nightmarish terms, with fearful tusks *"Like to a mortal butcher, bent to kill... His eyes like glow-worms shine when he doth fret; / His snout digs sepulchres where'er he goes; / The thorny brambles and embracing bushes, / As fearful of him, part, through whom he rushes."* (V&A ln 618-630, Abridged, "sepulchres" meaning graves) But what Venus finds most frightening of all is that the boar can't appreciate Adonis's beauty:

> *"Alas! he naught esteems that face of thine,*
> *To which love's eyes pay tributary gazes;*
> *Nor thy soft hands, sweet lips, and crystal eyne,*
> *Whose full perfection all the world amazes;*
> *But having thee at vantage, wondrous dread!*
> *Would root these beauties as he roots the mead."* (V&A ln 631-636)

The boar cannot distinguish between Adonis's facial features and a weedy meadow, its tusks will rend either one indiscriminately. Shakespeare's boar is an agent of Nature that doesn't differentiate between a beautiful boy and a blade of grass and a pile of pig-droppings. It's all life energy in various states of continual metamorphosis.

Venus uses male pronouns for the boar, perhaps because she knows Adonis wants to prove his manliness in battle against it.[127] But when she finally sees the boar after the boy's been gored, it is Mother Nature herself, *"whose frothy mouth bepainted all with red, / Like milk and blood being mingled both together."* (V&A ln 901-902) The description links the milk of nurturance with the blood of slaughter (and the menstrual blood of renewed fertility). We will sift through Nature's foam of milk and blood later.

Nature manifests itself as the boar, but also as the horses who court each other. Nature is the vegetation, the ground on which Venus glides, and yet is trampled by the horses' lust. Nature is the tall trees that hide Venus and Adonis from the sun and moon. She is the brambles that recoil in fear from the boar, and the thorns that grasp at Venus as she runs toward the bloody scene: *"And as she runs, the bushes in the way / Some catch her by the neck, some kiss her face, / Some twine about her thigh to make her stay: / She wildly breaketh from their strict embrace."* (V&A ln 871-874) Nature is also the forest floor which *"with purple tears that his wound wept, was drench'd. / No flower was nigh, no grass, herb, leaf or weed, / But stole his blood and seem'd with him to bleed."* (V&A ln 1054-1056) Nature drinks his blood, then grants him a sort of immortality.

The poem, it turns out, has a large cast. And then there's the narrator—it's hard to say exactly how the poet fits into this ensemble. The narrator speaks twice directly to Venus, but she doesn't seem to hear him. When Adonis has scorned the offer of her body as a park, the narrator says, *"Poor queen of love, in thine own law forlorn, / To love a cheek that smiles at thee in scorn!"* (V&A ln 251-252) And during Adonis's unseen battle with the boar, as Venus wavers between hope and despair, the narrator addresses her again:

> *"O hard-believing Love, how strange it seems*
> *Not to believe, and yet too credulous;*
> *Thy weal and woe are both of them extremes;*
> *Despair and hope make thee ridiculous,*
> *The one doth flatter thee in thoughts unlikely,*
> *In likely thoughts the other kills thee quickly."* (V&N ln 985-990)

The narrator stays with Venus during Adonis's climactic fight scene and then allows her to narrate the crime by deduction. In this way, the narrator lets us know whose story it is. Although the reader is invited to identify with Adonis, Venus is the story's protagonist.

Slings and Eros
VENUS AND ADONIS

What we call "myths" are old explanations for how the world got to be this way. What was the intentional plan for the earth (and how did it go off the rails)? How does humanity fit in? How did such-and-such animal, mineral, or vegetable get such-and-such a characteristic? That part of an old myth can sound pretty silly later on, but all of the fanciful who-what-where-when-hows are really just shiny decorations on the core tree–why? What does this tell us about how to be a human being in relation to the rest of creation? And in relation to the creators? Myth situates humanity in relation to the earth around us, the cosmos above us, and sometimes to a realm of death below. In some ways, myth separates: you are here with the land below and the sky above, these are the boundaries between you and the dirt and the divine. And in other ways myth integrates: you are made of soil and spirit.

Ovid didn't create the myths in the *Metamorphoses*. He was more like a DJ remixing a mash-up of popular stories, spinning the greatest hits of Greek mythology on a consistent beat. And the myths that held the most appeal to Ovid personally were the ones about boundaries between animals/minerals/vegetables, mortals, and gods. He explored the frontiers by looking at places where they had been crossed: lofty gods overtaken by lowly desires to have sex with humans (let's remember this would be the equivalent of a Rhodes Scholar smitten with lust for an orangutan), and people being transformed into trees, bucks, birds, or boulders.

In Ovid's *Metamorphoses*, Adonis's blood transforms the anemone—he is essentially resurrected or reincarnated as this fragile flower. That sounds a bit paltry. The myth had originated as an explanation of the annual Adonia ritual. Catherine Belsey explains, "This festival, the rite of Adonis, appears to have taken place in spring or summer all over the Mediterranean region. It seems that on the first day of the Adonia, the reciprocal love of

Venus and Adonis was celebrated, with ripe fruit and sweet cakes, in the presence of their images as lovers, while on the second, the body of the hero was ritually consigned to the waves with bitter lamentation. Love and death were thus brought into close conjunction."[128] The Adonia was itself a copy of an ancient Anatolian festival for the goddess Cybele and her son/lover Attis, who was disemboweled by a boar, mourned by his mother, and annually reincarnated. The Venus and Adonis myth—and we should keep in mind here that in every version *except* for Shakespeare's they totally get it on before he's killed—explains how the fertility of the world requires a blend of natural and supernatural energies.

Nature is mortal in the sense that winter annually invades, and every individual living thing will someday die. But nature is immortal in the sense that spring will always rise again, and life in general does go on (hard to believe after being rejected or losing a loved one, but it's true). The immortal Venus will meet another Adonis. On the mythic/ritualistic level, this Adonis is one in a series of thousands or millions of Adoni, stretching into the past and the future; this scene plays out every year. To borrow an image from Kurt Vonnegut, he's a link in a Tralfamadorian chain. Shakespeare's poem takes place over three days and two nights. It seems really long, but he's condensing time: in terms of nature, the story lasts half a year—from the dawning of spring to the darkening of autumn, then quickly skips ahead to the next spring.

Ovid used the myth to explain the coloring of this flower. Maybe he didn't care about the Adonia festival, but obviously he liked the story (and thank goodness—the *Metamorphoses* can become a bit monotonous with male gods assaulting maidens).

Shakespeare didn't care about the Adonia, except to the extent that he lived during the Protestant Reformation, when ritual was getting really dull and gloomy.[129] If he'd been born a century earlier, he would have been a Catholic priest performing the vibrant Mass, but in his day, the only refuge for flamboyant ritualists was the theater, and in this particular year the theaters were closed due to the plague. So, he opened up the naughty Bible and jazzed up this old tale where a guy becomes a flower. But Shakespeare didn't really care about the flower either. He spins the myth to explain why love is so difficult: the goddess of love herself is embittered by an old wound and suffers from Post-Traumatic Stress Disorder.

After Adonis has been gored to death, Venus paints her face with his blood and utters a curse:

"Since thou art dead, lo here I prophesy,
Sorrow on love hereafter shall attend:
It shall be waited on with jealousy,
Find sweet beginning, but unsavoury end;
Ne'er settled equally, but high or low,
That all love's pleasure shall not match his woe...

It shall suspect where is no cause of fear,
It shall not fear where it should most mistrust;
It shall be merciful, and too severe,
And most deceiving when it seems most just...
[Since] *in his prime death doth my love destroy,*
They that love best their love shall not enjoy."
(V&A ln 1135-1164, Abbreviated)

This dark dirge feels like it should be accompanied by a macabre parade of bloody cadavers: Juliet and her Romeo; Desdemona and Othello; Cleopatra and Antony; Goneril, Regan, and Edmund; Ophelia and Hamlet; yes, even Gertrude and Claudius (they really were a good couple, till the brat from her previous marriage messed it up); and, bringing up the rear, Falstaff holding a letter from Hal. But they should also be followed by the limping wounded veterans who made it: Beatrice and Benedick; the two young couples from *A Midsummer Night's Dream*; Hermione and Leontes from *The Winter's Tale*.

I abbreviated Venus's speech. It's thirty lines of curse, but it's hard to read without getting pulled into a game of 'name that play.' And it is indeed prophetic in the sense that most of Shakespeare's star-crossed love stories had not yet been written. Lysander's comment about Ovid and Plutarch is equally true of Shakespeare:

"Ay me! for aught that I could ever read,
Could ever hear by tale or history,
The course of true love never did run smooth." (MND I.i)

From now on, Venus declares, love will be plagued with jealousy and death—two of Shakespeare's favorite topics. Here she's not using the words as divine names (this is lower-case "j" jealousy and lower-case "d" death), but as infections that will poison love. A depressing thought, but on the bright side, without love's difficulties we wouldn't have the Evanescence *Synthesis* album.

Venus smashes a Pandora's jar, unleashing the toxic waste byproducts of love. But she also endows love with the anarchic energy that will animate Shakespeare's romantic comedies:

> *"The strongest body shall it make most weak,*
> *Strike the wise dumb, and teach the fool to speak."* (V&A ln 1145-1146)

> *"Put fear to valour, courage to the coward...*
> *And set dissension 'twixt the son and sire;"* (V&A ln 1158-1160)

> *"Pluck down the rich, enrich the poor with treasures;*
> *It shall be raging mad, and silly mild,*
> *Make the young old, the old become a child."* (V&A ln 1150-1152)

Here come Shakespeare's lunatics, lovers and poets, fops and fools, bumpkins and Sir Toby Belch. Venus hasn't completely scorched the earth. And actually, this part of the curse makes love sound fun, even potentially revolutionary.

Offspring
VENUS AND ADONIS

Magic always has a cost, and Venus's dark spell causes Adonis's dead body to dematerialize. It *"melted like a vapour,"* and where his blood spattered the ground, a purple flower is sprung (yes, she finally gets a rise out of him). She recognizes it by scent: Adonis has been reborn, or Adonis's blood has impregnated the earth and this blossom is their offspring. She picks this flower, *"but know, it is as good / To wither in my breast as in his blood."* Venus then talks to the anemone as Adonis's offspring:

'"Here was thy father's bed, here in my breast;
Thou art the next of blood, and 'tis thy right:
Lo in this hollow cradle take thy rest,
My throbbing heart shall rock thee day and night:
There shall not be one minute in an hour
Wherein I will not kiss my sweet love's flower.'

Thus weary of the world, away she hies,
And yokes her silver doves; by whose swift aid
Their mistress mounted through the empty skies, .
In her light chariot quickly is convey'd;
Holding their course to Paphos, where their queen
Means to immure herself and not be seen."
(V&A ln 1183-1194, "hies" meaning hurries)

The vibrant, exuberant love goddess becomes a world-weary goth girl, "the cropped flower becoming an emblem of unfulfilled desire and traumatic loss... Shakespeare's Venus, the first casualty of love's wound, retreats from the world to live in silence."[130] Venus has longed to possess Adonis, and at last she's got him, but not in the manner she expected. It's a bittersweet moment, and we can probably forego any wisecracks about how she finally does deflower him in the end.

The surprise twist is that Shakespeare's narrative is not about the transformation of Adonis, but about the metamorphosis of Venus. In archetypal terms, she has been the eternal virgin (in the sense that her youth is annually renewed), and also the whore. But in the tragic finale, she becomes maternal and a widow, even a wicked stepmother, as she poisons love and kills the flower. Venus has attained a maturity, and a totality. She has known love and now she knows loss, which broadens her understanding, enabling her to see a fuller spectrum. The poem has toyed with the comical reversal of the exalted Adonis and the earthy Venus, but she emerges from the poem more goddess than ever. And when the narrator says she *"means"* to hide and lament for all eternity, he knows she won't.

A similar blossom will bloom in *A Midsummer Night's Dream*, *"A little western flower, / Before milk-white, now purple with love's wound, / And maidens call it Love-in-idleness."* (MND II.ii)[131] Enchanted by its power, Titania will cradle and infantilize Bottom the weaver with poetry reminiscent of Venus, while Demetrius and Lysander reject Hermia like Adonis. But the *Venus and Adonis* story will continue in *Hamlet*, with the dejected Ophelia gathering psychopharmacological flora, drowning surrounded by blossoms, and rising again in blooms: *"Lay her i' the earth: / And from her fair and unpolluted flesh / May violets spring!"* *(HAM V.i)*

Nearing the end of his career, Shakespeare will give it a comic spin in *Cymbeline*, with Imogen awakening in a grave surrounded by flowers beside a decapitated body she assumes to be her lost husband. She later finds her husband is alive, and that headless cadaver was just some clod who stole his clothes. I guess it doesn't sound very funny, but once you've sat through *Cymbeline*, you'll laugh at just about anything. Shakespeare was pretty burned out by this point.

And yet he still gives it one last go in *The Winter's Tale*, and this time he finally gets it. The infant girl, referred to as a *"blossom,"* is abandoned to die on a seashore. But she's found, adopted by shepherds, and grows up to play the fertility goddess ., handing out flowers in a sheepshearing pageant. She weds the handsome prince Florizel, whose name means "flowers." And they actually do live happily ever after.

Venus's curse on love will reverberate throughout Shakespeare's literary career. The poet will denigrate Venus, perhaps a sign of his own embitterment as he suffered from venereal diseases. But in this early poem, Venus is arguably exonerated: Adonis's sexual anxiety (rejecting Venus) and masculine insecurity (stubborn will to fight the boar) get the better of him. This tragic flaw brings his downfall, traumatizing the goddess. The blight on love can be blamed on this rigid Puritan. Likewise, we'll see in Shakespeare's plays that heroines trash-talk Cupid, but it's the tragic heroes who really become dangerous in their jealousy.

The tragic romance of Venus and Adonis was not a botched one-night stand but a perpetual cycle. Shakespeare twisted the story into a tragedy, but the first generation of his readers also knew that these two would work it out. In Edmund Spenser's 1590 epic poem *The Fairy Queen*, Venus and Adonis have a special sanctuary, a sort of Kokomo vacation home outside of space and time, where they can rendezvous at leisure:

> "There wont fair Venus often to enjoy
> Her dear Adonis' joyous Company,
> And reap sweet Pleasure of the wanton Boy;

There yet some say in secret he doth lie,
Lappèd in Flowers and precious Spicery,
By her hid from the World, and from the Skill
Of Stygian Gods, which do her Love envy;
But she her self, when ever that she will,
Possesseth him, and of his Sweetness takes her Fill."
(Spenser, *The Fairy Queen*, Book 3, "Stygian" meaning "of the
river Styx," the threshold of death)

Venus & Diana

Love Triangle

THE TWO NOBLE KINSMEN

At the very end of his writing career, Shakespeare did some of his deepest explorations of Greek goddesses in *The Two Noble Kinsmen*, co-written with his protégé, John Fletcher. The two authors took turns composing sections; our focus will center primarily on Shakespeare's scenes.

The story takes place shortly after *A Midsummer Night's Dream*. Theseus and Hippolyta are ruling Athens, and a war with Thebes breaks out.[132] The two titular noble kinsmen are Theban cousins who distinguish themselves in battle (Theseus recalls *"By th' Helm of Mars, I saw them in the war, / Like to a pair of Lions, smeared with prey"*) but are taken captive.[133] As prisoners of war looking out a dungeon window, they see Hippolyta's sister Emilia picking flowers. Both fall in love with her and Palamon, the more romantic of the two, exclaims "Behold the wonder! By heaven, she is a goddess." His cousin Arcite smirks, "I will not, as you do, to worship her, / As [if] she is heavenly, and a blessed Goddess; / I love her as a woman, to enjoy her." (TNK II.ii, Fletcher)

Emilia is an Amazon, uninterested in marriage (fondly recalling her first love, *"'tween maid and maid"*[134]), she reveres the virgin huntress Diana and the war-goddess Bellona.[135] But Theseus and Hippolyta decide that she should marry one of the cousins, and the lucky groom must be determined by ritual combat as a means of revealing whom the gods have chosen:

Hippolyta says, *"He whom the gods / Do of the two know best, I pray them he / Be made your lot,"* and Theseus agrees to this *"divine arbitrament."* (TNK V.iii Shakespeare) The fight itself will be offstage, but the real dramatic action is in the characters' pre-fight prayers. Arcite prays to the war god Mars for victory:

> *"O, great corrector of enormous times,*
> *Shaker of o'er-rank states, thou grand decider*
> *Of dusty and old titles, that heal'st with blood*
> *The Earth when it is sick, and cure'st the world*
> *O' th' pleurisy of people, I do take*
> *Thy signs auspiciously, and in thy name*
> *To my design march boldly—Let us go."*
> *(TNK V.i, Shakespeare, "Pleurisy" meaning excess)*

This prayer to Mars has been greatly abbreviated, but the following prayers to goddesses will be reprinted at greater length. These are the most detailed theological statements in Shakespeare's plays and are largely unknown due to their placement in a collaborative script. The Romantic Palamon beseeches the love goddess Venus to unite him with the maiden he adores:

> *"Our stars must glister with new fire, or be*
> *Today extinct. Our argument is love,*
> *Which, if the goddess of it grant, she gives*
> *Victory too. Then blend your spirits with mine,*
> *You whose free nobleness do make my cause*
> *Your personal hazard. To the goddess Venus*
> *Commend we our proceeding, and implore*
> *Her power unto our party.*
> *Hail, sovereign queen of secrets, who hast power*
> *To call the fiercest tyrant from his rage*
> *And weep unto a girl; that hast the might*
> *Even with an eye-glance to choke Mars's drum*
> *And turn th' alarm to whispers; that canst make*
> *A cripple flourish with his crutch, and cure him*
> *Before Apollo; that mayst force the king*

To be his subject's vassal, and induce
Stale gravity to dance... What godlike power
Hast thou not power upon? To Phoebus thou
Add'st flames hotter than his; the heavenly fires
Did scorch his mortal son, thine him. The huntress,
All moist and cold, some say, began to throw
Her bow away and sigh. Take to thy grace
Me, thy vowed soldier, who do bear thy yoke
As 'twere a wreath of roses, yet is heavier
Than lead itself, stings more than nettles.
I have never been foul-mouthed against thy law,
...O, then, most soft sweet goddess,
Give me the victory of this question, which
Is true love's merit, and bless me with a sign
Of thy great pleasure.
(Here music is heard; doves are seen to flutter.)
O thou that from eleven to ninety reign'st
In mortal bosoms, whose chase is this world
And we in herds thy game, I give thee thanks
For this fair token, which being laid unto
Mine innocent true heart, arms in assurance
My body to this business.—Let us rise
And bow before the goddess. Time comes on." (TNK V.i, Shakespeare)

Palamon the lover has prayed to Venus, as Arcite the fighter has prayed to Mars. The young Amazon Emilia prays to Diana that she'll be married to the one who loves her more:

"O sacred, shadowy, cold, and constant queen,
Abandoner of revels, mute contemplative,
Sweet, solitary, white as chaste, and pure
As wind-fanned snow, who to thy female knights[136]
Allow'st no more blood than will make a blush,
Which is their order's robe, I here, thy priest,
Am humbled 'fore thine altar. O, vouchsafe
With that thy rare green eye, which never yet
Beheld thing maculate, look on thy virgin,

And, sacred silver mistress, lend thine ear—
Which ne'er heard scurrile term, into whose port
Ne'er entered wanton sound—to my petition,
Seasoned with holy fear. This is my last
Of vestal office. I am bride-habited
But maiden-hearted. A husband I have 'pointed,
But do not know him. Out of two I should
Choose one, and pray for his success, but I
Am guiltless of election. Of mine eyes,
Were I to lose one—they are equal precious—
I could doom neither; that which perished should
Go to 't unsentenced. Therefore, most modest queen,
He of the two pretenders that best loves me
And has the truest title in 't, let him
Take off my wheaten garland, or else grant
The file and quality I hold I may
Continue in thy band.
(Here the hind vanishes under the altar, and in the place ascends a
rose tree, having one rose upon it.)
See what our general of ebbs and flows
Out from the bowels of her holy altar
With sacred act advances: but one rose.
If well inspired, this battle shall confound
Both these brave knights, and I, a virgin flower,
Must grow alone unplucked.
(Here is heard a sudden twang of instruments, and the rose falls from
the tree.)
The flower is fall'n, the tree descends. O mistress,
Thou here dischargest me. I shall be gathered;
I think so, but I know not thine own will.
Unclasp thy mystery!—I hope she's pleased;
Her signs were gracious." (TNK V.i, Shakespeare)

Each of the prayers receives a sign of divine acceptance, and all three prayers will be granted. Arcite, more concerned with male competition, will be blessed by Mars with victory in the fight. However, as he mounts Emilia's horse, the animal goes wild and he's mangled to death in the reins.

Here we have a fascinating recollection of the renegade horse in *Venus and Adonis*, and like Adonis, Arcite, who obsesses over male rivalry, is killed by an animal. Plus, Theseus and Hippolyta (her name means Crazy Horse) are watching, and she may well be pregnant with their son, Hippolytus, destined to die strangled in the reins of maddened mares. Whether the horse who kills Arcite acts as an agent of Nature, Fortune, or Diana, is left open to interpretation. With his dying breath, Arcite the fighter assents to Palamon the lover marrying Emilia, and thus is Emilia's prayer to Diana answered as well—the one who loves her more becomes her husband.[137]

Venus and Diana are generally rivals in Shakespeare's plays. And yet, here at the end of his career, Shakespeare reveals that they have collaborated behind the scenes. And a close reading of Palamon's prayer to Venus shows that he attributes to her none of the lust and looseness that has characterized Shakespeare's career-long vilification of the love goddess. The Venus/Diana prayers in the fifth act, taken together, could signal a transcendence of the differences between these goddesses: no longer the huntress versus the whore, but a synthesis showing a fuller spectrum of the divine feminine.

PART II

Kupfenberger inuent. D.Dancker.iß sculp.

Fortune & Nature

The Housewife and the Whore: Fortune vs. Nature
As You Like It

In *As You Like It*, a French Duke has just been overthrown by his brother in a political coup, so he sets up a refugee camp in the forest. The daughters of the rival dukes are best friends, and we first encounter them sitting together on the lawn between the stolen palace and the enchanted woodland. They discuss their feelings about the mutiny. Rosalind, the banished Duke's daughter, attempts to change the topic to love, but Celia instigates a philosophical-theological debate about Fortune. This is Fortune with a capital "F," the goddess Fortuna, and the discourse will quickly turn to Fortune's uneasy peace with the goddess Nature.

> "CELIA. Let us sit and mock the good housewife Fortune from her wheel, that her gifts may henceforth be bestowed equally.
> ROSALIND. I would we could do so; for her benefits are mightily misplaced; and the bountiful blind woman doth most mistake in her gifts to women.
> CELIA. 'Tis true; for those that she makes fair she scarce makes honest; and those that she makes honest she makes very ill-favouredly.
> ROSALIND. Nay; now thou goest from Fortune's office to Nature's: Fortune reigns in gifts of the world, not in the lineaments of Nature.

(Enter TOUCHSTONE)

CELIA. No; when Nature hath made a fair creature, may she not by Fortune fall into the fire? Though Nature hath given us wit to flout at Fortune, hath not Fortune sent in this fool to cut off the argument?

ROSALIND. Indeed, there is Fortune too hard for Nature, when Fortune makes Nature's natural [the fool] *the cutter-off of Nature's wit.*

CELIA. Peradventure this is not Fortune's work neither, but Nature's, who perceiveth our natural wits too dull to reason of such goddesses, and hath sent this natural [fool] *for our whetstone; for always the dullness of the fool is the whetstone of the wits."* (AYL I.ii)

The Wheel of Fortune image here could have numerous meanings. Because she is described as a housewife, perhaps we're meant to imagine a wheel for spinning yarn, which would link her with images of the Fates determining the span of a human lifeline. Or it could be more like a carnival game or roulette wheel, which may be the implication in a debate in *Henry V: "Giddy Fortune's furious fickle wheel, that goddess blind, that stands upon the rolling restless stone...she is turning, and inconstant, and mutability, and variation."* (H5 III.vi)[138]

Touchstone, the court jester who they call *"Nature's natural,"* does not join in the debate. In this scene, he is a dull messenger, a stone they use to sharpen their razor wits. But later they'll drag him as baggage to the forest and the natural habitat will activate him, like an old leather suitcase resurrected as a goat. It's interesting that in this scene he stumbles into a discussion about maidens being "fair," meaning either pretty or honest, since he'll later meet a comely forest lass who'll openly say, *"Well, I am not fair; and therefore I pray the gods make me honest,"* (AYL III.iii) and he'll attempt to seduce her by staging a false wedding. His offer to "make an honest woman of her," as the old expression goes, is a lie. But, spoiler alert, Shakespeare will rig the game so she can make an honest man of him. Touchstone will be Nature's torchbearer in this play, ultimately foiled or reformed by Fortune, depending on how you look at it.

Rosalind and Celia are approximately equal by Nature (Rosalind is smarter), but a rough turn of Fortune's wheel has determined that Celia will be socially elevated and Rosalind an outcast. However, Celia will subvert her father's will, vowing to share in Rosalind's misfortune. Their debate about Fortune and Nature also illustrates the situation of their future husbands, who are brothers. Nature has made them sons of the same parents, and yet Fortune determined that one should be born first and inherit everything. So, Oliver has become a gentleman and raised his younger brother like livestock. But despite his lack of education, young Orlando has been gifted by Nature with eloquence, gentleness, and Herculean strength. Rosalind will venture into the forest disguised as a male and turn the boyish Orlando into the man of her dreams. Celia will marry his rehabilitated brother.

Rosalind's father, the banished Duke, having suffered misfortune, falls into the embrace of Nature. He starts a hippie commune in the woods.

> "*DUKE SENIOR. Now, my co-mates and brothers in exile,*
> *Hath not old custom made this life more sweet*
> *Than that of painted pomp? Are not these woods*
> *More free from peril than the envious court?*
> *Here feel we not the penalty of Adam,*
> *The seasons' difference; as the icy fang*
> *And churlish chiding of the winter's wind,*
> *Which when it bites and blows upon my body,*
> *Even till I shrink with cold, I smile and say*
> *'This is no flattery; these are counsellors*
> *That feelingly persuade me what I am.'...*
> *And this our life, exempt from public haunt,*
> *Finds tongues in trees, books in the running brooks,*
> *Sermons in stones, and good in everything.*
> *I would not change it.*
> *AMIENS. Happy is your Grace,*
> *That can translate the stubbornness of fortune*
> *Into so quiet and so sweet a style.*
> *DUKE SENIOR. Come, shall we go and kill us venison?*" (AYL II.i)

This is one of the most comical moments in all of Shakespeare. The forest is perfect, everyone is safe, come on let's go kill something... He doesn't even call it a deer, but "venison"; in his mind the running stag is already dead meat. He does feel a twinge of guilt over this, acknowledging that the stag is a citizen of the forest. And at just that moment he receives a report of his fellow exile, the melancholy philosopher, Jaques:

"And, in that kind, swears you do more usurp
Than doth your brother that hath banish'd you...
To fright the animals, and to kill them up
In their assign'd and native dwelling-place." (AYL II.i)

The Duke has been overthrown by his brother, and for all he knows, the meat on his plate may have been the deer-duke of this woodland. The merry refugees might find the forest *"free from peril,"* but Bambi could disagree. And apparently, the Duke has not yet encountered the man-eating lion that will soon attack Oliver.

Fortune can't smile on the deer and the hunter at the same time—one or the other must be disappointed. In this case, the deer who, if it could speak, might have cried, *"O, I am Fortune's fool!"* But to Nature, life goes on regardless. The hunter might starve and become fertilizer, or eat a deer and excrete fertilizer. Either way the grasses are fed.

Sitting by a river, Jaques spies a stag wounded by the hunter's arrow, how it *"Stood on th' extremest verge of the swift brook, augmenting it with tears...weeping into the needless stream."* (AYL II.i) Jaques sees only meaningless loss, like tears in the rain; it's too bad he doesn't have Krishna or Yoda to explain this to him. Life force is fluid, flowing from one form to another, never lost. The deer has been a temporary carrier of water and life. Jaques is as well, and so is the river. The sophomoric philosopher is confused by the *"hairy fool"* deer and the horny fool Touchstone, death and sex. He'll be particularly impressed by how the exiled jester *"rail'd on Lady Fortune in good terms."*[139] (AYL II.vii) Jaques will briefly consider enrolling in clown college, then wander off to become a hermit, but it's unlikely he'll emerge as a Brahman or a Jedi.

Ovid in Love'st..?
As You Like It

Commentators will generally focus on the melancholy philosopher Jaques because he is the character most like the playwright. Shakespeare inserted him into the preexisting narrative, and even gave him his own name, Jakes/Shakes.[140] But Jaques himself wishes to become a disciple of the fool

Touchstone. And it seems no coincidence that the banished Touchstone compares himself to the exiled Ovid, who Shakespeare himself strove to emulate.[141] Jaques admires Touchstone's ability to transform ideas through creative wordplay: *"In his brain, which is as dry as the remainder biscuit after a voyage, he hath strange places cramm'd with observation, the which he vents in mangled forms."* (AYL II.vii)

Touchstone is an agent of Nature, in the sense of genetic opportunism. *"We that are true lovers run into strange capers; but as all is mortal in nature, so is all nature in love mortal in folly."*[142] (AYL II.iv) All that lives will die, and so will the foolishness of love. Touchstone's cynical view of love might be best summed up by the English poet David Bowie: "Wham-bam-thank-you-ma'am." While young lovers have their heads in the clouds about romance, his goatish mind is in the gutter of animal imperative. Mocking a romantic poem about Rosalind as a jewel and a painting, he says:

> *"If a hart do lack a hind, let him seek out Rosalind.*
> *If the cat will after kind, so be sure will Rosalind...*
> *Sweetest nut hath sourest rind, such a nut is Rosalind.*
> *He that sweetest rose will find must find love's prick and Rosalind."*
> (AYL III.ii)

Rosalind calls him rancid[143] and he calmly answers, *"You have said; but whether wisely or no, let the forest judge."* (AYL III.ii) Touchstone is a sexual scavenger, but still considers himself superior to Orlando, who carves his sweetheart's name into trees and litters the woodland with scraps of poetry.

In Touchstone's view, sex is natural, but matchmaking and marriage are artificial. He calls the shepherd a pimp for pairing livestock: *"To get your living by the copulation of cattle; to be bawd to a bell-wether, and to betray a she-lamb of a twelvemonth to crooked-pated, old, cuckoldly ram, out of all reasonable match."* (AYL III.ii) His low opinion of animal husbandry applies to human husbandry as well. He explains wedlock in terms of subjugating animals: *"As the ox hath his bow, sir, the horse his curb, and the falcon her bells, so man hath his desires; and as pigeons bill, so wedlock would be nibbling."* (AYL III.iii) That's a pretty literal approach to the old expression "get hitched."

Believing marriage to be artificial, he'll set up a fake wedding to seduce a lovely goatherd. Instead of a stone church, he chooses Nature for a sanctuary: *"Here we have no temple but the wood, no assembly but horn-beasts,"* and he enlists a fellow called Martext (meaning faulty words) to perform the naughty nuptials, *"for he is not like to marry me well; and not being well married, it will be a good excuse for me hereafter to leave my wife."* (AYL III.iii)

He's about to get away with it too, but Shakespeare himself shows up in the form of Jaques and scolds him into lawful matrimony. Touchstone sighs, *"Come, sweet Audrey; We must be married or we must live in bawdry."* At the play's end, as the main characters pair off for a mass-wedding, he'll join *"the rest of the country copulatives, to swear and to forswear, according as marriage binds and blood breaks."* (AYL V.iv) The satyr-like Touchstone will be domesticated, appropriately enough, by a goatherd.

Touchstone is a trickster, a creature of appetite, and the trap he lays for a maiden in the woods would be right at home in Ovid's *Metamorphoses*. But this is a Shakespearean forest, not an Ovidian one, and the fool is soon ensnared into proper English marriage. We get a good laugh and pass gentle judgment on Touchstone. Yet, in another sense, we could say that the exiled clown who *"rail'd on Lady Fortune"* becomes an acolyte of Nature: he was first introduced as *"Nature's natural,"* his lust is sincere, and he considers the forest which Nature created more sacred than a Church made by human hands. Then, having discovered his true self in his natural habitat, he is snared and dragged back into culture.

This is not the only wacky wedding that takes place in the play. Rosalind, pretending to be the boy Ganymede pretending to be the girl Rosalind, lures her beloved Orlando into a wedding rehearsal, presided over by her friend Celia. In the gender-bending woodland wild of *As You Like It*, Nature herself can be the church of a clown's wedding, and a young lady can perform the marriage sacrament as a Catholic Priest.

Ganymede's Gameshow
As You Like It

In *A Midsummer Night's Dream*, as Helena chases Demetrius through the forest, she breathlessly pants out a series of shape-shifting and gender-bending metaphors:

> *"Run when you will; the story shall be chang'd:*
> *Apollo flies, and Daphne holds the chase;*
> *The dove pursues the griffin; the mild hind*
> *Makes speed to catch the tiger."*
> (MND II.i, "hind" meaning red deer)

But she can't catch him and slumps down in despair: *"Your wrongs do set a scandal on my sex. / We cannot fight for love as men may do; / We should be woo'd, and were not made to woo."* (MND II.i) Helena scowls at Nature, but Fortune will come to her aid: fairies drug Demetrius. Helena, we may recall, is a good deal taller than Hermia, just as Rosalind is taller than Celia (*"I am more than common tall"*). It's likely these paired roles were originally played by the same two performers, Helena recast as Rosalind. And in *As You Like It*, the story shall indeed be changed: Rosalind will scandalize her sex by cross-dressing, and she will woo the wooer.

Shakespeare wrote many cross-dressed girls; it tickled his funny bone to see a boy playing a girl playing a boy. But most of his transvestite heroines use this disguise to hide or spy, assuming mild-mannered alter-egos. Not so with Rosalind, who emulates a flamboyant youth, Jove's own boy-toy Ganymede. The shapeshifter Rosalind is aggressive and mischievous.

Nature has made her female, and Fortune has banished her. Rosalind calls herself *"one out of suits with Fortune,"* (AYL I.ii) so she switches suits. And as a saucy boy she grabs Fortune's steering wheel to take control of her own destiny. Having witnessed Orlando's strength in a wrestling match and heard his tongue-tied stuttering, she becomes determined to break him down and rebuild him into a partner who can suit her needs. And not just a suitor whose candle will burn out after the wedding night: *"Men are April when they woo, December when they wed. Maids are May when they are maids, but the sky changes when they are wives."* (AYL IV.i)

She's got her work cut out for her. He's a hopeless wallflower, hanging bad teenaged poetry from tree-limbs:

> *"Nature presently distill'd*
> *Helen's cheek, but not her heart, Cleopatra's majesty,*
> *Atalanta's better part, sad Lucretia's modesty.*
> *Thus Rosalind of many parts by heavenly synod was devis'd,*
> *Of many faces, eyes, and hearts, to have the touches dearest priz'd.*
> *Heaven would that she these gifts should have,*
> *And I to live and die her slave."*
> (AYL III.ii, "Synod" meaning committee)

Orlando is smitten with Rosalind but envisions her as some hybrid super clone devised by a focus group of mad celestial scientists, a Frankenstein monster of famous heroines glued together with stardust and moonbeams. Rosalind wants no such thing, and she doesn't want a love-slave either; she wants a partner and also apparently, a lover who can share her penchant for role-play: *"I will be more jealous of thee than a Barbary cock-pigeon over his hen, more clamorous than a parrot against rain, more new-fangled than an ape, more giddy in my desires than a monkey. I will weep for nothing, like Diana in the fountain, and I will do that when you are dispos'd to be merry; I will laugh like a hyen[a], and that when thou are inclin'd to sleep."* (AYL IV.i) Rosalind's ideal marriage is one that keeps the giddy excitement of courtship alive for a lifelong honeymoon and is also a relationship that affirms her gender fluidity: she compares herself to a male pigeon guarding a female hen.

Rosalind as Ganymede is a game show host. Not only does she take the wheel of her own marital destiny, but with the other hand she steers a hopeless shepherd and his haughty crush to the altar as well. By the last act of the play, the blind housewife Fortune's wheel is spinning wild, a series of twists that could be best performed with bumper cars and kazoo music. The bad guys get so dizzy that they forget to be bad; they just want to get off the roller-coaster. The usurping Duke wanders off to become a monk, Orlando's cruel brother turns nice and marries a perfect stranger, Celia. The swain weds his sweetheart—even the clown ties the knot with a nice country girl. In the midst of this, we could almost miss an honest-to-goodness *Deus ex Machina*.., god of the nuptial night, descends from the sky.[144] The Wheel of

Fortune finally stops, pretty much everyone's a winner, and the gameshow ends with a quadruple wedding. The Duke exclaims:

> *"First, in this forest let us do those ends*
> *That here were well begun and well begot;*
> *And after, every of this happy number,*
> *That have endur'd shrewd days and nights with us,*
> *Shall share the good of our returnèd fortune."* (AYL V.iv)

Fortune has put everyone where they belong. Nature has healed them of the toxic masculinity and dog-eat-dog competition of culture. Now the forest gives its blessing to these marriages, and the adventurers will bring some of this natural remedy back to the city. Fortune and Nature are in harmony, all is in order. Then, in a surprise twist, the gender-bending Rosalind steps out on the stage again and removes her wig to bid the audience goodnight. Like Pinocchio, she is transformed into a real boy.[145]

Shakespeare would recycle the basic premise of *As You Like It* in *King Lear*. Once again, the nobles are be usurped and banished into the wilderness, but this time it is a hellish no-man's-land. And the debate about Fortune and Nature continues in darker tones.

Nature

Götterdaughterung – or – Daughterdämmerung
KING LEAR

In *King Lear*, both Lear and Edmund pray to a goddess called "Nature," but they're actually praying to two very different goddesses by the same name. Edmund's divine Nature is the sadistic mistress of a cruel dog-eat-dog arena. Lear inherits Shakespeare's conception of Nature as hierarchical patriarchy, fortified by filial devotion and nurture (although ironically, Lear sees nurture as something a child should do for a parent). Edmund bleeds his own father dry; Lear expects to be nursed by his daughters—it all gets a bit messy. The debate about the nature of Nature runs through the full script, and the ending doesn't tie it off with a neat little bow; the topic is left in tatters. Lear and Edmund are like blindfolded men describing an elephant, each perceiving a different facet of Nature.

We in the audience see "nature" as a backdrop, theatrical scenery, or lack of scenery. In a low-budget *King Lear*, the poetry can paint it in our minds. But Nature in this play is more than a setting, she is a matrix interacting with each character, churning and thrashing and feeding. Nature takes center stage. Characters lie to each other, verbally creating false realities, but Nature stays true. This is kind of like calling climate change "fake news"; you can say it as loud as you want, Nature isn't listening. She's too busy giving *good* news to the cockroaches.

Fortune has foolishly crowned Lear, who has never really known himself and is therefore incapable of knowing anybody else. He's got a dragon's temper and a sweet tooth for saccharine flattery. Lear also fancies himself a gameshow host and, dividing his kingdom into thirds, he invites his three daughters to play in a bizarre love contest, a declarative decathlon. He already knows that his eldest, Goneril, gets what's behind Door Number One: scenic Scotland *"with shadowy forests...plenteous rivers and wide-skirted meads."* Regan is destined to receive Door Number Two: Wales and the West Country, *"no less in space, validity, and pleasure."* Woods and pastures and pleasure are very picturesque, a painter's paradise. But he's rigged the game, saving the breadbasket farmlands of southern England for his youngest daughter, Cordelia.[146] Then, in a surprise twist, Cordelia throws the game and the other two contestants get to split the grand prize.

Lear runs this big game with one hand behind his back, reserving the biggest jackpot for himself: a solid gold parachute. His retirement plan is a non-stop celebrity tour with an entourage of one hundred knights. He wants great power with no responsibility. Lear even insists on keeping the title of king, although he won't rule any land.

Catherine Belsey observes, "If Lear misunderstands the meaning of kingship, he also tragically misconstrues the nature of kinship."[147] He seems a bit befuddled about how babies are made; Queen Lear has been out of the picture for some time, or maybe Lear spilled his seed in the soil and it sprouted these three blossoms. He thought he could make Cordelia his mother, *"I lov'd her most, and thought to set my rest / On her kind nursery."* And when she refuses this strange arrangement, he retroactively makes her a bastard, calling the cosmos, sun, triple moon goddess Hecate and stars as his witnesses:

> *"For, by the sacred radiance of the sun,*
> *The mysteries of Hecate and the night;*
> *By all the operation of the orbs,*
> *From whom we do exist and cease to be;*
> *Here I disclaim all my paternal care,*
> *Propinquity and property of blood."*[148] (KL I.i)

Not only does Lear revoke Cordelia's legitimacy, he also encourages Mother Nature to forsake her as well, *"A wretch whom nature is asham'd / Almost t'acknowledge hers."*

Lear's command that Nature shun Cordelia is just the first domino of the "Daughtergate" downfall.[149] Goneril challenges her father's entitlement to an entourage of rowdy friends. In her defense, remember this is one hundred hungry knights plus their helpers, horses, hawks, hounds, and harlots. Lear was a traveling menagerie. Goneril was willing to feed this old man's ego, but it's quite another thing to feed his personal circus and zoo. In response, Lear hits below the belt:

> *"Hear, nature, hear; dear goddess, hear*
> *Suspend thy purpose, if thou didst intend*
> *To make this creature fruitful!*
> *Into her womb convey sterility!*
> *Dry up in her the organs of increase;*
> *And from her derogate body never spring*
> *A babe to honour her! If she must teem,* ["teem" meaning breed]
> *Create her child of spleen, that it may live*
> *And be a thwart disnatur'd torment to her!*
> *Let it stamp wrinkles in her brow of youth;*
> *With cadent tears fret channels in her cheeks;*
> *Turn all her mother's pains and benefits*
> *To laughter and contempt; that she may feel*
> *How sharper than a serpent's tooth it is*
> *To have a thankless child! Away, away!"* (KL I.iv)

If it weren't harsh enough to name her Goneril (you can bet the girls in school called her Gonerilla), now Lear curses her with full-blown gonorrhea. The king runs off to Regan, who also rejects his retinue, reasoning *"O, sir, you are old; Nature in you stands on the very verge of her confine."* (KL II.iv) Regan reasons that Lear's aging dirtbag body will soon be compost, releasing his chemicals back into the circle of life, so he needs no hundred bodyguards. Lear curses her as well, calling for hounds to *"anatomize Regan; see what breeds about her heart."* (KL III.vi) "Anatomize" here means dissection or vivisection.[150] Lear takes an axe to his own family tree.

Having cursed his daughters, Lear continues his misogynistic rampage, cursing his own feminine side: *"O, how this mother swells up toward my heart! /* Hysterica passio, *down, thou climbing sorrow, / Thy element's below!"* (KL II.iv) In his wild witch hunt, Lear accuses himself of *hysterica passio,* womb-panic (or perhaps we're to understand that some time ago he swallowed Queen Lear and she now resides in his belly). Then, ranting in a storm, he calls on the thunderlord to blight the whole kingdom:

> *"And thou, all-shaking thunder,*
> *Strike flat the thick rotundity o' the world!*
> *Crack nature's moulds, all germens spill at once,*
> *That make ingrateful man!"* (KL III.ii)

Nature's moulds are ovum and germens are sperm. He calls forth an apocalyptic tidal wave of generative materials and a miscarriage of whatever the earth may be rotundly pregnant with.[151] Lear's misogynistic tirades against women and Nature will ultimately make it hard for an audience not to sympathize with the daughters who threw him out.[152]

Better Nature Through Sexual Chemistry
KING LEAR

After the wealthy Earl of Gloucester has been blinded, deprived of his lands, and cast out as a beggar, he gains a Marxist insight about material wealth and poverty: *"Distribution should undo excess, and each man have enough."* (IV.i) There's a dark, comical irony in this, coming from a man who distributed his seed at both ends of the social spectrum, but is determined that only one son inherit all of his property.

Nature gave the *"goatish"* Earl of Gloucester two sons (that we know of), but Fortune played favorites. Edgar, the firstborn legitimate son gets the title and lands, while Edmund the second-born bastard gets nothing but dirty jokes. Edmund challenges the patriarchal pantheon of Olympian gods, calling upon primal Nature to be his guide:

"Thou, Nature, art my goddess; to thy law
My services are bound. Wherefore should I
Stand in the plague of custom, and permit
The curiosity of nations to deprive me?
For that I am some twelve or fourteen moonshines
Lag of a brother? Why bastard? Wherefore base?
When my dimensions are as well compact,
My mind as generous, and my shape as true
As honest madam's issue? Why brand they us
With base? With baseness? bastardy? Base, base?
Who, in the lusty stealth of nature, take
More composition and fierce quality
Than doth within a dull stale tired bed
Go to the creating a whole tribe of fops
Got 'tween asleep and wake? ...Edmund the base
Shall top the legitimate. I grow, I prosper.
Now, gods, stand up for bastards!"
(KL I.ii, "curiosity" meaning unnatural behavior)

The bastard argues that Edgar, conceived at lazy leisure, inherited the name and lands, but Edmund inherited the *"lusty stealth* [and] *fierce quality"* of the passionate affair by which he was conceived. Edmund speaks for the ancient belief that better sex produces stronger children (these are the ritual origins of Comedy, bawdy performances as a type of foreplay so that couples would go home, get wild, and sprout strong citizens). Apparently, the sex that produced Edmund was so exciting that twenty years later Gloucester still fondly recalls *"this knave came something saucily to the world...there was good sport at his making."* (KL I.i) He jokes that he's blushed so many times thinking about the encounter that he now looks permanently suntanned.[153]

Edmund is societally branded with *"baseness,"* meaning that he springs from the lower appetites, as opposed to the honest heart and lofty mind that produced his legitimate brother. He'll use his baseness and lusty stealth to fight dirty, and he'll almost win, but Shakespeare fixes the fight. Shakespeare considered patrilineal legitimacy to be natural, and bastardy to be unnatural (Angelo in *Measure for Measure* compares bastards to counterfeit money). We can see Edmund as a rags-to-riches, self-made man, the rugged individual pulling himself up by the bootstraps with the Protestant work ethic and the spirit of capitalism. In this sense he would be a great tragic hero—except Shakespeare hated all that. He fixes Edmund up on a double date with Goneril and Regan but makes them all as sterile as mules.

In an angry fit of insecure patriarchalism, Shakespeare puts Edmund in his place. The bastard loses to the legitimate heir in ritual combat, a form of divination to let the gods decide who is more honest. As a bonus, the crown of England will go to the victor. Edgar stands over his defeated bastard brother and crows:

> *"The gods are just, and of our pleasant vices*
> *Make instruments to plague us:*
> *The dark and vicious place where thee he got*
> *Cost him his eyes."* (KL V.iii, "got" meaning begot or sired)

The moral of Shakespeare's Gloucester story is that you should always put all your eggs in one basket. For the crime of heresy against patriarchalism, the master puppeteer forces Edmund to recant; his dying words are a wish to be helpful: *"Despite of mine own nature."* (KL V.iii)[154]

Edmund is arguably the most driven and goal-directed character in *King Lear*, which should rightfully make him the protagonist. Plus, he is the play's most charismatic character, deserving a place among Shakespeare's great tragic heroes. Actor Anthony Alcocer, who was playing Edmund in a 2018 outdoor production of *King Lear* at Shakespeare in Delaware Park in Buffalo, New York, told me that the first step in developing the character is to forget the title of the script. "This play is called *Edmund*." I couldn't agree more. The land and legitimacy are poetic illusions; Edmund's real job is to steal the show. In fact, he did so in spades one evening that season. The king called for thunder and thunder arrived—the heavens opened, torrential rain fell, and the production had to shut down twenty minutes before the end. Edmund won! He got both queens and all the lands. Mother Nature had answered his prayer: *"Now, gods, stand up for bastards!"*

Edmund may have been originally played by William's little brother Edmund Shakespeare, who tagged along to London, becoming an actor. The youngest of the eight Shakespeare siblings, he was apparently a bit of a scamp, was involved in some scandals. He died a few years after *King Lear* at the rock star age of twenty-seven.

Sound and Fury—or—Nature vs "Fake News"
KING LEAR

In *King Lear*, Mother Nature's rival is not the housewife Fortune, but the human ability to create a virtual reality through speech, something akin to our modern phenomenon of decrying "Fake News." Lear himself is a news junky, born too soon for cable and social media updates. He starts the play asking his daughters who he is, and then goes around asking *everybody* who he is: *"O, you, sir, you, come you hither, sir: who am I, sir? ...Doth any here know me? ...Who is it that can tell me who I am?"* (KL I.iv) At first, he'll believe lies but reject the truth, then he just refuses to believe anything, it's all "fake news."

Lear gives up being a real king because he wants to be a fake king; he insists on keeping the title without the responsibilities or lands. He's king of nothing, and like the old story of The Emperor's New Clothes, he'll wind up naked. He longed to live a lie, and when his daughters reject his unrealistic expectations, he accuses them of being witches, *"unnatural hags;"* animals, *"she-foxes;"* and mythical monsters, *"centaurs."* He puts them on trial in absentia (appropriate since it's a dispute in which neither foster mother wants custody) with a madman as the judge and a clown as the jury. Then he runs off into a storm and rails at Nature herself.

It's sad to see how Lear becomes increasingly pathetic and unsympathetic. Remember in *As You Like It*, when the Duke, banished to the forest, grooved with Nature? *"Are not these woods / More free from peril than the envious court?"* And shivering in icy breezes, *"This is no flattery; these are counsellors / That feelingly persuade me what I am."* (AYL II.i) Lear doesn't do that. He's an old windbag, full of sound and fury, sputtering and spitting at the wind.

What makes Edgar a legitimate heir and Edmund a nobody are magic words: vows spoken in a wedding service. But Gloucester perjured his marital oath by committing adultery. Edgar was three months old and at his mother's breast when his father went out slumming *"in the lusty stealth of nature.*" Edmund forges a letter to fool his father about Edgar, then uses one of Gloucester's own letters to overthrow him. By this point in the play, nobody can trust anybody, and Cornwall shrugs, *"True or false, it hath made thee Earl of Gloucester."*

If we expect greater honesty from Edgar, we're in for disappointment. He lies to his father in the guise of Poor Tom, and after the old man is blinded, Edgar misleads and deceives him as a redneck at the top of the Dover cliffs and as a fisherman at the bottom. Except there was no cliff. Edgar hoodwinks the audience: on a bare stage, his description creates the optical illusion of a precipice, but then the old man leaps and lands with a thud. The joke is on Gloucester. He's the funniest fool in Shakespeare, but the joke is also on us.

Gloucester is honest, but tragically blind. The removal of his eyes is just a formality, and even his blinding becomes a dark slapstick comedy. Then, just when we expect him to gain some *in*-sight, he blasts off like a rocket in the opposite direction, thinking he's gained a cosmic view of a human flea circus: *"As flies to wanton boys are we to the gods, / They kill us for their sport."* (KL IV.i) So he decides to end his miserable life and fails with a farcical pratfall. Jan Kott writes, "The blind Gloucester falls over on the empty stage. His suicidal leap is tragic...but the pantomime performed by actors on the stage is grotesque and has something of a circus about it. The blind Gloucester who has climbed a non-existent height and fallen over on flat boards, is a clown... In Shakespeare, clowns often ape the gestures of kings and heroes, but only in *King Lear* are great tragic scenes shown through clowning."[155] Gloucester should have had his own play, Polonius would have loved it, a *"tragical-comical-historical-pastoral,"* it could have been called *Clownfall.*

Lear's daughters, Goneril and Regan, start the play as a tag team of liars, indulging Lear's taste for artificial sweeteners. Then they paddle their dispossessed father back and forth like a king-pong ball. Or perhaps it would be more accurate to say he declared himself the royal couch potato and they toss him around like a hot potato. But it's only a matter of time before their sibling rivalry turns deadly. They start bidding in the bachelor auction for Edmund. Regan has the advantage because her husband was killed during the half-time intermission of Gloucester's blinding. And she's all in:

"Take thou my soldiers, prisoners, patrimony;
Dispose of them, of me; the walls are thine:
Witness the world that I create thee here
My lord and master...
Let the drum strike, and prove my title thine." (KL V.iii)

That drumbeat never drops, because Edmund is immediately ensnared in an accusation of treason (Yes, "ensnared" was a pun I couldn't resist, but at least I didn't use the puns about baseness, Poor Tom, and symbolism. Moving on). Regan not only bids to be Edmund's wife, but to *"create thee here"* as a divine mother who'll retroactively fix his legitimacy issue. That is some genuine royal hocus-pocus. But Regan's magic words are just air, undermined by her bellyful of death; Goneril has already poisoned her. And soon their three stiff bodies will be stacked like firewood. Edmund sighs, *"I was contracted to them both, all three / Now marry in an instant."*

Traditionally, Cordelia is the one character we can trust. Or is she? The *Manga Shakespeare* team of Richard Appignanesi and Ilya presented a very convincing assertion that the banished Cordelia dons a disguise and becomes the Fool.[156] We never see the two of them together—the Fool doesn't show up until she's gone, and then mysteriously vanishes just before she returns. Then, when Lear carries Cordelia's body from the prison gallows he says, *"My poor fool is hang'd!"* (KL V.iii) Cordelia as the Fool creates a balance with Edgar as Poor Tom and proves her legendary loyalty. It also fixes the problem of having her jet to France and back overnight. It's possible that one of Shakespeare's greatest transvestite heroines has fooled us all for centuries.

King Lear in performance always ends so badly, which is too bad. Instead of a corpse-cart bell and the chant of "bring out your dead," the curtain call should be a festive Sondheim jig, "Bring on the lovers, liars, and clowns." This is a story in which lies, written and spoken, have thrashed and shattered these slapstick marionettes. But that doesn't mean Shakespeare's lies, written and spoken, need to bludgeon the audience. We're in on the joke, we have a divine omniscient view of how speech has distorted reality. Lear's daughters sell him bridges of emotional connection that evaporate, a madman leads a blind man up a mountain that fades in the air, Lear gets lost in a mirage wilderness of self-deception. But no matter how much people lie, Nature remains honest and true.

The real tragedy of *King Lear* is that some of the funniest lines in all of Shakespeare get mangled and contorted into sentimental drivel. The sour jawbreaker comedy that's meant to grind your teeth is all homogenized into bland baby food. We should be wiping away tears of laughter. Terry Gilliam, the Monty Python animator who made the *Fisher King*, could make a great comedy with the script of *King Lear*. Or I guess an editor could remix it from his pre-existing films and call it *Lear and Loathing in La Munchausen*.[157]

Mother and Daughter Nature
KING LEAR

Lear blusters a lot. Like a sad white man grasping for victimhood, he points the finger at everyone and never mind how many of his fingers point back at him. Lear feels he's been betrayed by his daughters and by Nature herself. That's all in his mind. His daughters did what he raised them to do, Goneril and Regan told him exactly what they knew he wanted to hear, and Cordelia told him the truth.

Finding shelter, he pitifully whines that *"the rain came to wet me once, and the wind to make me chatter; when the thunder would not peace at my bidding,"* but he hadn't been out there commanding the storm to stop. Very much the opposite. *"Blow, winds, and crack your cheeks! Rage! Blow!"* He commanded the storm to rage and it did. If we look past Lear's self-pity, we'll actually see that Nature still considers him king and follows his commands.

Lear gives away his crown, and Nature gives him a better one. It's not some shiny ring of fool's gold, but a medicinal poultice of herbal remedies. This is a bit confusing because the stage direction tells us he's *"fantastically dressed up with flowers."* However, this was a later insertion, copied from Hamlet: *"Re-enter Ophelia, fantastically dressed with straws and flowers."* Cordelia gives us the pharmaceutical breakdown of Lear's new headgear: *"Crown'd with rank fumiter and furrow weeds, with harlocks, hemlock, nettles, cuckoo-flowers, darnel, and all the idle weeds that grow in our sustaining corn."* (KL IV.iv) He's wearing a pharmacopeia on his head. As Jayne Elisabeth Archer and others have noted, "The crown of 'idle weeds' contains plants that expel toxins from the body: fumitory was used as a diuretic to cleanse the skin, liver, and spleen; hemlock and darnel were taken as purgatives and for their narcotic power."[158]

Nature prescribes these remedies, and then we get a second opinion from a doctor:

> "PHYSICIAN. There is means, madam:
> Our foster nurse of nature is repose,
> The which he lacks; that to provoke in him
> Are many simples operative, whose power
> Will close the eye of anguish.
> CORDELIA. All bless'd secrets,
> All you unpublish'd virtues of the earth,
> Spring with my tears! Be aidant and remediate
> In the good man's distress! Seek, seek for him." (KL IV.iv)

The physician prescribes rest and "simples," meaning herbal remedies. Cordelia prays to Nature to produce medicinal plants that she will water with her tears. King Lear insists that he has been betrayed by Mother Nature and his daughter Cordelia. Actually, both remain quietly loyal and obedient to him. None of the main characters can see this, but in the fourth act a nameless gentleman observes on behalf of the audience: "Thou hast one daughter who redeems nature." (KL IV.vi)

Lear's embitterment toward Nature is contagious. His brain is a wasteland, and all his ranting may create the optical illusion that he's wandering through the blasted heath of Macbeth's Scotland. Actually, the trustworthy Cordelia tells us he's been wandering in a "high-grown field" of "sustaining corn," which in Shakespeare's day would mean wheat stalks two meters tall, corn as high as an elephant's eye. Darnel, one of the weeds in his crown, will only grow when the grains are healthy. Despite Lear's blighting curses, the land remains abundantly fertile, but political intrigues have everyone too busy to weed or harvest it. Shakespeare knew this well, having grown up in the countryside. He was a city slicker, but let's not forget he was a land baron too, and only wrote King Lear for funds to buy grain plantations.

Womb, Tomb, and Infinite Breast
ROMEO AND JULIET | TIMON OF ATHENS

Shakespeare's personified Nature is one of his most complex and nuanced characters.[159] She is ever-present in the background, but frequently leaps into the foreground in the form of a forest, storm, plant, or animal interacting with the characters. A country boy and farmer, William Shakespeare knew that "the environment" is not just a backdrop or piece of scenery, but a matrix, an interconnected web of life in which humans are just one of many active factors.

Nature is the land that kings marry. The crown is a wedding ring signifying a special relationship with the earth and elements. Many of his royal plays explore this relationship. For example, Nature loves Lear (a stormy marriage but a strong one) and hates the usurper Macbeth. Shakespeare's Nature is the mystical and mysterious forest that can alleviate the toxic masculinity of patriarchal culture. She is also the blood-drinking pit that swallows children. Within this web, the lover, lunatic, and poet are brief carriers of a life force in constant flux: *"So, from hour to hour, we ripe and ripe / and then, from hour to hour, we rot and rot."* (AYL II.vii)

Shakespeare's clearest sermon in praise of maternal Nature is delivered by a Friar in *Romeo and Juliet*. He describes the earth as mother to diverse plants and creatures, good, bad, and ugly, and how even the vilest of poisons has its virtues:

> *"The earth that's nature's mother, is her tomb;*
> *What is her burying grave, that is her womb:*
> *And from her womb children of divers kind*
> *We sucking on her natural bosom find.*
> *Many for many virtues excellent,*
> *None but for some, and yet all different.*
> *O, [mighty] is the powerful grace that lies*
> *In plants, herbs, stones, and their true qualities.*
> *For naught so vile that on the earth doth live*
> *But to the earth some special good doth give;*
> *Nor aught so good but, strain'd from that fair use,*
> *Revolts from true birth, stumbling on abuse.*

Virtue itself turns vice being misapplied,
And vice sometime's by action dignified." (R&J II.iii)

Lawrence is talking about the plants in his cell, a greenhouse in an Italian city. But he will also be the proponent of natural human love, letting nature take its course in human pairing. When he learns that Romeo and Juliet have bonded instinctively, he accepts that Nature has produced this love as the antidote for a poisonous cultural feud.

Friar Lawrence's sermon on the diverse bounties of Nature has its flipside in a tirade delivered in *Timon of Athens*. This is the bitter story of a gentleman who has squandered his wealth on rented friends who then offer no assistance when he goes bankrupt. Timon blames everyone except himself for his downfall, even castigating Nature, *"damn'd earth, thou common whore of mankind,"* for having produced humans in the first place. Then he goes foraging: *"The bounteous housewife Nature on each bush / Lays her full mess before you."* (TA IV.iii) There's a rancid irony here that Timon delivers a screed while digging in the dirt for edible roots, and in a darkly comical moment the earth gives him a root to eat, he absent-mindedly thanks her, then goes right on telling her to stop feeding humanity.

> *"That nature, being sick of man's unkindness,*
> *Should yet be hungry! Common mother, thou,*
> *Whose womb unmeasurable and infinite breast*
> *Teems and feeds all; whose self-same mettle,*
> *Whereof thy proud child, arrogant man, is puff'd,*
> *Engenders the black toad and adder blue,*
> *The gilded newt and eyeless venom'd worm,*
> *With all th' abhorrèd births below crisp heaven*
> *Whereon Hyperion's quick'ning fire doth shine-*
> *Yield* [me], *who all thy human sons doth hate,*
> *From forth thy plenteous bosom, one poor root!*
> *Ensear thy fertile and conceptious womb,*
> *Let it no more bring out ingrateful man!*
> *Go great with tigers, dragons, wolves, and bears;*
> *Teem with new monsters whom thy upward face*
> *Hath to the marbled mansion all above*
> *Never presented!- O, a root! Dear thanks!-*

Dry up thy marrows, vines, and plough-torn leas,
Whereof ingrateful man, with liquorish draughts
And morsels unctuous, greases his pure mind,
That from it all consideration slips."
(TIM IV.iii, "Hyperion" is the personified sun, "go great" and
"teem" mean conceive)

Timon of Athens is Shakespeare's most rancid creation. The play has
no female characters, except for a brief cameo by two prostitutes. And yet,
even at his most bitter, Timon acknowledges Nature as *"Common mother...*
Whose womb unmeasurable and infinite breast / Teems and feeds all" creatures
from *"thy fertile and conceptious womb."* He's also surprisingly scientific in his
understanding of Nature generating new life by recycling from droppings
and decay: *"The earth's a thief, that feeds and breeds by a composture stol'n from*
gen'ral excrement." (TA IV.iii) The topic of Nature as the blood-drinking
tomb will be further explored in the chapters on *Titus Andronicus.*[160]

In Lawrence's sermon and Timon's tirade, Nature is self-sufficient
and self-sustaining (she even recycles). Shakespeare can, at times, be
remarkably modern in his biology lectures. But we must keep in mind that
he was steadfastly medieval in his belief that Nature must be husbanded by
a human king. Shakespeare's ideal Nature is patriarchal and hierarchical.
Perhaps the best illustration of this is a sermon given by the Archbishop
in *Henry V*, in which Nature taught monarchy and the division of labor to
bees, so that humans could learn from this example:

"Obedience; for so work the honey bees,
Creatures that by a rule in nature teach
The act of order to a peopled kingdom.
They have a king, and officers of sorts,
Where some like magistrates correct at home;
Others like merchants venture trade abroad;
Others like soldiers, armèd in their stings,
Make boot upon the summer's velvet buds,
Which pillage they with merry march bring home
To the tent-royal of their emperor;
Who, busied in his majesty, surveys
The singing masons building roofs of gold." (H5 I.ii)[161]

Ironies abound here. Shakespeare, following Aristotle, assumes that a hive is ruled by a king (this was written ten years before the release of Charles Butler's 1609 apiary exposé, *The Feminine Monarchy*).[162] The other irony is that this priest's speech is the perfect opposite of Jesus' advice to "consider the lilies" who don't have to work for a living. In this homily, the lilies exist to be plundered by an army of fascist bees.

Shakespeare's ideal Nature was medieval and monarchic. And he was unabashedly nationalistic in his belief that Nature's masterpiece was England, whose peace and prosperity were protected by oceans.

> *"This royal throne of kings, this scept'red isle,*
> *This earth of majesty, this seat of Mars,*
> *This other Eden, demi-paradise,*
> *This fortress built by Nature for herself*
> *Against infection and the hand of war,*
> *This happy breed of men, this little world,*
> *This precious stone set in the silver sea...*
> *This blessèd plot, this earth, this realm, this England,*
> *This nurse, this teeming womb of royal kings."* (R2 II.i)[163]

The Missing English Goddess
A Midsummer Night's Dream | Romeo and Juliet | The Merry Wives of Windsor

Milton called Shakespeare "Fancy's child" who could "warble his native wood-notes wild," but Shakespeare took little interest in native English deities. The indigenous peoples of Britain had gods and goddesses before the Romans arrived, but these have been largely lost to history. There was a bit of syncretism, the identification of such-and-such native English deity with such-and-such Roman deity. Then, during the Christianization of Rome and England, all these goddesses were hidden behind the masks of saints and the Virgin Mary. The Protestant Reformation shoved the sacred women of Christianity further into the margins, and in Elizabethan poetry and plays they had to be hidden behind Roman goddess masks again. It all gets a bit confusing.

While all of this was going on, indigenous English deities did get to run wild in the forest preserve of fairy lore—as long as it was firmly agreed that fairies were strictly "old wives' tales" for children's amusement and not in any way to be confused with serious adult religion. We continue this tradition today, with Santa Claus and the Tooth Fairy harmlessly hovering on the sidelines of Christianity. William Shakespeare does not appear to have taken fairies very seriously–his fairy-ology is neither consistent nor comprehensive. He borrows from various traditions (published poems and whatever stories he heard from his own granny or nanny) and fits each fairy to a particular story.

A study of the divine feminine in Shakespeare cannot ignore the two fairy queens: Titania in *A Midsummer Night's Dream* and Mab in *Romeo and Juliet*. Plus, his presentation of Titania, the supernatural forest spirit, is as close as we'll get to a representation of an indigenous English goddess on the Shakespearean stage. Ironically, he places her in a forest near Athens, but really all of Shakespeare's forests are the English forest.

Titania is clearly distinguished from the Greco-Roman goddesses. In *A Midsummer Night's Dream*, Diana is the watery moon and Venus is *"Aurora's harbinger,"* the morning star. Both are distant and celestial whereas Titania is down-to-earth and natural. Catherine Diamond observes that

"Titania reigns over the biodiverse forest minutiae: butterflies, bees, fireflies, medicinal herbs, and flowers,"[164] whereas Oberon rules the predatory bear, leopard, and boar. The fairy queen and king are in a custody dispute over a foster child, and Oberon's stubborn refusal to play his part in lunar rituals is causing an environmental catastrophe. *"The ploughman lost his sweat, and the green corn / Hath rotted ere his youth attain'd a beard."* (MND II.i) As a Nature goddess, Titania's concern for a single grain of wheat dying in its youth is as great as her compassion for a farmer, or for a whole nation dependent on agriculture.[165]

This play was written during what climatologists call a "little ice age," a time of cooling and crop loss. It was also a time when seasonal fertility rituals were in decline. Gary Day writes, "The discipline demanded by a new economic order, Puritan attacks on traditional customs and pastimes, the new individualism, and a more scientific understanding of nature, all contributed to a weakening of man's connection to the world of flora and fauna."[166] Shakespeare takes a playfully satirical jab at the Protestant work ethic and the spirit of capitalism, standing up for the magical aspects of Nature, personified by Titania. This is ironic since Shakespeare himself was a Citizen Cain land baron, convicted of hoarding wheat during famine to manipulate grain prices (yes, "C-a-i-n," in reference to the Biblical cutthroat ploughman).

Titania as a personification of Nature is maternal, yet she apparently cannot have children of her own. She has adopted a child, or stolen one depending on how we read the script. Her strong maternal feelings are at the core of her discord with Oberon. Feeling entitled to this kid as a kind of exotic knick-knack, the fairy king is willing to hold all-natural fertility hostage, and Titania's defiance sparks a standoff of mutually assured destruction. To restore fertility to the land, Titania is essentially being ordered to sacrifice a child.[167]

Oberon commands Puck to redirect her affections to a boar or leopard but the playful trickster encounters a childish jackass and uses him instead. Externalizing Bottom's ass-ness satisfies Oberon's command to substitute a beast, and then Titania externalizes his childishness by infantilizing him. Drugged with juice from Venus's son Cupid, Titania babies Bottom with poetry reminiscent of *Venus and Adonis*, but she's more maternal than sexual.[168]

Bottom is an ass, yet Titania sees an angel. Whatever he is, she knows he's not a fairy, and uses interspecies metaphors as she wraps herself around him:

> "Sleep thou, and I will wind thee in my arms...
> So doth the woodbine the sweet honeysuckle
> Gently entwist; the female ivy so
> Enrings the barky fingers of the elm." (MND IV.i)

In this, his most Ovidian play, Shakespeare comes closest to the *Metamorphoses* theme of encounters between mortals and gods in the midst of woodland Nature. And like Ovidian victims, Bottom will be unable to tell the tale. Titania does give Oberon the changeling child, but the victory is soured because he couldn't win without cheating. Perhaps the two will share half-year custody, the child spending the colder months with the subterranean king and the warmer months the forest goddess.

At the same time that he was writing *A Midsummer Night's Dream*, Shakespeare was also working on *Romeo and Juliet*. With fairies still flitting through his mind, he created an imaginary one for Mercutio's speech about dreams:

> "O, then, I see Queen Mab hath been with you.
> She is the fairies' midwife, and she comes...
> Her chariot is an empty hazelnut,
> Made by the joiner squirrel or old grub,
> Time out o' mind the fairies' coachmakers.
> And in this state she gallops night by night
> Through lovers' brains, and then they dream of love;
> O'er courtiers' knees, that dream on curtsies straight;
> O'er lawyers' fingers, who straight dream on fees;
> O'er ladies' lips, who straight on kisses dream,
> Which oft the angry Mab with blisters plagues,
> Because their breaths with sweetmeats tainted are." (R&J I.iv)

While Titania is a woodland nymph concerned with cobwebs, moths, and blossoms, this Mab is a metropolitan busybody visiting courtiers, lawyers, ladies, and soldiers. Titania is an embodiment of Nature, and Mab is a resident of culture, cruising the urban jungle in her hotrod chariot.[169] Titania doesn't share Oberon's concern for nuptial propriety—he conspired with Puck in a matchmaking scheme while she reclined with a mechanic, lamenting enforced chastity. But Mab angrily leaves cold sores on the lips of loose maidens.

Despite scholarly efforts to reconcile or relate them, Titania and Mab are two very distinct manifestations of a Fairy Queen, each with different habits from different habitats. But later, Shakespeare himself synthesizes the two into a single Fairy Queen in *The Merry Wives of Windsor*. Like Titania, she is a forest fairy leading circle dances to bless fertility, and like Mab, she is vindictive about *"sluttery"* (sloppiness and looseness).

> *"FAIRY QUEEN. About, about;*
> *Search Windsor castle, elves, within and out...*
> *The several chairs of order look you scour*
> *With juice of balm and every precious flower;*
> *Each fair instalment, coat, and sev'ral crest,*
> *With loyal blazon, evermore be blest!*
> *And nightly, meadow-fairies, look you sing,*
> *Like to the Garter's compass, in a ring;*
> *Th' expressure that it bears, green let it be,*
> *More fertile-fresh than all the field to see...*
> *Fairies use flow'rs for their charactery.*
> *Away, disperse; but till 'tis one o'clock,*
> *Our dance of custom round about the oak*
> *Of Herne the Hunter let us not forget...*
> *Corrupt, corrupt, and tainted in desire!*
> *About him, fairies; sing a scornful rhyme;*
> *And, as you trip, still pinch him to your time."* (MWW V.v)

Significantly, while Shakespeare situates Titania near Athens and Mab in Italy, the Fairy Queen in *The Merry Wives of Windsor* inhabits an English forest in Windsor. And Herne, the horned hunter, bears a certain resemblance to the indigenous English antlered god, Cernunnos. It's doubtful Shakespeare made this connection, but the name "Herne" must have come from somewhere. In this scene, the Fairy Queen is played by a local gossip and Herne is played by Falstaff (wearing antlers and expecting illicit sex in the woods, for which he'll be pinched in punishment).

William Shakespeare does not seem to have intentionally or consciously set out to present an indigenous English Nature goddess, but by coincidence he cobbles together this interesting constellation of characteristics, just enough for a clouded composite portrait.

Monster Nature
Titus Andronicus

We may think of Shakespeare's woodland as a magical playground, a *kindergarten* in the German sense of a haven for childish sprites in *A Midsummer Night's Dream*, even a fountain of youth for the refugees of *As You Like It*, as if Shakespeare inherited Ovid's jungle and did some expert forestry, clearing the dank underbrush, deadly critters, and supernatural sexual predators. But in the beginning, Shakespeare's forest had been a dangerous place, a seething cesspool of Nature with a heart of impenetrable darkness.[170]

One of Shakespeare's first forays into forest Nature was in *Titus Andronicus*, an atrocity exhibition written during a dark time for drama, when the emerging English stage had to lure in the fans of street duels, bearbaiting, and the gallows. Why would peasants pay a penny to see players pretend when they could watch criminals get maimed, hanged, beheaded, or burned alive for free? So, for a time, playwrights competed to write the bloodiest scripts, and the hungry young William Shakespeare made his bid to outdo them all with the shock and schlock of *Titus*.

While the principle characters go out on a merry hunt, the play's villains plot mischief in the wood. The wicked Aaron instructs two barbaric brothers to prey upon Titus's daughter, whom he likens to a deer.

> *"My lords, a solemn hunting is in hand;*
> *There will the lovely Roman ladies troop;*
> *The forest walks are wide and spacious,*
> *And many unfrequented plots there are*
> *Fitted by kind for rape and villainy.*
> *Single you thither then this dainty doe,*
> *And strike her home by force if not by words...*
> *The Emperor's court is like the house of Fame,*
> *The palace full of tongues, of eyes, and ears;*
> *The woods are ruthless, dreadful, deaf, and dull...*
> *There serve your lust, shadowed from heaven's eye."* (TA II.i)

Aaron describes the city as a hive of eyes and ears and lies, the body politic as a demonic entity.[171] In the city of Rome, someone is always watching, and Aaron's lover has just become the empress, so to be caught with her would certainly mean his gruesome execution. But the woods are an ideal scene for his crimes, a place where surveillance is impossible, even for the gods.

The Goth Queen Tamora takes the stage. In the first act she was hauled to Rome in chains, a prisoner of war forced to watch helplessly as her eldest son was sacrificed and dismembered in vengeance for the fallen soldiers who sacked her homeland. Maybe her husband was killed in this war, but he is never mentioned. Perhaps Tamora herself has been ruling the nation as an Amazon queen bee. She has been dragged through the streets as a humiliated captive, and by Roman custom she will soon have her neck broken in a triumphal parade before a howling crowd. But when Titus's daughter evades the new emperor's marriage proposal, Tamora seizes the day and grabs him on the rebound, becoming empress.

The next morning, having prostituted herself to seal the deal, she celebrates her costly liberation with a walk in the woods. Here in the wild, outside the patriarchal city, she blossoms into her full strength. She will soon use this savage power to take over the city, but first she needs to recharge. Reuniting with her chosen lover Aaron, Tamora poetically describes how their union will transform the wilderness into an enchanted forest:

> "The birds chant melody on every bush;
> The snakes lie rollèd in the cheerful sun;
> The green leaves quiver with the cooling wind
> And make a chequer'd shadow on the ground;
> Under their sweet shade, Aaron, let us sit,
> And while the babbling echo mocks the hounds,
> Replying shrilly to the well-tun'd horns,
> As if a double hunt were heard at once,
> Let us sit down and mark their yellowing noise;
> And after conflict such as was suppos'd
> The wand'ring prince and Dido once enjoyed,
> When with a happy storm they were surpris'd,
> And curtain'd with a counsel-keeping cave
> We may, each wreathèd in the other's arms,
> Our pastimes done, possess a golden slumber,
> Whiles hounds and horns and sweet melodious birds

Be unto us as is a nurse's song
Of lullaby to bring her babe asleep." (TA II.i)

Tamora speaks of the park as a primeval paradise, as if she and her illicit lover could sit beneath a bough with a flask of wine and take turns reading from the *Rubaiyat*.[172] She compares herself to that other famous barbarian queen Dido, who seduced the wandering Aeneas in a cave during a storm (this, like Aaron's description of Fame, comes from the fourth book of Virgil's *Aeneid*). The forest will shelter them and keep their secrets, so they can lie in each other's arms. Lovers *"wreathed"* like plants together is an image Shakespeare will use again in *A Midsummer Night's Dream*, when Titania wraps herself around Bottom like the ivy on an elm tree.

But their bliss will be interrupted by Titus's daughter Lavinia and her husband Bassianus. They'll playfully banter about Actaeon stumbling into Diana's forest grove, then the Goth queen reveals her full horrifying power. She will transform the woodland paradise into a Roman wilderness of pain. The melody of horns, horses, hounds, and birds is replaced by a symphony of swarming scavengers, spawns, and serpents. The safe haven cavern degenerates into a foul and fetid crevice:

> *"TAMORA. A barren detested vale you see it is:*
> *The trees, though summer, yet forlorn and lean,*
> *Overcome with moss and baleful mistletoe;*
> *Here never shines the sun; here nothing breeds,*
> *Unless the nightly owl or fatal raven.*
> *And when they show'd me this abhorrèd pit,*
> *They told me, here, at dead time of the night,*
> *A thousand fiends, a thousand hissing snakes,*
> *Ten thousand swelling toads, as many urchins,*
> *Would make such fearful and confusèd cries*
> *As any mortal body hearing it*
> *Should straight fall mad or else die suddenly."* (TA II.i)

Tamora's two sons emerge from seething shadows. They murder Bassianus, dump his body in a pit, and drag his young bride Lavinia off to do something unspeakable. Lavinia appeals to Tamora as a woman, requesting execution and burial, but the Goth Queen sees Lavinia only as Titus's soft target (and by extension, this chaste bride represents the vaunted purity of Rome), so she shows no mercy. This is the first time in the script that Tamora is called a *"tiger,"* and it won't be the last—she'll turn Rome into a *"wilderness of tigers."* (TA III.i)

Later, two of Titus's sons will wander by the scene of the crime, and one of them will stumble into the pit of dark Nature:

> *"QUINTUS. What, art thou fallen? What subtle hole is this,*
> *Whose mouth is covered with rude-growing briers,*
> *Upon whose leaves are drops of new-shed blood*
> *As fresh as morning dew distill'd on flowers?...*
> *MARTIUS. Why dost not comfort me, and help me out*
> *From this unhallow'd and blood-stainèd hole?...*
> *Lord Bassianus lies beray'd in blood,*
> *All on a heap, like to a slaughtered lamb,*
> *In this detested, dark, blood-drinking pit.*
> *QUINTUS. If it be dark, how dost thou know 'tis he?*
> *MARTIUS. Upon his bloody finger he doth wear*
> *A precious ring that lightens all this hole...*
> *And shows the ragged entrails of this pit;*
> *So pale did shine the moon on Pyramus*
> *When he by night lay bath'd in maiden blood.*
> *O brother, help me with thy fainting hand-*
> *If fear hath made thee faint, as me it hath-*
> *Out of this fell devouring receptacle,*
> *As hateful as Cocytus' misty mouth.*
> *QUINTUS. Reach me thy hand, that I may help thee out,*
> *Or, wanting strength to do thee so much good,*
> *I may be pluck'd into the swallowing womb*
> *Of this deep pit, poor Bassianus' grave."* (TA II.i)

Commentators have long noted the misogynistic description of this crevice, it sounds like Georgia O'Keeffe on a bad acid trip. The ground is bloody and bloodthirsty, Martius describes it like the yawning mouth of Hell itself, *"Cocytus"* being the Roman name of the river Styx, gutter to the underworld. Sinking the dead Emperor's son Bassianus into the soil of Rome is a horrible reverse birth. The description of a womb-as-tomb echoes Titus's description of his familial crypt as he laid his battle-slain sons to rest:

"O sacred receptacle of my joys,
Sweet cell of virtue and nobility,
How many sons hast thou of mine in store
That thou wilt never render to me more!" (TA I.i)

Titus is presumably a widower—someone bore him twenty-five sons and a daughter, but this mother (like so many dead mothers in Shakespeare) is never mentioned. We could almost imagine that his children sprouted from the maternal soil of Rome itself.

And we can't ignore the fact that Roman culture, with all its patriarchal grandeur, was built on the back of Mother Earth. In a sense, Nature herself is a hostage and forced bride of the patriarchal city, like Tamora. And the Goth Queen as a manifestation of shackled and exploited Nature will have her revenge. Furthermore, having become mother figure and puppeteer of the childish emperor Saturninus, "a sort of fascist Pee-wee Herman,"[173] Tamora has gained the imperial might of a living goddess.

Grinning from the sidelines, her acolyte Aaron says:

"Now climbeth Tamora Olympus' top,
Safe out of Fortune's shot, and sits aloft,
Secure of thunder's crack or lightning flash,
Advanc'd above pale envy's threat'ning reach...
Upon her wit doth earthly honour wait,
And virtue stoops and trembles at her frown....
I will be bright and shine in pearl and gold,
To wait upon this new-made emperess.
To wait, said I? To wanton with this queen,
This goddess, this Semiramis,[174] this nymph,
This siren that will charm Rome's Saturnine,
And see his shipwreck and his commonweal's." (TA II.i, Semiramis was a legendary queen who murdered her lovers)

In *Titus Andronicus*, Nature is personified as a sociopath: good, bad, and ugly. Ascending to the throne of Rome, Tamora will become Nature's semi-divine high priestess. And this special relationship will emphasize and empower those aspects of Nature that are most like the vengeful, vicious Tamora.

Titus Android
TITUS ANDRONICUS

When we meet Titus, the play's titular character, he is essentially an android, a wind-up killing machine. As a conquering general, he has spent his life mechanically marching centurions into meat-grinders of war. Twenty-one of his twenty-five sons have been butchered in battle, two of them casualties of this latest campaign against the Goths. With four sons and a daughter left, he decides it's time to lay down his Energizer battle drum and retire.

In stiff ceremony, Titus dispatches his dead sons to lie among their ancestors in the family tomb. He orders the Goth Queen's eldest son to be sacrificed so that his blood can appease the angry ghosts and keep them from disturbing the Roman peace. In this scene we meet Tamora as helpless mother, appealing to Titus's humanity, but her passionate words are in vain. This terminator cannot be bargained or reasoned with, he is without pity or remorse. Titus triggers a chain reaction of escalating retaliation; he sees a helpless prisoner, but soon she'll have her finger on the buttons of Rome.

The play opens with civil strife in the streets. The Emperor has died and his two sons vie for the throne while the citizens wish to install Titus. With simple clockwork logic, the automaton announces that the son who was born first automatically succeeds. The newly crowned Emperor Saturninus rubs in his victory by publicly proposing to his younger brother's girlfriend, Titus's daughter Lavinia. Like a vending machine, the general dispenses her and when his children protest, he executes one of his surviving sons for rebellion against patriarchalism. Disgusted by this dissent within the Andronicus household, Saturninus instead marries the Goth queen, Tamora.

The very next day, Tamora mobilizes for revenge, a *quid pro quo*. As Titus mercilessly sent her firstborn son to be butchered and dismembered (*"lopp'd"*), Tamora sics her dogged sons on Titus's only daughter. Lavinia pleads with Tamora as Tamora pleaded with Titus, but to no avail—the Queen responds mechanically. Lavinia is ravished and dismembered, her tongue cut out and her hands *"lopp'd"* off. Tamora has rightly identified her opponent Titus as a cyborg, and deduces that his weak spot, his beating human heart, is his daughter. Tamora will later trick Titus into chopping off his own hand as well. She'll offer to accept this in exchange for two of his sons, framed for Bassianus's murder, but then she'll send only their severed heads.

Titus is totally overwhelmed. He quotes Ovid in Latin, *"Terras Astrea reliquit"* (the goddess of Justice has abandoned the earth), writes angry letters to the editors of fate, ties them to arrows, and fires them into the sky. But the gods don't hear, and his letters are intercepted by Tamora the nemesis-goddess on earth. Then she appears to him, dressed as the Roman goddess Revenge, with her two sons disguised as the henchmen Murder and Rape.

> *"TAMORA. Know thou, sad man, I am not Tamora:*
> *She is thy enemy and I thy friend.*
> *I am Revenge, sent from th' infernal kingdom*
> *To ease the gnawing vulture of thy mind*
> *By working wreakful vengeance on thy foes.*
> *Come down and welcome me to this world's light;*
> *Confer with me of murder and of death;*
> *There's not a hollow cave or lurking-place,*
> *No vast obscurity or misty vale,*
> *Where bloody murder or detested rape*
> *Can couch for fear but I will find them out;*
> *And in their ears tell them my dreadful name-*
> *Revenge, which makes the foul offender quake."* (TA V.ii)

There's nothing in Titus's instruction manuals about how to deal with a living death-goddess who can pull the levers and turn the screws of Rome itself to break him. The Queen has gone Goth-Industrial, and he can't beat her as a chess machine. Coppélia Kahn writes, "The play can be seen as the story of Titus's transformation from Roman hero to revenge hero, which he accomplishes by hacking and hewing his way through the tangled matrix of outrages and injuries that Tamora spawns."[175] As a vengeful mother whose powers extend over the metropolis and wilderness alike, Tamora indeed becomes the matrix and state domina—a sadistic dominatrix.

This is when Titus becomes interesting, in a roundabout way. Of all the shocking and distasteful elements of this play, perhaps the most offensive to our modern sensibilities is how Titus discovers his humanity. As patriarch, guardian of the Andronicus family honor, he appropriates his daughter's victimhood as his own. In doing so, he discovers his feminine side and unleashes his own inner Goth-Queen. First, the rusty tin-man Titus learns to weep:

> *"I am the sea; hark how her sighs do blow.*
> *She is the weeping welkin, I the earth;*
> *Then must my sea be movèd with her sighs;*
> *Then must my earth with her continual tears*
> *Become a deluge, overflow'd and drown'd;*
> *For why my bowèls cannot hide her woes,*
> *But like a drunkard must I vomit them."*
> (TA III.i, "welkin" meaning sky)

He goes off into his study, the man-cave he's renamed *"revenge's cave,"* symbolic of the earth's womb, and emerges with a page from Ovid's playbook, the *Metamorphoses*. His muted and mutilated daughter has used Ovid's story of Philomel to report the crimes against her (Philomel was raped by the husband of her sister Procne, who retaliated by killing their son). Titus sheds the manly rules of engagement and becomes Procne: *"For worse than Philomel you us'd my daughter, / And worse than Progne I will be reveng'd."* (TA V.ii) By this he means he'll lay down his armor, tie on an apron, and play the psycho housewife.[176]

Combining the grim determination of Sweeney Todd with the chirpy cheer of Mrs. Lovett, he butchers Tamora's rapacious sons, bakes them into a pastry, and invites their mother over for a dinner-party. With her mouth full she asks where her children are, and the chef replies,

> *"Why, there they are, both bakèd in this pie,*
> *Whereof their mother daintily hath fed,*
> *Eating the flesh that she herself hath bred."* (TA V.iii)

Before she can digest the news that she's got her sons' dainties (testicles) in her teeth, Titus lunges across the table and stabs her to death. He preemptively silences her response and the obscene cuckoo clockwork of Looney Toons escalation comes to an end. Like a replicant who dreams of becoming a real boy, Titus has finally found his own humanity. Or *in*humanity, if you're not into the whole brevity thing.

Lavinia is not just an accessory to Titus's revenge. In this play, she is the soul of Rome, and we'll look closely at her role later in this chapter. But for now, we'll continue on the theme of Nature's death aspect in *Titus*.

She's a Man-eater
TITUS ANDRONICUS

Starhawk, a modern practitioner of the Earth-goddess religion Wicca, cautions against confining "Mother Nature" to the role of cookie-baking housewife or kind old granny. "She has a thousand names, a thousand aspects. She is the milk cow, the weaving spider, the honeybee with its piercing sting. She is the bird of the spirit and the sow that eats its own young. The snake that sheds its skin and is renewed; the cat that sees in the dark; the dog that sings to the moon—all are Her."[177]

The goddess Nature is good, bad, and ugly. And she's not distant in the sky but present in the web of life. "She is the reality behind many metaphors. She *is* reality, the manifest deity, omnipresent in all life, in each of us. The Goddess is not separate from the world–She *is* the world, and all things in it: moon, sun, earth, star, stone, seed, flowing river, wind, wave, leaf and branch, bud and blossom, fang and claw, woman and man."[178] We can see some aspects of this nature goddess in *A Midsummer Night's Dream*, but the picture is incomplete without the Midsummer nightmare, *Titus Andronicus*.

Nature in this play is a sow that eats her own young. In the opening scene, Titus brings two dead sons to be laid in the earth, returned to the maternal soil of Rome. Being a good Roman citizen, he does not bury them where they fell on the Black Sea but drags their dead bodies home to lie in the motherland with their patriarchal ancestors. Bassianus is thrown into a *"blood-drinking pit,* [a] *swallowing womb."* Nature is the death-goddess and Tamora acts as her sacrificial priestess. Having been dragged to Rome in chains, she's exhausted, but Titus's sacrifice of her eldest son activates and energizes her. In a sense, she'll take the infantile emperor Saturninus as his replacement and devour him to gain political strength. Then, at the play's end, she'll unknowingly eat her other two sons, a gruesome reverse birth: *"Like to the earth, swallow her own increase."* (TA V.ii)

Roman soil can also be picky in its appetite. Titus kills one of his sons for defying him, and then refuses him burial in the family crypt: *"Traitors, away! He rests not in this tomb... / Bury him where you can, he comes not here."* Titus believes the burial of a traitor would pollute the resting place of the patriarchs.

While others debate who gets to go *into* the earth, Tamora's henchman Aaron is pulling people out to play ghastly pranks on their mourning relatives:

> *"Oft have I digg'd up dead men from their graves,*
> *And set them upright at their dear friends' door*
> *Even when their sorrows almost were forgot,*
> *And on their skins, as on the bark of trees,*
> *Have with my knife carvèd in Roman letters*
> *'Let not your sorrow die, though I am dead.'"* (TA V.i)

The lovechild of Tamora and Aaron, born in the middle of the play, is nearly sacrificed to cover up the affair. Then, when Aaron escapes with the baby, he is caught and the infant is sentenced to hanging, suspension between sky and land. But ultimately, the young life is spared. Titus's son Lucius, who will become Emperor, departs from his father's merciless rigidity, and that's as close as we get to a hopeful ending. Aaron himself is half-buried:

> *"Set him breast-deep in earth, and famish him;*
> *There let him stand and rave and cry for food.*
> *If any one relieves or pities him,*
> *For the offence he dies. This is our doom.*
> *Some stay to see him fast'ned in the earth."*
> (TA V.iii, "doom" here meaning death-sentence)

And the Goth Queen's cadaver is unceremoniously dumped to rot:

> *"As for that heinous tiger, Tamora,*
> *No funeral rite, nor man in mourning weed,*
> *No mournful bell shall ring her burial;*
> *But throw her forth to beasts and birds to prey.*
> *Her life was beastly and devoid of pity,*
> *And being dead, let birds on her take pity."* (TA V.iii)

Lavinia had called Tamora a *"tiger,"* and Titus observed that she turned Rome into a *"wilderness of tigers"* (assisted by Aaron, whom Lucius called a *"ravenous tiger"*), so she's left to be eaten by tigers. There's a dark poetic justice to this. As Lavinia was desecrated by beasts, Tamora will be desecrated, and defecated. There's also a concern for the ecology, that Tamora's body is toxic waste. As a wild foreigner, killer, and cannibal, her septic biomatter is not allowed to become part of Roman soil until it has been processed as animal droppings. She's put the whole circle of life on a tilt, and it must be righted again. Tamora embodied the darkest sides of the divine feminine spectrum as widow, whore, and wicked stepmother, so her royal bond with Nature must be completely severed if Rome is to recover its honor and virtue.

Domina / Mother Roma
TITUS ANDRONICUS | CORIOLANUS

In *Titus Andronicus*, Lavinia functions as her father's external heart, but she also personifies the soul of Rome. Her chastity and conscience are the measure of civilization, and she is destined, through matrimony and maternity, to become a living embodiment of the city's patron goddess, Roma. This destiny takes a cruel detour, civilization melts in chaos, and Lavinia is a casualty of a gruesome blood-feud. After being violated, she becomes a vengeful nemesis.

Lavinia's womb is Titus's prized possession, and he'll give it to whomever he chooses. When Lavinia informs him that she's chosen Bassianus, he accuses the suitor of attempting to sexually violate him, and when Saturninus asks for Lavinia, Titus assents, handing his daughter off to be legally raped. He is willing to sacrifice his virgin daughter to the Pax Romana.[179] She narrowly evades this, and at great cost: one of her brothers sacrifices his life to cover her escape.

Lavinia has very few words in the script, just enough lines for a composite character sketch. She is fierce in her determination to choose her own partner, even in defiance of her father's wishes. Her beloved Bassianus is a contender for the crown, but she stands by him after he's been passed by. Catching Tamora and Aaron, she mocks the empress for having an affair, contrasting her own chastity with Tamora's promiscuity. She remains defiant when her husband is murdered, and as the rapists close in, she demands death before dishonor. Her last words are a dehumanizing insult, and she is cut off in the middle of a curse upon Tamora: *"No grace? no womanhood? Ah, beastly creature, / The blot and enemy to our general name! / Confusion fall—"* (TA II.iii)

Like Philomel and other Ovidian victims of sexual violence, Lavinia is silenced. She is the only character in all of Shakespeare's plays to be raped, and in a sense, the poet shields his audience from the emotional interiority of this trauma.[180] She can still read and write—we get the facts but not the feelings. And she learns to communicate through body language, from which her father can *"wrest an alphabet"* to translate her *"martyr'd signs."* (TA III.ii)[181] Then, in assisting Titus with the slaughter of her attackers, Lavinia becomes not just an accessory to murder, but a sacrificial priestess holding a bowl to catch the blood. Once her honor is avenged, Titus grants her last wish, assisting in her suicide.

Lavinia is deprived of her destiny, Roman motherhood: women bear sons so sons can bear arms. Were she not so horrifically interrupted, she would have bloomed into Volumnia, the ideal Roman mother in Shakespeare's *Coriolanus*. Volumnia has named her only son Martius, after the war god Mars, who may be his father for all we know. And she explains her philosophy of Roman motherhood to his wife Virgilia while Martius is single-handedly besieging a city, carving Corioli a new one (for this he'll win a title meaning A-hole of Corioli).

> *"VOLUMNIA. If my son were my husband, I should freelier rejoice in that absence wherein he won honour than in the embracements of his bed where he would show most love. When yet he was but tender-bodied, and the only son of my womb...to a cruel war I sent him, from whence he return'd his brows bound with oak. I tell thee, daughter, I sprang not more in joy at first hearing he was a man-child than now in first seeing he had proved himself a man.*
> *VIRGILIA. But [what if] he died in the business, madam, how then?*
> *VOLUMNIA. Then his good report should have been my son; I therein would have found issue [offspring]. Hear me profess sincerely: had I a dozen sons, each in my love alike, and none less dear than thine and my good Marcius, I had rather had eleven die nobly for their country*

than one voluptuously surfeit out of action...
VIRGILIA. His bloody brow? O Jupiter, no blood!
VOLUMNIA. Away, you fool! It more becomes a man
Than gilt his trophy. The breasts of Hecuba,
When she did suckle Hector, look'd not lovelier
Than Hector's forehead when it spit forth blood
At Grecian sword, contemning."
(COR I.iii, "contemning" means mocking)

The debate, rising in drama, shifts gears from prose to poetry as Volumnia reverently cites Virgil's *Aeneid*, the myth of Rome's descent from Troy. She compares the Trojan queen Hecuba's lactating breasts to the pulsing wounds of her son Hector, slain on the battlefield. From Volumnia's perspective, the greater beauty was Hector's forehead spewing forth acidic curses upon Achilles's blade.

Volumnia is a stone-cold battle-axe, the Spartan ideal of motherhood. She is the strongest character in the play and is further fortified by solidarity with other women: Volumnia is always accompanied by Coriolanus's wife Virgilia, and sometimes by her young friend Valeria, whom Coriolanus describes as *"The moon of Rome, chaste as the icicle / That's curdled by the frost from purest snow, / And hangs on Dian's temple."* (COR V.iii) Together they make a trinity of virgin, wife, and mother/widow. The triplicate of "V" names conjures Vesta, the Roman goddess of home and hearth, and her temple priestesses, the Vestal Virgins, who tended an eternal flame representing the continuity of Rome.[182] Valeria is a minor role; she's missing from the three middle acts of the play. But we may note that people only argue with Volumnia when Valeria is not around, and in the scenes in which the three are bonded together, they are unstoppable.

Returning victorious, the celebrity general is pressured toward the popularity contest of politics. *"The people are the city,"* Coriolanus is told, yet he has nothing but contempt for the crowd: *"Who deserves greatness deserves your hate. And your affections are a sick man's appetite."* (COR I.i) Coriolanus only loves the motherland as he identifies it with his own mother.

Coriolanus is not a great public speaker; he seems to have a kind of Tourette's syndrome. However, he doesn't need lofty oratory to impress the masses.[183] They want to see his battle-scars, his *"marks of merit,"* which are his medals and memoirs. These taxpayer-funded documents are in the public domain, but the soldier considers them his private parts: no one yet has seen him bleed and lived to tell, *"every gash was an enemy's grave."* Coriolanus refers to his wounds as *"nothings,"* not in the sense of "Oh, it was nothing," but "nothing" in the sense of the womb: he has been penetrated for Rome.

As Lavinia's womb is her father's possession in *Titus Andronicus,* Coriolanus's wounds are his mother's prized possessions. When his mother tries to pimp him out as a politician, encouraging him to show some skin so all of Rome can see his/her scars, "draped in a gown of humility he himself describes as a *'womanish toge,'*"[184] Coriolanus refuses to bear a *"harlot's spirit."* He objects to being objectified, subjected to the hungry eyes of the mob's piercing male gaze. Volumnia retorts: *"Thy valiantness was mine, thou suck'dst it from me; / But owe thy pride thyself."* (COR III.ii)

Coriolanus's refusal to peddle his flesh in this burlesque gets him booed off the political stage. Then, in a bizarre twist, some pundits whip up the mob to banish him; he is *"whoop'd out of Rome."* Cursing the city, he runs to the arms of the one person he really respects, his long-time adversary Aufidius. It almost seems as though Shakespeare created Coriolanus by resurrecting Antony as a zombie golem—he's lost his cosmic vision and poetry, and his Cleopatra is a bearded biker warlord. Their (I can't believe I'm using this word) bromance blossoms into a genuine homoerotic romance.[185]

Coriolanus returns to Rome, and the city is defenseless. He stands at the gate, the sexual portal, at the head of a savage horde ready to ravage the city to death. Against all odds, Volumnia strides out to meet them, bringing Coriolanus's wife, Virgilia, their young son, and her friend Valeria. Volumnia defiantly hisses, *"Thou art my warrior; I holp to frame thee"* (I built you), and shames him for the very idea of *"Making the mother, wife, and child, to see / The son, the husband, and the father, tearing / His country's bowels out."* (COR V.iii) Reversing the custom of a son bowing before his mother, Volumnia kneels before Coriolanus and the barbarian army. And something of a miracle occurs:

> *"CORIOLANUS. O mother, mother!*
> *What have you done? Behold, the heavens do ope,*
> *The gods look down, and this unnatural scene*
> *They laugh at. O my mother, mother! O!*
> *You have won a happy victory to Rome...*
> *Ladies, you deserve*

To have a temple built you. All the swords
In Italy, and her confederate arms,
Could not have made this peace." (COR V.iii)

With this passive-aggressive action, Volumnia has defeated the whole army, and Coriolanus declares her a goddess worthy of praise for the salvation of the city. As the peace treaty is signed, the First Senator echoes this, "*Behold our patroness, the life of Rome!*" But there is no salvation without sacrifice, Coriolanus will be stabbed to death by the vandals, furious that he accepted tears instead of blood. Coppélia Kahn notes the tragic irony that "the mother who lives only through her son survives while he is sacrificed so that she and the city with which she is identified may live."[186]

Titus Andronicus and *Coriolanus* are both stories about barbarians at the gate, hungry hordes threatening to "*plough Rome and harrow Italy*." This would be the Roman equivalent of a zombie apocalypse. At stake is civilization itself, held together by feminine virtue and hyper-masculine *virtus* (in the Roman dystopia, *virtus* meant forced colonial and sexual conquest, the opposite of modern "virtue"). Both plays complicate the issue by putting barbarians on both sides of the gate, within and without. In *Titus Andronicus*, the Goth Queen and her acolytes infiltrate the city and take it over from the inside. Finally, Titus's son Lucius must enlist a Goth army to threaten the city. In *Coriolanus*, the general is exiled by a mindless mob of childish seesaw voters—Shakespeare considered democracy unnatural— and the rejected general leads an army of barbaric Volscians to the city gates. In both plays the city is narrowly saved.

Lavinia and Volumnia both represent the soul of Rome. Lavinia is Rome's conscience, and after being brutalized, she becomes vengeful. Deprived of her destiny to bear soldiers, she will feed sons to their own mother. Volumnia has greater power, especially in her trinitarian form, and manages to defeat a whole howling horde with a single gesture of grace, kneeling before the city gate. Volumnia says numerous times that Coriolanus's power comes from her, that she nursed and built him into a warrior, and "*There's no man in the world more bound to's mother.*" But she also gains her power from him: by birthing a warrior she has attained full Roman personhood. And when Coriolanus arrives as the angry father, son, and ghost of Mars, the sacred mother intercedes on behalf of the people, saving the city from his apocalyptic wrath.

In Shakespeare's time, everybody knew (spoiler alert) that Rome did fall to barbarians several centuries after these stories take place. It was inevitable. More significantly, in the 1500s, Rome was in a sense "besieged" by Germanic peoples during the Protestant Reformation. At the heart of Catholic resistance was the love of the goddess in her Virgin Mary manifestation: the Reformers were determined to strip her of the divine power to maternally intercede with the angry father God. Shakespeare was wisely silent on the topic of the Reformation but was clearly drawn to stories about Rome and its goddess under siege.

Crowning
MACBETH

We've been looking at Nature as a sentient entity, not just a scenic backdrop mural, but a living matrix, a manifestation of the divine feminine. As wild lands go, the land of the Scots seems to be particularly wild. Maybe the Scottish Mother Nature is a redhead. Anyway, Nature is very active in *Macbeth:* she's angry, defiant, and dangerous. Deservedly so, since the *"butcher and his fiend-like queen"* commit so many outrages against all forms of maternalism.

The play opens with brave sons of Scotland being thrown into a slaughter. In a report of the battle, the armies are described like tigers thrashing in the water, and the poetic imagery presents a murky primeval chaos:

> *"As two spent swimmers that do cling together*
> *And choke their art. The merciless Macdonwald*
> *Worthy to be a rebel, for to that*
> *The multiplying villainies of nature*
> *Do swarm upon him...*
> *And Fortune, on his damnèd quarrel smiling,*
> *Show'd like a rebel's whore. But all's too weak;*
> *For brave Macbeth –well he deserves that name–*
> *Disdaining Fortune, with his brandish'd steel,*
> *Which smoked with bloody execution,*
> *Like Valor's minion carvèd out his passage...*

Till he unseam'd him from the nave to the chaps,
And fix'd his head upon our battlements." (MAC I.i)

Macdonwald surges with the seething powers of Nature, and Lady Luck follows him like a barracks prostitute. But Macbeth arises in berserker fury and opens him from his navel to his mouth–from one orifice to another. Macbeth, who is called *"Valor's minion,"* bravery's baby, disses the housewife Fortune and quickly weds a war goddess, becoming *"Bellona's bridegroom, lapp'd in proof."*

Childbirth and infanticide are major themes in *Macbeth*, and they're introduced before we even meet the title characters. Macbeth and Macdonwald fight like Biblical twins in the womb, with the bloody mud of Scotland as amniotic fluid. Like an alien spawn, Macbeth then delivers himself by C-section, *"carved out his passage"* through Macdonwald's navel, the scar from his umbilical cord. He emerges *"bathe*[d] *in reeking wounds,"* *"lapp'd in proof,"* baptized in the blood of his enemies. Macbeth is an unnatural born killer. And he displays Macdonwald's severed head as a trophy.

Macbeth may be great on the battlefield, but he's got insecurities in the bedroom (his marriage bed is a barren heath), and he's no master strategist. Fortunately, or unfortunately, he's got Lady Macbeth to nurture his nascent serial killer instinct by renouncing her own biological fertility. She's been his wife but really blossoms as his partner in crime, worrying that he's *"too full o' the milk of human kindness,"* not "kindness" in the sense of friendliness, but in the sense of human nature. She calls on spirits of death to *"unsex"* her, turn her breasts into spray-flowers of acid, and activate early menopause so *"that no compunctious visitings of nature / Shake my fell purpose."* (MAC I.v) When her husband wavers from a rash and bloody deed, she says that she would kill a nursing infant rather than back down.

Mary McCarthy wrote, "She has to wear the pants... She is aware of Macbeth; she *knows* him (he does not know her at all, apparently), but she regards him coldly as a thing, a tool that must be oiled and polished."[187] The curse of casting the Scottish Play is that the title character needs to be a bad actor. Macbeth is an understudy at best, in a show written by witches and directed by his wife, and once he starts improvising, he's a hack.

Symbols of gruesome birth and infanticide abound. Slinking toward Duncan, Macbeth hallucinates a *"naked new-born babe,"* a heavenly cherub decrying his guilt. Later, he'll envision a bloody child, then a crowned child, symbols of the future he cannot control.[188] The witches' potion contains the *"finger of birth-strangled babe"* and the blood of a sow who has eaten nine of her own offspring. Then, in a trance, Macbeth sees a procession of future Scottish kings, motherless in the sense that the crown is passed from father to son. The patrilineal line culminates in King James, whose mother, Mary Queen of Scots, is omitted even though she reigned as sole monarch for a quarter century. Mary had been beheaded by order of Queen Elizabeth, and James politically distanced himself from his Mom in the hope of gaining the crown.

The Macbeths are grim reapers of mothers and babies. He will cast suspicion upon the children of Duncan and Banquo for killing their own fathers. When he sends assassins to Macduff's house, the young son will defiantly defend his mother, but both will be slaughtered. And like a Tolkien wraith-king, Macbeth receives a Nazgul-riddle that *"none of woman born shall harm Macbeth."* Little does he know his nemesis Macduff was *"untimely ripp'd"* from his mother's womb. And here we should note that in Shakespeare's time, caesarean delivery was only performed on women who were already dead or dying: "No record exists of a mother surviving one in Britain before the end of the eighteenth century."[189] Macduff was not born, but torn from a dead mother, and thus the play will end with another repudiation of biological maternity.

Macbeth is filled with shocking atrocities against motherhood, and the female characters can be unsettling, disturbing, or downright dastardly. But there is a deeper conflict with a more powerful mother who might escape our notice because she's lurking, not just in the background, but under the boards of the stage: the maternal mud of the land.

Slouching Toward MacBethlehem
MACBETH

In the natural matrix of *Macbeth*, men spring from the soil of Scotland. Banquo understands this when the witches announce his genetic destiny and he questions: *"If you can look into the seeds of time, / And say which grain will grow and which will not."* (MAC I.iii) King Duncan promotes

Macbeth as Thane (tax-collector) of Cawdor, saying, *"I have begun to plant thee, and will labor / To make thee full of growing."* (MAC I.iv)

The killing of Duncan is a crime against Nature, in the Shakespearean sense, where Nature is wedded to a king. On his way to the kill, Macbeth prays that the land be deaf and mute: *"Thou sure and firm-set earth, / Hear not my steps, which way they walk, for fear / Thy very stones* [tell] *of my whereabout."* (MAC II.i) He tries to enlist Nature as an accessory to this murder, or at least not to stand witness against him. Macbeth steps toward the sleeping king with *"Tarquin's ravishing strides,"* reminding us of the sexual predator in Shakespeare's poem, *The Rape of Lucrece,* and when the deed is done, he's stuck with the image of the slain king, *"His gash'd stabs look'd like a breach in nature / for ruin's wasteful entrance."* (MAC II.iii) There's plenty of killing onstage in *Macbeth,* but this central murder is not shown, perhaps because it verges on sexual violence. Macbeth symbolically kills his own father and marries his own motherland. He penetrates the crown with his unworthy head.

Biologically and economically speaking, royalty is a parasite, something that saps the habitat and its inhabitants with a greed bounded only by a self-serving caution not to kill the host. But Shakespeare believed in an elemental connection between monarchs and the land. He grew up in the time of Queen Elizabeth who explained her refusal to marry by saying she was already wedded to the king*dom,* the terrain of England. Duncan, like Lear, is supposedly a widower whose wife is never mentioned, but symbolically they are husbands of the soil. When Duncan is slain, the land cries out in the many voices of Nature:

> *"The night has been unruly. Where we lay,*
> *Our chimneys were blown down, and, as they say,*
> *Lamentings heard i' the air, strange screams of death,*
> *And prophesying with accents terrible*
> *Of dire combustion and confused events*
> *New hatch'd to the woeful time. The obscure bird*
> *Clamor'd the livelong night. Some say the earth*
> *Was feverous and did shake."* (MAC II.iii)

The land, widowed and traumatized, becomes barren. The trick-or-treat murder plunges Scotland into a winter so bleak that Hell freezes over: *"This place is too cold for hell."* The agrarian economy collapses, a Porter playing Hades's gatekeeper reports, *"Here's a farmer that hanged himself on th' expectation of plenty."* Scotland veils herself in mourning, the land is shrouded in primeval darkness. Birds and beasts churn in a widening gyre of chaos:

> *"ROSS. Thou seest the heavens, as troubled with man's act,*
> *Threaten his bloody stage. By the clock 'tis day,*
> *And yet dark night strangles the traveling lamp.*
> *Is't night's predominance, or the day's shame,*
> *That darkness does the face of earth entomb,*
> *When living light should kiss it?*
> *OLD MAN. 'Tis unnatural,*
> *Even like the deed that's done. On Tuesday last*
> *A falcon towering in her pride of place*
> *Was by a mousing owl hawk'd at and kill'd.*
> *ROSS. And Duncan's horses...beauteous and swift...*
> *Turn'd wild in nature, broke their stalls, flung out,*
> *Contending 'gainst obedience, as they would make*
> *War with mankind.*
> *OLD MAN. 'Tis said they eat each other.*
> *ROSS. They did so, to the amazement of mine eyes*
> *That look'd upon't."* (MAC I.iv)

Horse-cannibalism is never a good omen.

Scotland lurches into a full-blown climate catastrophe. The weather had been a mix of *"fair and foul,"* but turns decidedly foul as the land rebels against the toxic monarch:

> *"MALCOLM. I think our country sinks beneath the yoke;*
> *It weeps, it bleeds, and each new day a gash*
> *Is added to her wounds...*
> *ROSS. Alas, poor country,*
> *Almost afraid to know itself! It cannot*
> *Be call'd our mother, but our grave."* (MAC IV.iii)

Macbeth interrogates the witches for more information, demanding answers even if *"bladed corn be lodged and trees blown down,"* even if *"the treasure / of nature's germaines tumble all together."* (MAC IV.i) The answer he gets is grim: he is shown the line of future kings descended from Banquo (which will include King James himself, smiling smugly in the audience). When his barren wife has gone mad with guilt and the physician is helpless, Macbeth sarcastically asks if he could test a urine sample from Scotland herself and find the cause of her infertility: *"If thou couldst, doctor, cast / The water of my land, find her disease / And purge it to a sound and pristine health."* (MAC V.iii)

Macbeth realizes too late that his crime against nature has sterilized him: *"Upon my head they placed a fruitless crown / And put a barren sceptre in my grip."* (MAC III.i) There will be no branches on his family tree, and he finally recognizes himself as *"the yellow leaf,"* withered foliage bound for the fall. He clings to a prophecy that he cannot be overthrown unless Birnam forest should uproot itself and march against him. But this too shall come to pass. We can view the walking woods as Nature's uprising against her rapacious captor.[190] Macbeth's head, which forcefully penetrated the crown, will be severed and suspended between earth and sky where it cannot further pollute the climate or the countryside. Scottish Nature will emerge from barren winter to a fertile spring.

Hecate, Circe, & Medea

Scapegoat

Samuel Johnson bitterly describes how King James fed the fad of witch-hunting:

> "The king, who was much celebrated for his knowledge, had, before his arrival in England, not only examined in person a woman accused of witchcraft, but had given a very formal account of the practices and illusions of evil spirits, the compacts of witches, the ceremonies used by them, the manner of detecting them, and the justice of punishing them, in his dialogues of *Demonologie*... And as the ready way to gain king James's favour was to flatter his speculations, the system of *Demonologie* was immediately adopted by all who desired either to gain preferment or not to lose it. Thus the doctrine of witchcraft was very powerfully inculcated, and as the greatest part of mankind have no other reason for their opinions than that they are in fashion, it cannot be doubted but this persuasion made a rapid progress, since vanity and credulity co-operated in its favour, and it had a tendency to free cowardice from reproach... Thus, in the time of Shakespeare, was the doctrine of witchcraft at once established by law and by the fashion, and it became not only unpolite, but criminal, to doubt it; and as prodigies are always seen in proportion as they are expected, witches were every day discovered."[191]

Shakespeare lived in a time of witch mania.

There was a climate crisis in the late Medieval and Renaissance periods, unusually low temperatures and high rainfall caused crop failure, with resultant loss of livestock and surges of plague. Some climatologists call this the "Little Ice Age." Europeans sought scapegoats to blame, spawning an age of catastrophic witch hunts. As the climate cooled, the response was to burn women alive. This may sound silly and superstitious to us, but anthropologists in the future (if there are any) will no doubt look back on the early 21st century as a time when politicians avoided conversations about climate change by focusing on persecuting women for being women.

There were other factors involved in the old witch-craze. After a thousand years of Rome's totalitarian control of the European intellect (the Church limited literacy and punished heresy/thought-crime), advancements in shipbuilding and international trade ushered in an era of globalization. Along with jewels and spices, the new trade routes also brought in ideas–international ideas and Classical Greco-Roman texts preserved by the Muslims. This sudden influx of information awakened a curiosity about human potential, the age we know as the Renaissance. Obviously, a budding conversation about human potential and dynamics would spark a debate about one of the most fundamental dynamics in society: the balance or imbalance of gender. Curious intellectual young ladies who were wondering if it was time for a feminist movement could look out their windows and see women being publicly hanged or burned, sometimes in steel cages full of live cats. The message was clear: if you can't take the heat, stay in the kitchen.

The appropriation of Greek and Muslim medical science also led to the rise of a male medical establishment. Medieval medicine was mostly practiced by women, particularly the old herbalist/midwife who lived on the edge of the village. She was essentially the equivalent of Planned Parenthood (the only other local gynecologist was the parish priest). The rising male medical establishment determined to destroy the competition by discrediting or lynching them. This might be the most effective smear campaign in history, branding the village midwife as a sinister witch.

The shamans, midwives, and medicine women who were labeled "witches" had traditionally been devotees of the trinitarian goddess of youth, fertility, and wisdom. But in Shakespeare's time, the official belief was that "witches" were in league with the Christian Devil: women who had been unwittingly seduced into the service of a malevolent male demon. This carried the degrading implication that women were gullible and susceptible to both sexual and spiritual temptation. Records of witch trials from the period contain confessions about "witches" as servants of Satan, but these confessions were obtained under torture, making them unreliable. Plus, the priests who conducted the trials and wrote up the confessions had their conclusions set from the start and would not have documented any testimony that disagreed.

The first witch that Shakespeare portrayed, and the only one he brought to trial, was the historical Joan of Arc in *Henry VI, Part 1*. This French military commander would later be canonized as Saint Joan, but from the English perspective she was a sorceress, and they burned her alive. Adding insult to injury, the English attributed this maiden's battlefield brilliance to the Christian Devil.[192] So Shakespeare's first witch is in league with Lucifer, whom she calls *"the lordly monarch of the north,"* and his last witch, Sycorax, in *The Tempest*, had been a devotee of the satanic Setebos.

King James himself wrote a witch hunt manual, the *Daemonologie*, which Shakespeare used as a research source for *Macbeth* as a way of kissing up to his new patron. But Shakespeare did not assign the "weird sisters" a male manager, and they are never brought to trial. There is actually a fascinating pattern in Shakespeare's writing: witches who work for devilish male deities must die (Joan is burned alive, Sycorax is dead), while witches who don't declare allegiance to a male deity survive (the witches in *Macbeth*, *The Merry Wives of Windsor* and Paulina in *The Winter's Tale*).

I wrote at length about the variety of Shakespearean "witches" in *Supernatural Shakespeare* and won't repeat all of that here. For the purpose of this book, however, it's worth taking a quick look at Shakespeare's references to some witches from Classical mythology, some of whom are goddesses or demigoddesses.

But some caution is in order. First, Shakespeare created different witches to function in different ways in different stories. My kids ask me if such-and-such is true about all zombies, and I have to answer that different filmmakers have different zombie-ologies. Second, Shakespeare's plays are a product of his time, when women were considered pawns in a patriarchal satanic corporation, and it may not have occurred to him that "witchcraft" could be a goddess religion.

Shadowplay
Macbeth

Hecate is named in Ovid's *Metamorphoses*, and the translator Arthur Golding introduced her with a parenthetical "Hecate (of whom the witches hold as of their goddess)." Shakespeare makes numerous references to Hecate as the goddess of the waning moon, or the waning-moon aspect of the triple moon-goddess, Diana. In *A Midsummer Night's Dream*, Puck refers to nocturnal fairies as *"We fairies, that do run / By the triple Hecate's team / From the presence of the sun."* (MND V.i, her chariot was drawn by a team of *"night's swift dragons,"* MND III.ii) Lear swears by *"the mysteries of Hecate and the night,"* (KL I.i), and during the players' performance in *Hamlet,* the assassin uses a poison that has been strengthened by the light of a dying moon: *"Thou mixture rank, of midnight weeds collected, / With Hecate's ban thrice blasted, thrice infected."* (HAM III.ii)

Macbeth contains numerous séance scenes, and the play is itself a séance in the sense of conjuring spirits of the dead to appear on a stage. Macbeth will refer to Hecate twice. As he approaches the sleeping king by moonlight he mentions *"pale Hecate,"* and later when Scotland is shrouded in darkness, he'll call her *"black Hecate."*[193] She will also make two brief cameos onstage, appearing as a supervisor to the Weird Sisters. They are "weird" in the sense of *Wyrd,* an old Anglo-Saxon word for destiny or fate. And as we see in the play, they function like the Greek Fates, predicting births and deaths. Note that they never tell Macbeth to kill anyone; they say he'll be king, and then his wife proposes assassination and serial killing as a snakes-and-ladders shortcut.

Significantly, Hecate never reveals herself to Macbeth, and this is likely the reason she is usually cut from productions. She shows up once to scold the sisters and once to commend them but leaves when Macbeth approaches. Hecate is also distinct from the sisters in that they are morally ambiguous, but she is malevolent: *"I, the mistress of your charms / The close contriver of all harms."* The sisters tell Macbeth he'll be king regardless of what he does, but Hecate intends for him to become reckless and ruthless. After castigating the sisters for coaching him on their own, she returns to her home on the dark side of the moon, to prepare further sorcery:

> "*HECATE. I am for the air; this night I'll spend*
> *Unto a dismal and a fatal end.*
> *Great business must be wrought ere noon:*
> *Upon the corner of the moon*
> *There hangs a vaporous drop profound;*
> *I'll catch it ere it come to ground.*
> *And that distill'd by magic sleights*
> *Shall raise such artificial sprites*
> *As by the strength of their illusion*
> *Shall draw him on to his confusion.*
> *He shall spurn fate, scorn death, and bear*
> *His hopes 'bove wisdom, grace, and fear.*
> *And you all know security*
> *Is mortals' chiefest enemy.*" *(MAC III.v)*

Hecate says that she will mold illusions from moonbeams in order to spur Macbeth into rash and bloody deeds. When next he meets the witches, he'll demand information and they will ask if he wants it from them or from their masters, (*"FIRST WITCH. Say, if thou'dst rather hear it from our mouths, / Or from our masters'? / MACBETH. Call 'em, let me see 'em."*). Macbeth will then see a floating head, two phantom babies, and a line of eight future kings. Perhaps these are the *"artificial sprites"* (spirits) that Hecate promised.[194] And indeed these visions will encourage him toward further atrocities leading to his downfall and the fulfillment of the witches' prophecy that royalty will pass from Duncan to the line of Banquo. Although why witches would want Banquo's witch-hunting descendant James on the throne is anybody's guess.

Circe and Medea
THE MERCHANT OF VENICE | THE TEMPEST

Some of Shakespeare's earliest plays contain references to the sorceress Circe, a demigoddess (daughter of the sun god Helios and the sea nymph Perse, or some sources say she was the daughter of Hecate and the Colchian King Aeetes). Shakespeare was familiar with Circe from the fourteenth book of Ovid's *Metamorphoses* and may have also heard about her role in *The Odyssey*, transforming some of Odysseus's sailors into swine.

In *Henry VI, Part 1*, a duke looks in on Joan in prison and remarks, *"See how the ugly witch doth bend her brows / As if, with Circe, she would change my shape!"* (1H6 V.iii) *A Comedy of Errors* contains numerous references to a male fear of being transformed by a sorceress, and as an exasperated duke tries to sort through the identity crises, he mutters, *"I think you all have drunk of Circe's cup."* (COE V.i) This might just be a joke about how wine can turn people into swine.

These were two of Shakespeare's earliest plays, and he won't explicitly name Circe again. After this he'll become more interested in Circe's niece (or sister) Medea. Shakespeare was not familiar with Euripides's play *Medea*, but knew the story from the seventh book of Ovid's *Metamorphoses*. A Colchian princess was charmed by an adventurer named Jason, who "swore to take her as his wife / By triple Hecate's holy rites"[195] *if* she would assist him in stealing the legendary Golden Fleece. So she betrayed her father, and to cover their escape, she dismembered her brother (Shakespeare refers to this in *2 Henry VI*, when a soldier vows that if he gets his hands on a son of York, *"Into as many gobbets will I cut it / As wild Medea young Absyrtus did."* 2H6 V.ii[196]). Arriving home, Jason was saddened to find his father dying, but Medea used magic herbs to revive him. Later, when Jason tried to weasel out of their marriage and wed a younger princess, the scorned Medea went on a killing spree, murdering the young bride and her father, as well as her own children by Jason, then flew off in Hecate's chariot drawn by *"dragons of the night."* (CYM II.ii)[197]

Shakespeare puts numerous Medea references into *The Merchant of Venice*. In the opening scene, Bassanio tells Antonio that he needs a loan so that he can voyage in quest of Portia, whose hair he likens to the Golden Fleece, and whose island Belmont he compares to Colchis:

> *"In Belmont is a lady richly left,*
> *And she is fair and, fairer than that word,*
> *Of wondrous virtues. Sometimes from her eyes*
> *I did receive fair speechless messages...*
> *Nor is the wide world ignorant of her worth;*
> *For the four winds blow in from every coast*
> *Renownèd suitors, and her sunny locks*

Hang on her temples like a golden fleece,
Which makes her seat of Belmont Colchos' strond,
And many Jasons come in quest of her."
(MOV I.i, "Colchos' Strond" meaning Colchis' beach)

He will soon stumble into the irony that she has some things in common with the Colchian princess Medea. Portia betrays her father by giving Bassanio certain hints about how to win the shell game for her hand in marriage.[198] More significantly, when Bassanio's father-figure Antonio faces certain death, Portia will revive him with legalistic incantations. Then, in an attorney's disguise, she tricks Bassanio into betraying their marriage vows, surrendering his wedding ring as a legal fee. Later, when Bassanio admits that he gave up the ring, Portia threatens him with a sexless marriage (devoid of offspring) and vows to be as liberal with her sexuality as he has been with her gift. Only when he grovels like a worm does she reveal the trick and return the ring.

This may all sound a bit mean, and certainly Portia has a predatory sadism about her, but it's important for the play. Like Jason, Bassanio is a gigolo, and he has objectified Portia as the Golden Fleece (his idiotic manservant even gloats: *"We are the Jasons, we have won the fleece"* right in front of her!). Having been alerted to the plot, she must preempt any further parallels with a trophy or garment. As a lawyer she proves her intelligence, and by the ring trick she shows she can be menacing.[199] Meanwhile, in a subplot, Shylock's daughter Jessica elopes with Lorenzo. They take a midnight stroll, and she says that on a night like this, *"Medea gathered the enchanted herbs / That did renew old Aeson."* (MOV V.i) Like Medea, Jessica has betrayed and robbed her father to elope, so the name-drop may contain a veiled threat.

A slim case could be made that Lady Macbeth's references to royal assassination, infanticide, and unsexing herself were inspired by Medea.[200] And Helena in *All's Well That Ends Well* revives a dying king with mysterious medicine, is abandoned by her husband, then entraps him and threatens to kill him if he cheats on her. But we should be cautious about witch-hunting Medea through the Shakespearean canon: many of his heroines are rebellious and menacing.

Ovid loved stories of sex and sorcery, and Medea may have been his favorite femme fatale. Besides starring in numerous episodes of the

Metamorphoses, she was also featured in his *Heroides* and *Tristia*, and was the leading lady in his stage play, *Medea*, unfortunately lost. In the *Metamorphoses*, while gathering herbs to revive a dying man, she gives a moonlit monologue. Jonathan Bate observes, "She emphasizes inversion—streams running backward to their sources, darkness at noon—because what she is preparing herself for is an inversion of the aging process."[201]

> "Upon the bare hard ground, she said: O trusty time of night
> Most faithful [keeping secrets, and] O golden stars whose light
> Doth jointly with the Moon succeed the beams that blaze by day
> And thou three headed Hecatè who knowest best the way...
> Ye Charms and Witchcrafts, and thou Earth which both with herb and weed
> Of mighty working furnishest the Wizards at their need:
> Ye Airs and winds: ye Elves of Hills, of Brooks, of Woods alone,
> Of standing Lakes, and of the Night approach ye everyone.
> Through help of whom (the crooked banks much wondering at the thing)
> I have compellèd streams to run clean backward to their spring.
> By charms I make the calm Seas rough, and make the rough Seas plain,
> And cover all the Sky with Clouds and chase them thence again.
> By charms I raise and lay the winds, and burst the Viper's jaw.
> And from the bowels of the Earth both stones and trees do draw.
> Whole woods and Forests I remove: I make the Mountains shake,
> And ev'n the Earth itself to groan and fearfully to quake.
> I call up dead men from their graves: and thee O lightsome Moon
> I darken oft, though beaten brass abate thy peril soon.
> Our Sorcery dims the Morning faire, and darks the Sun at Noon."
> (Book VII, Golding translation, updated)

Ovid's love for the character comes through, even in Golding's translation. And Shakespeare combined elements of Golding's translation and Ovid's original Latin to write one of his most powerful monologues:

> *"Ye elves of hills, brooks, standing lakes, and groves...*
> *Weak masters though ye be—I have be-dimm'd*
> *The noontide sun, call'd forth the mutinous winds,*

And 'twixt the green sea and the azur'd vault
Set roaring war. To the dread rattling thunder
Have I given fire, and rifted Jove's stout oak
With his own bolt; the strong-bas'd promontory
Have I made shake, and by the spurs pluck'd up
The pine and cedar. Graves at my command
Have wak'd their sleepers, op'd, and let 'em forth,
By my so potent art." (TEM V.i)[202]

This is the wizard Prospero, at the climax of *The Tempest*. As Medea used her magic to revive the aging Aeson, now Prospero uses this power to restore himself from island hermit to Duke of Milan. He decides to drown his book, which may well be a copy of Ovid's *Metamorphoses*, since clearly he's just been reading it. Perhaps Medea has been on Prospero's mind because of his anxiety that his daughter Miranda might betray him and rush into a relationship with the adventurer, Ferdinand.[203]

There might be an additional reason he thinks of Medea on the day of his departure. He inherited this island from Sycorax who, like Medea, was *"a witch, and one so strong / That could control the moon, make flows and ebbs."* (TEM V.i) We know little of Sycorax, only what we hear from Prospero, and they never met—she was dead before he arrived. The name Sycorax means something like swine-crow, although Ted Hughes points out that the Coraxi were a tribe in Colchis, home of Circe and Medea[204] (in which case the name could mean Circe of Coraxi). And Prospero seems to have gained some of her power. Like Circe, he can transform people *"to barnacles, or to apes / with foreheads villainous low,"* (TEM IV.i) and symbolically turns his enemies into pigs in the scene of the vanishing banquet. Prospero does not repeat Medea's reference to the "three headed Hecate," the moon-goddess in her trinitarian form, although he does conjure a triple goddess lightshow for Miranda and Ferdinand's engagement ceremony: Juno, Ceres, and Iris.

It's tough to make a case for whether Shakespeare believed in the supernatural powers of witchcraft. As a storyteller, he was flexible with the roles and functions of "witches" in his different plays, and there's a mix of Shakespearean witches empowered by devilish male deities or infernal goddesses. In his time, as in our own, witches make for good popular entertainment. Fitting various witches to various scenarios, Shakespeare was pretty willy-nilly about witchcraft.

Egypt

Vortex
ANTONY AND CLEOPATRA

Shakespeare's *Antony and Cleopatra* is based on Plutarch's *Life of Marcus Antonius*, from which he inherits a lengthy description of how Cleopatra first appeared to Antony:

"Therefore when she was sent unto by diverse letters, both from Antonius himself and also from his friends, she made so light of it and mocked Antonius so much that she disdained to set forward otherwise but to take her barge in the river of Cydnus, the [deck] whereof was of gold, the sails of purple, and the oars of silver, which kept stroke in rowing after the sound of the music of flutes, howboys, cithernes, viols, and such other instruments as they played upon in the barge. And now for the person of herself: she was laid under a pavilion of cloth of gold of tissue, appareled and attired like the goddess Venus commonly drawn in picture; and hard by her, on either hand of her, pretty fair boys appareled as painters do set forth god Cupid, with little fans in their hands, with the which they fanned wind upon her. Her ladies and gentlewomen also, the fairest of them were appareled like the nymphs Nereides (which are the mermaids of the waters) and like the Graces, some steering the helm, others tending the tackle and ropes of the barge, out of which there came a wonderful passing sweet savour of perfumes, that perfumed the wharf's side, pestered with innumerable multitudes of people."[205]

The scene of Cleopatra meeting Antony is so spectacular that Shakespeare couldn't stage it. As a company board member he must have known it would bankrupt the theater. Besides, no boy actor could carry this scene as Cleopatra, and Dave Gahan hadn't yet been born to play Antony.[206] The topic of her grand entrance comes up in a conversation between two Roman soldiers:

"ENOBARBUS. *When she first met Mark Antony she purs'd up his heart, upon the river of Cydnus.*
AGRIPPA. *There she appear'd indeed! Or my reporter devis'd well for her.*
ENOBARBUS. *I will tell you."*

And here, without warning, the rugged, cynical Enobarbus bursts into melodic verse:

"*The barge she sat in, like a burnish'd throne,*
Burn'd on the water. [Deck] was beaten gold;
Purple the sails, and so perfumèd that
The winds were love-sick with them; the oars were silver,
Which to the tune of flutes kept stroke, and made
The water which they beat to follow faster,
As amorous of their strokes. For her own person,
It beggar'd all description. She did lie
In her pavilion, cloth-of-gold, of tissue,
O'erpicturing that Venus where we see
The fancy out-work nature. On each side her
Stood pretty dimpled boys, like smiling Cupids,
With diverse-colour'd fans, whose wind did seem
To glow the delicate cheeks which they did cool,
And what they undid did...
Her gentlewomen, like the Nereides,
So many mermaids, tended her i' th' eyes,
And made their bends adornings. At the helm
A seeming mermaid steers. The silken tackle
Swell with the touches of those flower-soft hands

That yarely frame the office. From the barge
A strange invisible perfume hits the sense
Of the adjacent wharfs. The city cast
Her people out upon her; and Antony,
Enthron'd i' th' market-place, did sit alone,
Whistling to th' air; which, but for vacancy,
Had gone to gaze on Cleopatra too,
And made a gap in nature.
AGRIPPA. Rare Egyptian!
ENOBARBUS. Upon her landing, Antony sent to her,
Invited her to supper. She replied
It should be better he became her guest;
Which she entreated. Our courteous Antony,
Whom ne'er the word of 'No' woman heard speak,
Being barber'd ten times o'er, goes to the feast,
And for his ordinary pays his heart
For what his eyes eat only.
AGRIPPA. Royal wench!
She made great Caesar lay his sword to bed.
He ploughed her, and she cropp'd.
ENOBARBUS. ...Age cannot wither her, nor custom stale
Her infinite variety. Other women cloy
The appetites they feed, but she makes hungry
Where most she satisfies; for vilest things
Become themselves in her, that the holy priests
Bless her when she is riggish." (A&C II.ii, "riggish" meaning aroused)

Cleopatra appears wrapped in Venus imagery, surrounded by boys representing Venus's son Cupid. Plutarch says Cleopatra looks like "the goddess Venus commonly drawn in picture," but Shakespeare amps this up, insisting it would take an exceptional painting that looked more real than reality itself. But though he uses Venus as a point of reference, he doesn't confine Cleopatra to just looking like Venus, he also presents her as the Egyptian goddess Isis.[207] Shakespeare probably didn't know of Isis from Egyptian texts but was familiar with a description of Isis from the second century Roman novel *The Metamorphoses of Apuleius* (better known by its smirky nickname *The Golden Ass*).

In this book, an amateur magician who has accidentally transformed himself into a donkey calls out to all the goddesses at once.

"And by and by appeared unto me a divine and venerable face, worshipped even of the Gods themselves. Then by little and little I seemed to see the whole figure of her body, mounting out of the sea and standing before me, wherefore I purpose to describe her divine semblance, if the poverty of my human speech will suffer me, or her divine power give me eloquence thereto. First she had a great abundance of hair, dispersed and scattered about her neck, on the crown of her head she bore many garlands interlaced with flowers, in the middle of her forehead was a compass in fashion of a glass, or resembling the light of the Moon, in one of her hands she bore serpents, in the other, blades of corn, her vestment was of fine silk yielding diverse colors, sometime yellow, sometime rose, sometime flaming, and sometime (which troubled my spirit sore) dark and obscure, covered with a black robe in manner of a shield... Round about the robe was a coronet or garland made with flowers and fruits. In her right hand she had a timbrel of brass, which gave a pleasant sound, in her left hand she bore a cup of gold, out of the mouth whereof the serpent Aspis lifted up his head, with a swelling throat... Thus the divine shape breathing out the pleasant spice of fertile Arabia, disdained not with her divine voice to utter these words unto me...

"'I am she that is the natural mother of all things, mistress and governess of all the Elements, the initial progeny of worlds, chief of powers divine, Queen of heaven! The principal of the Gods celestial, the light of the goddesses: at my will the planets of the air, the wholesome winds of the Seas, and the silences of hell be disposed; my name, my divinity is adored throughout all the world in diverse manners, in variable customs and in many names, for the Phrygians call me the mother of the Gods: the Athenians, Minerva: the Cyprians, Venus: the Candians, Diana: the Sicilians, Proserpina: the Eleusians, Ceres: some Juno, others Bellona, others Hecate: and principally the Ethiopians which dwell in the Orient, and the Egyptians which are excellent in all kinds of ancient doctrine, and by their proper ceremonies accustom to worship me, do call me Queen Isis. Behold I am come to take pity of thy fortune and tribulation... behold the healthful day which is ordained by my providence.'"[208]

This is quoted at some length because the first paragraph contains numerous parallels with Shakespeare's narration of Cleopatra's entrance, including "the poverty of human speech," the goddess emerging from the sea, the silk of many colors, and the perfume. In the second paragraph, the goddess explains that she is one deity known by many names in different cultures, but because the Egyptians hold the divine feminine in highest reverence, she ultimately identifies as Isis.

Cleopatra emerges as an elemental being. *"The winds were love-sick"* with her perfume, the waters rippled to follow her boat, and the fans meant to cool her were like bellows arousing flame: "She is in heat."[209] The script will bear out a pattern of water, wind, and fire obeying her, but the element of land belongs to Caesar and Rome. This report of Cleopatra barging in sounds like a divine feminine version of a Roman triumphal parade, and she elaborately stages the whole extravaganza for an audience of one: Antony, who doesn't even show up. Sitting at a deserted sidewalk cafe, he sends a message that she should come to meet on his turf and terms. She politely responds that he can come begging.

Agrippa, salivating over his mental image of Enobarbus's description, fumbles to guide it into the gutter of pornographic fantasy. Overcome by this supernatural splendor, even in secondary report, he must objectify this idol or worship her as a goddess. Insecure of his own manhood, he projects the phallic sword of deified Julius Caesar himself, and uses the degrading euphemism *"he ploughed her." "And she cropp'd"* is, itself, a double-edged sword. On one side, the harvest of a child born of their union, on the other, she *"cropp'd"* meaning castrated or whipped a dominated Caesar. And now she's come for Antony.

In the world of Shakespeare's comedies, as Beatrice wryly observes:

> *"Wooing, wedding, and repenting is as a Scotch jig, a measure, and a cinquepace: the first suit is hot and hasty, like a Scotch jig, and full as fantastical; the wedding, mannerly modest, as a measure, full of state and ancientry; and then comes Repentance, and with his bad legs, falls into the cinquepace faster and faster, till he sink into his grave."*
> (MAAN II.i)

The lively dance becomes a wedding procession and finally a funeral march. For Shakespearean lovers, the maidenhead is a prize to be won, then comes a baby, and all the rest is epilogue. Not so with Cleopatra; her supernatural eroticism is a renewable resource: *"She makes hungry where most she satisfies."* Agrippa thinks that a hero like Caesar or Antony could consume her and move on, but Enobarbus knows that she can turn men into love-slave heroine addicts. She leaves them ragged and worn and wanting more.

Enobarbus's description of Cleopatra on the barge overflows with luscious sensations: sights, sounds, smells, the feeling of heat, electricity and magnetism in the air. And yet never in the speech does he describe what she actually looks like. The description doesn't show us her beauty, it shows her sophistication: she has planned and managed and executed this immersive theatrical spectacle so masterfully that her physical appearance becomes unimportant. Antony declines to attend, so through messengers she uses her wit and intelligence to control the situation.

At the play's end, Caesar walks into a room, sees three women, and asks, *"Which is the queen of Egypt?"* She's indistinguishable from two servants, at least in the eyes of this cold bureaucrat. Then she starts talking, and another Roman soldier glazes over, his gaze tinted with adoration.

The World Stage
ANTONY AND CLEOPATRA

Antony and Cleopatra is Shakespeare's infinite variety show. Polonius and Hamlet would call it *"tragical-comical-historical-pastoral...a jig* [and] *a tale of bawdry."* Harold Bloom writes that *"Antony and Cleopatra* surges on, prodigal of its inventiveness, daemonic in the varied strength of its poetry. Critics rightly tend to argue that, if you want to find everything that Shakespeare was capable of doing, and in the compass of a single play, here it is."[210] It is also the most cinematic of his scripts, with fast cuts between scenes, like a music video, and the poet's jumpy excitement gives it a "hand-held camera" feel.[211] Rightly so, since the play is about two celebrities born too soon for constant selfies and tweets that would blow up the internet every ten minutes. The two title characters, each with public and private personae, are in a bizarre love trapezoid: Cleopatra loves the man Antony, the celebrity Antony, and the celebrity Cleopatra. Antony loves the woman Cleopatra, the celebrity Cleopatra, and the celebrity Antony. That's six romances, with just two people!

The play is a magical mystery tour with stops all over the Roman world, jet-setting from Egypt to Rome, Sicily, Actium, Athens, then back to Rome and Egypt. The story takes a decade, but Shakespeare makes it all feel like one long week. There's a constant buzz of information overload, which gives the play a very modern feel: ten years' worth of messenger voyages, but it sounds like an instant twitter-fight, "The air is thick with information and news, but nothing much seems to be getting communicated, although when something does happen it affects the whole world at once."[212]

Shakespeare surrounds the superstars with a swarming Where's Waldo page full of "generals, proconsuls, soldiers, messengers, eunuchs, court ladies, parades of slaves and military parades."[213] And yet the world is not big enough for Caesar and this power-couple. Shakespeare's *Antony and Cleopatra* is a massive globe-trotting escapade, and yet as Jan Kott notes, "*Antony and Cleopatra* is a tragedy about the smallness of the world... The sun still circles the earth, but the earth has already become a tiny globule, lost and of no importance in the universe... The world is small because it can be won."[214] Shakespeare renders unto Caesar what is Caesar's, but it's worthless, an empire of dirt (and not in any poetic sense). He's king of the mountain, but it's all garbage.

In Roman history, *Antony and Cleopatra* is really the second act of a great winnowing. Rome had been a republic, theoretically ruled by all its citizens, represented by senators. Then, as Rome focused on imperial conquests, three celebrity generals became major political players, forming the First Triumvirate: Julius Caesar, Pompey Magnus, and Marcus Crassus. But in an Empire, there can be only one, and Julius Caesar was the last man standing. Then the senate killed him and civil war broke out. Julius Caesar's right hand man, Antony, and nephew (posthumously adopted as a son) Caesar Augustus, united to crush the assassins and invited Marcus Lepidus to form the Second Triumvirate. That's prologue. In this play, Antony and Caesar Augustus angle to overthrow each other. Lepidus is a joke; he can't hold his stature or his liquor, and when he passes out at a party, a soldier sarcastically comments that, carrying this wasted general, he bears one third of the world.

In Egyptian history, Cleopatra was the last in the Ptolemy line of colonial rulers who had been installed in Egypt by Alexander the Great three hundred years earlier (the capital city in which she lived, Alexandria, was named after Alexander). Combining Greek and Egyptian cultures, she was a cosmopolitan Renaissance woman fluent in seven languages and she ruled Egypt for twenty-one years as an unmarried queen. Shakespeare leaves out her Greek side, making her the living embodiment of Egypt, the *"serpent of old Nile."* Cleopatra's suicide will be the end of Ptolemy rule, after which Rome will install puppet rulers to tabulate taxes and dispatch shipments of grain.

The play ends with Caesar Augustus alone; this was always inevitable. This is not just Trivial Pursuit. Caesar's defeat of Antony and Cleopatra will turn him into a living god.[215] That had been an Egyptian thing, deified kings and god-queens like Hatshepsut and Cleopatra, but Rome would be seduced by this power. Caesar Augustus couldn't get Cleopatra sexually, but he did grasp her theologically. Godhood sort of worked for Augustus because he didn't enjoy it, and his successor Tiberius didn't enjoy it either. But after them came emperors who did, and their decadent revels rivaled those of Cleopatra's Alexandria, and imperial Rome melted into the Tiber (a resurgence of the revels in Renaissance Rome would spark the Reformation, another disaster for the Empire). A poet could make the case that Cleopatra's lavish lust for life stealthily conquered Rome and brought the Empire down, not once but twice.

The Serpent of Old Nile
ANTONY AND CLEOPATRA

Shakespeare presents Cleopatra through a shifting kaleidoscope of differing perspectives: Egyptian perspectives, Roman perspectives, Egyptian Antony's perspective, and Roman Antony's perspective. She is at the height of her power when she's performing, in public or in private, but we never get to see her conducting grand rituals before Egyptian throngs, or alone with Antony.[216] Shakespeare likely sensed the limitation of a boy actor to show the full spectrum of sacred and profane. Cleopatra herself sneers that if a boy tried to play her onstage it would look ridiculous. All her onstage scenes are, in a sense, behind-the-scenes. Shakespeare shows us the diva backstage between performances, Cleopatra the person who plays Cleopatra the goddess (or goddess*es*: the public Isis and the private .). The temperamental prima donna is alternately taciturn, tender, and tempestuous.

Our glimpses of Cleopatra's celebrity persona are indirect, like Medusa reflected in a shield. Sometimes she is the dark star whose presence can only be determined by the way objects swirl in her orbit. Enobarbus's description of her dramatic entrance on the barge is twenty-seven lines about bodies and air and water gyrating and gravitating around her, but when he tries to stare into the center of this vortex he can only say *"For her own person, / It beggar'd all description."* He's been generous with description, two hundred and eleven words, but her actual physical appearance gets eight words of evasion, no number of syllables would be enough.

Romans spend the entire play searching for the right word, one single label to sum her up. Whore, trull, boggler, filth, error, nag, cow, confusion, witch, gypsy ("gypsy" as a racial slur on Egyptians). But these heaps of trashy insults become her pedestal: the more they belittle her, the grander they reveal her to be. She was the one person in the world whom they really feared. Her very existence is a threat to Roman masculinity, and in their insecurity, they keep trying to hit below the belt. The worst of these epithets spew from Antony himself in those moments when Antony's Roman ego fleetingly emerges, gasping for breath before submerging again into Egyptian Antony. But Antony also knows her true name; both Antonys know it, in reverence and in rage: *"Egypt."*

When Antony is away on business, Cleopatra affectionately recalls his playful pet name for her, *"my serpent of old Nile."* In ancient Egyptian mythology, there was a subterranean snake called Apep who represented the subconscious longing for matriarchal egalitarianism. The Egyptians considered this a threat to the patriarchal hierarchy, a dark chaos roiling below the surface of *Maat*, totalitarian order. Every day this serpent had to be suppressed by the sun god Atum Re. It's unlikely Shakespeare had studied this, but he stumbles onto it when his Romans badmouth matriarchy as a sign of order melting into murky muck, which must finally be paved over by the Apollonian Augustus Caesar.

The Greek tourist Herodotus famously called Egypt a "gift of the Nile," his way of explaining the curious anomaly of an agricultural breadbasket where it doesn't rain. Mud surges upward in annual menstrual swells of the river. This is why Egypt is hundreds of miles long but only five miles wide, a swampy orifice in the desert. Herodotus would have been closer to the truth had he said that Egypt is the Nile, the Nile is Egypt. Ovid described the Nile as the source of all life, a primordial stew in which earth and water met sun and air, causing spontaneous generation of life:

> "The lusty earth of own accord soon after forth did bring
> According to their sundry shapes each other living thing,
> As soon as that the moisture once caught heat against the Sun,
> And that the fat and slimy mud in moorish grounds begun...
> As in their mother's womb, began in length of time to grow,
> To one or other kind of shape wherein themselves to show.
> Even so when that seven mouthed Nile the watery fields forsook,
> And to his ancient channel aft his bridled streams betook,
> So that the Sun did heat the mud, the which he left behind,
> The husbandmen that tilled the ground, among the clods did find
> Of sundry creatures sundry shapes: of which they spièd some,
> Even in the instant of their birth but newly then begun...
> And therefore when the miry earth bespread with slimy mud,
> Brought over all but late before by violence of the flood."
> (Book I, Golding Translation, Updated)[217]

The description of diverse organisms forming in a primordial ooze makes it sound like Ovid was reading Darwin, but *The Origin of Species* would not appear until fifteen centuries later. But time is fluid here. In Shakespeare's play, Lepidus seems to have been reading Ovid's *Metamorphoses,* which would not appear for another forty years. Antony attends a yacht party, and his fellow rulers are curious about how the life of Egypt springs from the desert. Antony explains:

> *"ANTONY. They take [measure] the flow o' th' Nile*
> *By certain scales i' th' pyramid; they know*
> *By th' height, the lowness, or the mean, if dearth*
> *Or foison follow. The higher Nilus swells*
> *The more it promises; as it ebbs, the seedsman*
> *Upon the slime and ooze scatters his grain,*
> *And shortly comes to harvest.*

LEPIDUS. Y'have strange serpents there.
ANTONY. Ay, Lepidus.
LEPIDUS. Your serpent of Egypt is bred now of your mud by the
operation of your sun; so is your crocodile... What manner o' thing is
your crocodile?
ANTONY. It is shap'd, sir, like itself, and it is as broad as it hath
breadth; it is just so high as it is, and moves with its own organs. It
lives by that which nourisheth it, and the elements once out of it, it
transmigrates... And the tears of it are wet." (A&C II.vii, "dearth or
foison" meaning barrenness or bounty)

In this scene, Lepidus is hopelessly sloshed and Antony plays with
him, slurring the Nile, the serpent, the crocodile, and Cleopatra. The queen
is consubstantial with the floodland and its wildlife. Antony's anatomy of
Cleopatra and the crocodile are the same: it is what it is, she is what she
is. And the tears of neither can be trusted. The creature that spontaneously
generates from the mud will return its biomass to the slime, but its spirit
will be reincarnated. Shakespeare makes numerous references in his plays
to metempsychosis, the transmigration of souls, which he'd read about in
the last book of Ovid's *Metamorphoses* (and he himself was said to have
been a reincarnation of Ovid).[218]

Like the mysterious Nile, Cleopatra is a "force of nature that can
neither be contained nor controlled, and that has in it the capacity to
engulf and the power to overwhelm, submerge and annihilate."[219] Drunk
at this yacht party, the aging rockstar Antony plays the lizard king, but
the Romans know that he is melting into the Nile and into Cleopatra
(and in those moments when Antony's Roman self emerges, he'll thrash in
terror). Rome is solid, fixed, and bounded, while Egypt is liquid, a place of
shapeshifting and loss of self. It would be limitless except that, in this story,
it is surrounded by Rome.

Cleopatra's identification with the Nile is symbolic of her own fluidity
and generative power. She can produce biological children, although in this
play her offspring, fathered by Julius Caesar and Antony, are only fleetingly
mentioned. Her true productive power is represented by Egypt itself, and
her ability to unmake and remake Antony. The serpent with which she is
equated is an ancient symbol of self-generation and shapeshifting: the snake
that sheds its skin to renew its youth was long believed to be immortal, and

to possess the wisdom that comes with immortality. There was an old belief that a snake could not die of old age, but would someday swallow its own tail, constrict in a spiral and blink itself out of existence. Cleopatra's own death will be by snakebite. She'll cradle a young serpent of the Nile at her breast, shuffle off her mortal , and ascend into timeless legend.

Everybody Knows She's a Femme Fatale
ANTONY AND CLEOPATRA

Cleopatra is Shakespeare's ultimate prima donna, and there's simply no way around saying it: she's a drama queen. Her generative strength and sexuality are counterbalanced by a violent temper, and a tendency toward tirades of apocalyptic wrath.

When a messenger arrives with news of Antony, she showers him in gold, then warns if the news is bad, she'll melt the gold and pour it down his throat.[220] When he tells her that the role of Antony's bride will be played by a dull understudy, Caesar's sister Octavia, the scorned queen explodes in hellish fury. She thrashes the messenger, pulls a knife, and threatens *"I'll unhair thy head; / Thou shalt be whipp'd with wire and stew'd in brine / Smarting in ling'ring pickle."* (A&C II.v) A servant stage-whispers *"Good madam, keep yourself within yourself."* But Cleopatra erupts in rage, *"Melt Egypt into Nile! and kindly creatures / Turn all to serpents! ...So half my Egypt were submerg'd and made / A cistern for scal'd snakes!"* (A&C II.v) Her tongue is a weapon of mass destruction, and she'll turn it on Rome as well: *"Sink Rome, and their tongues rot / That speak against us!"* (A&C III.vii)

When Antony accuses his beloved *"Serpent of old Nile"* of being reptilian, she recoils from being called cold-blooded:

> *"ANTONY. Cold-hearted toward me?*
> *CLEOPATRA. Ah, dear, if I be so,*
> *From my cold heart let heaven engender hail,*
> *And poison it in the source, and the first stone*
> *Drop in my neck; as it determines, so*
> *Dissolve my life! The next Caesarion smite!*

Till by degrees the memory of my womb,
Together with my brave Egyptians all,
By the discandying of this pelleted storm,
Lie graveless, till the flies and gnats of Nile
Have buried them for prey." (A&C III.xiii)

In this speech she summons an Exodus-style storm of poisoned hailstones that will kill her and her children (the son Caesarion that she bore with Julius Caesar, as well as the children she's had with Antony), and leave their cadavers in a pile for the insects. When she's cornered at the end of the play, she'll return to this image of being eaten by bugs; she would rather rot by the Nile than live in captivity.

"Be gentle grave unto me! Rather on Nilus' mud
Lay me stark-nak'd, and let the water-flies
Blow me into abhorring! Rather make
My country's high pyramidès my gibbet,
And hang me up in chains!"
(A&C V.ii, "blow" meaning bloat, "gibbet" meaning gallows)

Cleopatra can be over-the-top, but even the cynical critic Enobarbus admits that she is not over-acting.

"ENOBARBUS. I have seen her die twenty times upon far poorer
moment. I do think there is mettle in death, which commits some
loving act upon her, she hath such a celerity in dying.
ANTONY. She is cunning past man's thought.
ENOBARBUS. Alack, sir, no! Her passions are made of nothing
but the finest part of pure love. We cannot call her winds and
waters sighs and tears; they are greater storms and tempests than
almanacs can report. This cannot be cunning in her; if it be, she
makes a show'r of rain as well as Jove." (A&C I.ii)

His comment that she has a talent for theatrically dying will prove true at the play's end, when she elaborately stages and costumes her suicide to produce a defiant diorama, an unforgettable image of power to sear into Caesar's brain.

This Corrosion
ANTONY AND CLEOPATRA

There's an old proverb that "behind every great man is a great woman," but Cleopatra won't stay behind Antony, except to the extent that she's always upstaging him. Shakespeare's Cleopatra is theatricality incarnate, fatally fascinating in her *"infinite variety."* She's a master of self-expression, but it's a bit patronizing for us to evaluate her only by the public image she cultivates. If we want to know the artist, we need to look at the art, and Cleopatra's masterpiece is right there onstage: Antony himself.

Cleopatra is a performance artist who elaborately costumes, choreographs, and stars in an interactive, immersive theatrical experience for an audience of one. Her object is to transform a murder machine into a human being. The Roman critics don't get this. The Roman idea of masculine perfection is a robot, a terminator (and not the liquid metal kind). So, they can only judge Cleopatra's work in terms of degrading something useful into something frivolous, turning a weapon into a piece of arm candy. The opening lines of the play are delivered by soldiers discussing how Antony has gone soft, becoming putty in the hands of an enchantress. They can't appreciate what she's sculpting, only that Egypt has been corrosive to Antony's mettle.

> *"Nay, but this dotage of our general's*
> *O'erflows the measure. [And] his captain's heart,*
> *Which in the scuffles of great fights hath burst*
> *The buckles on his breast, reneges all temper,*
> *And is become the bellows and the fan*
> *To cool a gipsy's lust.*
> *(Flourish. Enter ANTONY, CLEOPATRA, her LADIES, the train,*
> *with eunuchs fanning her)*
> *Look where they come!*
> *Take but good note, and you shall see in him*
> *The triple pillar of the world transform'd*
> *Into a strumpet's fool. Behold and see."* (A&C I.i)

The soldiers describe Antony as a phallic pillar whose hard heart could break bronze armor, but now he's become a windbag blowing words at Cleopatra. Overflowing the measure is a metaphor of too much grain for a sack to hold, but the word *"o'erflows"* also introduces the play's central metaphor for Antony's disintegration—the monumental man is liquifying.

Antony delivers his first speech *to* Cleopatra but performs it *for* the Roman ambassadors. He argues that the problem is not with him but with Rome, the city of toxic masculinity should dissolve itself into the feminine river:

> *"Let Rome in Tiber melt, and the wide arch*
> *Of the rang'd empire fall! Here is my space.*
> *Kingdoms are clay; our dungy earth alike*
> *Feeds beast as man. The nobleness of life*
> *Is to do thus (embracing), when such a mutual pair*
> *And such a twain can do't, in which I bind,*
> *On pain of punishment, the world to weet*
> *We stand up peerless."* (A&C I.i, "weet" meaning admit)

Cleopatra judges this speech to be melodramatic. But Antony challenges the world to admit that the two of them, hyper-masculinity and hyper-femininity, in balanced union, have attained perfection.

The Romans continue to insist that Antony is on shore leave, taking a vacation from himself, and will return at any moment. Caesar misses the Antony of the good old days, a battlefield butcher who, during famine, could feast on tree bark and berries, drink horse piss and eat carrion.[221] But now he hears that Antony is *"not more manlike / Than Cleopatra, nor* [is] *the queen of Ptolemy / More womanly than he." (A&C I.iv)*

Antony was supposedly descended from Alcides, Hercules himself, who famously cross-dressed as a love slave to the queen Omphale. And Cleopatra refers to a time when she got Antony drunk in the morning and traded clothes with him: "Then put my tires and mantles on him, whilst / I wore his sword." It's even possible that Cleopatra wears his clothes in the second scene of the play; when she enters, a servant says, *"Hush! Here comes Antony"* and another responds, *"Not he; the queen."* (A&C I.ii)[222] Antony's soldiers will mutter in indignation at her influence, *"We are women's men." (A&C III. vii)* There are moments when Antony's Roman consciousness emerges from the deep, and he fears that he's lost his grip on manhood, blaming Cleopatra: *"You did know / How much you were my conqueror, and that / My sword, made weak by my affection, would / Obey it on all cause."* (A&C III.xi) Antony's penetrative weapon has gone flaccid, and he later rails that he has been castrated: *"She has robb'd me of my sword."*

Antony is Shakespeare's most charismatic tragicomic and romantic hero, but the age of heroes is coming to an end. He is fading out of existence, and worries that he has become translucent:

> *"ANTONY. Eros, thou yet behold'st me?*
> *EROS. Ay, noble lord.*
> *ANTONY. Sometime we see a cloud that's dragonish;*
> *A vapour sometime like a bear or lion,*
> *A tower'd citadel, a pendent rock,*
> *A forkèd mountain, or blue promontory*
> *With trees upon't that nod unto the world*
> *And mock our eyes with air. Thou hast seen these signs;*
> *They are black vesper's pageants.*
> *EROS. Ay, my lord.*
> *ANTONY. That which is now a horse, even with a thought*
> *The rack dislimns, and makes it indistinct,*
> *As water is in water.*
> *EROS. It does, my lord.*
> *ANTONY. My good knave Eros, now thy captain is*
> *Even such a body. Here I am Antony;*
> *Yet cannot hold this visible shape."*
> (A&C IV.xiv, "vesper" meaning evening)

Antony has been melting into the Nile, and now fears that he has evaporated into mist. His cloud-busting vision shapeshifts from flying dragons to predatory lions, from bears to the tamed horse, from an Olympian temple to a mountain to trees bowing toward the soil. A dream interpreter would tell him he's on the right track for self-discovery, but Antony can't see that. He's a middle-aged alcoholic straining to suck in his gut and hold the shape of a bronze Hercules.

Antony's suicide is sometimes seen as a comically botched affair. But the scenes it takes for him to bleed out can also be viewed as the final stages in his liquidation. The poet Ted Hughes writes that Antony must "free himself, wholly and finally, from that obsolete Herculean Roman Antony, and emerge as his true self... It ends with the crushed, empty armor of the former Herculean warrior, like an empty chrysalis, while the liberated love god, like an iridescent new winged being, lies in the lap of the Goddess."[223] Cleopatra's masterpiece is the metamorphosis of an android into a human being, and then into a sort of demigod. And, as an old expression goes, the proof is in the pudding: two thousand years later, Antony is remembered more as a lover than a fighter.

Soap Opera
ANTONY AND CLEOPATRA

Antony and Cleopatra were Western history's first celebrity power-couple. We would call them Cleopantony, except it would make us squirmy about who wears the pants (and in this play, we're told they sometimes play dress-up in each other's clothes). They genuinely enjoy being larger than life. Macbeth never gets to enjoy being Macbeth, Hamlet doesn't enjoy being Hamlet, but Antony enjoys being Antony. He savors his own musk. He's equally at home drinking horse urine on a military campaign and drinking fine wine at Alexandrian revels. Caesar is Caesar because that's the logical thing to be, but he doesn't enjoy it. Cleopatra loves being Cleopatra.

Set in an exotic land of sensuality and sensationalism, Shakespeare's play condenses ten years of soap opera episodes (Antony ages from 43-53, and Cleopatra from 29-39). Cleopatra's star-studded reality show had allegedly included prior celebrity contestants Pompey Magnus, Herod the Great, and Julius Caesar. But at last, in the climactic final season, the insatiable Cleopatra who *"makes hungry where most she satisfies"* met her match in *"the ne'er lust-wearied Antony."* Antony and Cleopatra were idols in both senses, celebrities and demigods. And their glam decade of decadence was a pop trash movie worthy of a hundred Duran Duran videos.

> *"ENOBARBUS. Ay, sir; we did sleep day out of countenance and made the night light with drinking.*
> *MAECENAS. Eight wild boars roasted whole at a breakfast, and but twelve persons there. Is this true?*
> *ENOBARBUS. This was but as a fly by an eagle. We had much more*

monstrous matter of feast, which worthily deserved noting."
(A&C II.ii)

Cleopatra loves both the man and the monumental myth of Antony; Antony loves both the lady and the legend of Cleopatra. And they both love their own public personae. A drop in ratings leads Antony into an identity crisis: "*If I lose mine honor, I lose myself.*" (A&C III.iv) Antony in defeat is not really Antony, and Cleopatra in captivity is not really Cleopatra. When she manages to prop him up after a loss, Cleopatra sighs in relief: "*Since my lord is Antony again, I will be Cleopatra.*" (A&C III.xiii)

Antony the living legend is also a politician, and Caesar scoffs in disgust at how he can elevate Cleopatra, both politically and theologically:

"*CAESAR. Contemning Rome, he has done all this and more...*
I' th' market-place, on a tribunal silver'd,
Cleopatra and himself in chairs of gold
Were publicly enthron'd [and] unto her
He gave the stablishment of Egypt; made her...
Absolute queen.
MAECENAS. This in the public eye?
CAESAR. ...In th' habiliments of the goddess Isis [she] appear'd."
(A&C III.vi)

Cleopatra is the producer of her own show, and her worst fear is being cast in someone else's scene. When Antony fears she will betray him to Caesar, he warns her of what it would be like to be a caged oddity in Caesar's carnival train:

"*ANTONY. Vanish, or I shall give thee thy deserving*
And blemish Caesar's triumph. Let him take thee
And hoist thee up to the shouting plebeians;
Follow his chariot, like the greatest spot
Of all thy sex; most monster-like, be shown
For poor'st diminutives, for doits, and let
Patient Octavia plough thy visage up
With her preparèd nails."
(A&C IV.xii, "doits" meaning coins of very low value)

This ghastly parade ends with a sort of bearbaiting, a catfight with Caesar's sister (Antony's scorned wife). When Antony is dead and Caesar shows up, Cleopatra must play the hardest role of all, an aging southern belle willing to depend on the kindness of strangers. But she knows that the cost of his kindness will be an immortality in burlesque parody:

> "CLEOPATRA. Mechanic slaves,
> With greasy aprons, rules, and hammers, shall
> Uplift us to the view; in their thick breaths,
> Rank of gross diet, shall we be enclouded,
> And forc'd to drink their vapour... Saucy lictors
> Will catch at us like strumpets, and scald rhymers
> Ballad us out o' tune; the quick comedians
> Extemporally will stage us, and present
> Our Alexandrian revels; Antony
> Shall be brought drunken forth, and I shall see
> Some squeaking Cleopatra boy my greatness
> I' th' posture of a whore." (A&C V.ii, "lictors" meaning officers)

This was gutsy for Shakespeare to write, since the speech was delivered by a boy in drag. But the scene works because, well, he's William Shakespeare. And the improv comedians enacting The Tedious Brief Tragical Mirth of Antony and Cleopatra sound a lot like the bumbling amateurs in *A Midsummer Night's Dream*.

Cleopatra the celebrity brand can't stand the idea of being parodied by her enemies. She runs her own show, as the executive producer and star of a great soap opera watched by the whole western world. Amidst all the gossip, glitz and glamor, we can even lose sight of the genuine human connection between these legendary lovers. Harold Bloom ponders, "Are Antony and Cleopatra 'in love with each other,' to use our language, which for once is not at all Shakespearean? ...We can certainly say that Cleopatra and Antony do not bore each other, and clearly they are bored, erotically and otherwise, by everyone else in their world."[224] Their first scene is like an arms race of romantic poetry:

> "CLEOPATRA. If it be love indeed, tell me how much.
> ANTONY. There's beggary in the love that can be reckon'd.

CLEOPATRA. I'll set a bourn how far to be belov'd.
ANTONY. Then must thou needs find out new heaven, new earth."
(A&C I.i, "bourn" meaning boundary marker)

These grand declarations are part performance—they're being watched by Roman critics and Egyptian groupies. But there's also something real in this, the expression of a love that transcends boundaries of gender, space, and time. A love that is too big for this world.

Mother Nature vs. Lady Luck
ANTONY AND CLEOPATRA

History tells us that Caesar defeated Antony. Poetry tells us that *Antony* defeated Antony. Either way, this great warrior must have been brought low by a man, and in both tellings he was weakened by a woman. But Shakespeare gently twists the story of Antony's downfall, and he does it so subtly that we can miss a major player lurking in the background. Antony is allied with Nature, personified onstage by Cleopatra. But Caesar is allied with Fortune, whom we hear about but never see, and ultimately, this goddess will bring Antony down. Antony was a force of Nature, but he was Fortune's fool.

Early in the play, Antony asks a palm reader, *"Whose fortunes shall rise higher, Caesar's or mine?"* The soothsayer warns him, *"If thou dost play with him at any game, / Thou art sure to lose; and of that natural luck / He beats thee 'gainst the odds."* Antony is a better player, but Caesar has Fortune on his side, *"The very dice obey him."* They have gambled on lotteries, quail, literal cock fights, and *"my better cunning faints under his chance."* (A&C II.iii)[225] When Antony and Caesar send fleets of ships or legions of soldiers to slaughter one another, they talk about it like another roll of the dice. Antony is better by land, hand-to-hand, or with an army, but Caesar challenges him by sea and Antony can't resist. When his soldiers tell him it's a bad idea, he answers:

"ANTONY. For that [because] he dares us to't.
ENOBARBUS. So hath my lord dar'd him to single fight.

CANIDIUS. ...But these offers,
Which serve not for his vantage, he shakes off;
And so should you." (A&C III.vii)

Caesar only plays when he will win, and he preys upon Antony's gambling addiction. When the fleet has been defeated, Antony knows his luck has run out, saying *"Fortune and Antony part here."* (A&C IV.xii)[226] Antony's suicide is the last move in his match with Caesar, not to throw the game, but to deprive his rival of victory (and spare himself the *"penetrative shame"* of being dominated). Enlisting an intern to assist, he says, *"Thou strik'st not me, 'tis Caesar thou defeat'st."* (AC IV.xiv)[227]

It's Cleopatra who best understands the battle of Fortune and Nature that has raged in Antony's downfall. As he lies dying in her arms, she promises a eulogy so loud and bitter *"that the false huswife Fortune break her wheel, / Provok'd by my offence."* (A&C IV.xv) When Antony is dead and Caesar is set to be deified, Cleopatra declares him a common thug in the service of Lady Luck:

"CLEOPATRA. 'Tis paltry to be Caesar:
Not being Fortune, he's but Fortune's knave,
A minister of her will... Nature wants stuff
To vie strange forms with fancy; yet t' imagine
An Antony were nature's piece 'gainst fancy,
Condemning shadows quite." (A&C V.ii)

Cleopatra laments that Nature lacks the imagination to compete with human fantasy but did its best in the creation of Antony. Now Nature's masterpiece has been brought down by bad luck. In *Antony and Cleopatra*, Fortune doesn't favor the bold or the beautiful, but the bland and bureaucratic. Antony is a romantic champion and compulsive gambler; Caesar runs the casino. If we look for Cleopatra's barge today, we'll find it bolted in the entryway of Caesars Palace in Las Vegas. But in her final moments, she'll perceive great Antony's ghost, still defiant: *"I hear him mock the luck of Caesar."* (A&C V.ii)

A Dead End..?
ANTONY AND CLEOPATRA

In Shakespeare's Roman plays we see numerous variations on the theme of barbarians at the gate, besieging the city, threatening to reduce Rome to rubble, and turn "order" into chaos. "Order" has to be in quotes here, because we're talking about an Orwellian dystopia: Roman "order" was fascism. In *Coriolanus*, the urban rabble was barbaric. Then the exiled general led a horde of barbarians to tear it all apart and the city was saved by a female trinity. In *Julius Caesar*, republican senators slaughtered the king (Shakespeare was a romantic royalist who considered democracy to be anarchic mob rule). In *Titus Andronicus*, the barbaric Goths infiltrated the city, despoiled its purest maiden, and then an exiled soldier vengefully led a horde to the city.

Antony and Cleopatra flips this around. Instead of barbarians threatening to turn Roman order into chaos, Egypt is besieged by bureaucrats. The play ends with its title characters cornered, seeking sanctuary in a tomb. Although he's stabbed himself, Antony is too tough to die and takes several scenes to bleed out. The image of Cleopatra and her servants hoisting him up can look comical; as a final indignity, the flaccid warrior must be hauled up like luggage. But in original performances this was likely accomplished with a platform and pulley system, the technological apparatus used for a *Deus ex Machina*, God from the Machine. Antony is not being lowered into a hole, he is ascending.

Reunited, they speak of Antony's suicide as a rare species of victory:

> "*ANTONY. Not Caesar's valour hath o'erthrown Antony,*
> *But Antony's hath triumph'd on itself.*
> *CLEOPATRA. So it should be, that none but Antony*
> *Should conquer Antony; but woe 'tis so!*" (A&C IV.xv)

Cleopatra briefly considers living in a world without Antony:

> "*CLEOPATRA. Shall I abide*
> *In this dull world, which in thy absence is*
> *No better than a sty? O, see, my women,*

The crown o' th' earth doth melt. My lord!
O, wither'd is the garland of the war,
The soldier's pole is fall'n! Young boys and girls
Are level now with men. The odds is gone,
And there is nothing left remarkable
Beneath the visiting moon." (A&C IV.xv, "sty" meaning pigpen)

Cornered in a tomb, besieged by Roman soldiers, Cleopatra decides to turn the tables—she and Antony will invade the realm of the dead: *"To rush into the secret house of death / Ere death dare come to us."* (A&C IV.xv) It's likely a coincidence, but in this bold pronouncement she resembles the Babylonian goddess Ishtar storming the underworld.[228] Once resolved for suicide, Cleopatra brightens and in a darkly comical moment chirps, *"Let's do it after the high Roman fashion, / And make death proud to take us."* There's the obvious joke that Cleopatra will approach death like a beauty pageant, making her grand exit in style. But the core meaning here is that suicide is the trendy way to go, all the chic Greek and vogue Roman heroines were doing it. Of course, Cleopatra adds her own distinctive flair. In Classical drama women committed suicide offstage by sword or hanging, but the queen of Egypt will dramatically die before our very eyes by snakebite.

Cleopatra is theatricality incarnate and refuses to be an understudy or a prop in Caesar's production. Northrop Frye wrote, "her suicide is motivated by her total refusal to be a part of someone else's scene, and she needs the whole fifth act to herself for her suicide show."[229] It must be elaborately costumed and stage managed for maximum impact; she sets it up like a fashion photo shoot. By killing herself, she will steal the show from Caesar. She even gives the snake a line, the funniest punchline in the play, coaching it to call Casear an *"Asssssss."*

. writes, "Finally, as a spectacle executed with her elegant theatricality (no bungler she) and rich with imagistic suggestions of feminine fecundity and sensuality, her death seems to constitute a strong counterstatement to *virtus,"*[230] toxic masculinity. Caesar had planned to exhibit the exotic queen in a Roman triumph, a fascist march, and she rains on his pride parade. Cleopatra's suicide is not only an escape from Caesar, but a consummation of marriage with Mark Antony. It's classic Shakespearean irony to stage their wedding in a tomb, but poetically it's a portal between this world and the next, and Cleopatra escapes to where they met when she barged into his life on the river Cydnus: *"I am again for Cydnus / To meet Mark Antony"* (AC V.ii)

Ted Hughes writes that their deaths are not tragic but transcendent. Rome entrapped them in a dead end, but the lovers escaped into legend: "Though they carve up the living body, with suffering in every stroke of the blade, they cannot touch the divine nature—they can only liberate it."[231] Caesar is the *"universal landlord,"* but Cleopatra cannot be claimed or colonized: *"I am fire and air; my other elements / I give to baser life."* Caesar is left to rule over a landfill, "and the world has become flat."[232]

Shakespeare becomes flat too; he's deflated by these deaths. After this he'll slog into his bleak midwinter period with *Coriolanus, Timon of Athens, Pericles, Prince of Tyre,* and *Cymbeline,* a creative period where (taking a line from Shakespeare himself) *"This borrowed passion stands for true old woe."* (PER IV.iv)

The great bardolator Harold Bloom writes that Shakespeare "was wary of further quests into the interior... The sublime music of Antony's self-destruction would be the play's largest poetic achievement, except that nothing could surpass the immense harmonies of Cleopatra's death scene, which can be said to have changed Shakespeare himself once and for all. After *Antony and Cleopatra,* something vital abandons Shakespeare."[233] In the character of Cleopatra he invests the full goddess spectrum, and maybe his muse abandons him. Or, Bloom surmises, perhaps he realized that the audience wanted less, not more.

Shakespeare idolized Queen Elizabeth, whose publicists wrapped her in goddess imagery. King James came packaged as a new Augustus Caesar. Shakespeare genuflected to James with *Macbeth,* then turned around and wrote a play in which King James symbolically strangled theatricality to death. Was Cleopatra's famous final scene an attempt at career suicide? If so, Shakespeare, like Antony, took a long time to bleed out. He started cranking out mediocre scripts on an assembly line for a company that had been ominously re-named the King's Men.

PART III

Risen Heroines

Blooming from the Tomb
MUCH ADO ABOUT NOTHING | ALL'S WELL THAT ENDS WELL

Antony and Cleopatra ends in gloom. The great hero has melted into mist, the drama queen has transformed into a cold statue of herself. Then the performers bow and we shuffle out of the theater to drink ourselves to death. We never get to see the ending Shakespeare intended, where the fallen heroes leap back onto the stage for a victory dance.

"Nowadays," a theater critic wrote in 1606, the year of *Antony and Cleopatra's* premiere, "they put at the end of every tragedy (as poison into meat) a comedy or jig." This is how a Shakespearean tragedy ended, as we may recall from the mechanics' tragedy performed within *A Midsummer Night's Dream*: Pyramus and Thisbe kill themselves, then jump up for a lusty *"Bergomask dance."*[234] Antony and Cleopatra's folksy jig would be the final victory over Caesar's foiled plot to drag the defeated lovers on a humiliating forced march; the swirling circle is the opposite of the linear triumphal procession. Death is defeated, love springs eternal.

The heroine's descent into the underworld to rescue or reunite with the hero is a running theme in Shakespearean tragedy. Juliet and Cleopatra both descend into a tomb expecting to reunite with their lovers, and in both cases a miscommunication spurs the hero to take his own life. Then the heroine pursues her lover into the realm of death (and brings him back onto the stage for a curtain-call jig). To this we should add Thisbe and Pyramus, whose tragic deaths take place next to Ninus's tomb. Cordelia descends with Lear into the subterranean dungeon, and the messenger sent to cancel the execution is just moments too late to save her, then Lear pursues her into the afterlife, and she leads him back onstage for a daddy-daughter dance.

These tragedies were interspersed with comedies in which the underworld rescue is successful. In *The Comedy of Errors*, Antipholus of Ephesus is dragged down into a dungeon due to a series of misunderstandings, then escapes and seeks sanctuary in a shadowy abbey. Meanwhile, his father is under a death sentence (and his twin brother will be as well, if it should be revealed that he comes from Syracuse). The abbess, emerging from the womb-like temple, rescues all three of them. In the meantime, there's been a comical subplot of the manservant Dromio mistakenly claimed by a hot wench in an underground kitchen.

Hermia's venture into the nocturnal forest co-ruled by a *"king of shadows"* in *A Midsummer Night's Dream* could be considered an underworld journey. In *The Merchant of Venice*, Portia descends from celestial Belmont into the deathly realm of the Venetian courtroom, where she defeats the grim, legal contract, rescuing the merchant Antonio from incarceration and execution. More significantly, she rescues her husband Bassanio from survivor's guilt.

In *Much Ado About Nothing*, a nasty prank transforms a wedding into a witch trial. The gullible groom Claudio becomes convinced that his blushing bride Hero is a whore.[235] She swoons, he runs off, and then, oddly enough, the Friar from *Romeo and Juliet* pops in, and once again his solution to the problem is for the heroine to play dead.[236] The prank works, and guilt-ridden Claudio is tasked with resurrecting her reputation. He leads a procession, singing to the virginal moon-goddess Diana:

> *"Done to death by slanderous tongues*
> *Was the Hero that here lies:*
> *Death, in guerdon of her wrongs,*
> *Gives her fame which never dies.*
> *So the life that died with shame*
> *Lives in death with glorious fame...*
> *Now, music, sound, and sing your solemn hymn.*

Pardon, goddess of the night,
Those that slew thy virgin knight;
For the which, with songs of woe,
Round about her tomb they go.
Midnight, assist our moan;
Help us to sigh and groan,
Heavily, heavily: Graves, yawn and yield your dead,
Till death be utterèd, heavily, heavily." (MAAN V.iii, "Death,
in guerdon of her wrongs" meaning Death, in recompense for
wrongs done against her.)

The song implies that the restoration of her reputation can resurrect
Hero. Claudio does not believe it will work, vowing to make this an annual
pilgrimage ritual, and accepting Beatrice as an alternate bride (a fairly
courageous move for the callow Claudio, considering that Beatrice has
threatened to *"eat his heart in the marketplace"*). But then he's most fortunate
that the disguised bride he blindly marries lifts her veil and reveals herself
to be Hero: *"One Hero died defil'd, but I do live, / And surely as I live, I am a
maid."* (MAAN V.iiv) Hero's descent into the underworld rescues Claudio
from the cancer of jealousy. It also rescues the audience from going home
sickened having seen Beatrice marry this clod.[237]

Hero and Claudio are really a sideshow in a play "known to many as
Beatrice and Benedick, [that] might as soon be called *As You Like Beatrice* or
What Beatrice Wills."[238] Beatrice is a force of nature, and Benedick fears she
is a living manifestation of the discord goddess Ate, *"possessed by a Fury,"*
a snake-haired gorgon monster, and calls her a *"harpy,"* a beastly chimera
combining a woman and a bird of prey. The battle-hardened Benedick is
terrified of this chthonic man-eating abyss, and yet, witnessing how his
friend flounders around, he finally overcomes his fear of being castrated
and cannibalized. Benedick realizes that the virginal Diana, the voluptuous
Venus, and volcanic, voracious Nature are all one in the spectrum of the
divine feminine. And if he is to be devoured, it's just part of the circle of
life: *"The world must be peopled."*

Shakespeare's most fearless adventurer into the netherworld is the
stonecold sociopath Helena of *All's Well That Ends Well.* She combines the
cunning of Shakespeare's supervillains, Richard III, Iago, and Edmund. As
a master strategist she stalks her prey, but unlike the transvestite heroines,

this supervixen does not need a masculine disguise to get close. Perhaps Helena's most distinguishing trait among Shakespeare's leading ladies is that she is not romantic. Robert Ornstein notes, "Even when she is alone her responses are guarded; instead of a spontaneous rush of feeling there is cautious appraisal of possibilities and practicalities."[239] A cool realist, she expects no help from the stars or the gods:

> "Our remedies oft in ourselves do lie,
> Which we ascribe to heaven. The fated sky
> Gives us free scope; only doth backward pull
> Our slow designs when we ourselves are dull." (AWTEW I.i)

Helena has set her sights on Bertram, a frivolous frat boy who can be best described with the modern half-word "bro." Flipflops and tank-tops hadn't been invented yet, but that's who this guy is. What Helena sees in this fop is a mystery for the ages. A servant reports having overheard Helena trashing on all the deities who have kept her from Bertram:

> "Fortune, she said, was no goddess, that had put such difference
> betwixt their two estates; Love [Cupid] no god, that would not
> extend his might only where qualities were level; Diana no queen of
> virgins, that would suffer her poor knight surpris'd without rescue in
> the first assault, or ransom afterward. This she deliver'd in the most
> bitter touch of sorrow that e'er I heard virgin exclaim in."
> (AWTEW I.iii)

Helena refers to herself as a *"knight"* (meaning a devotee of the virgin goddess Diana) who has been captivated since her first glance at Bertram, with no hope of release.[240] She's grimly determined to win him but makes no attempt to attract him. She wants to entrap him. And it works—she ensnares her prey early in the script. Approaching a king's darkened deathbed, she gambles on a cure: if successful in healing him she demands he give her the husband of her choosing, and if she fails, she'll be tortured to death. Having saved the king, she claims her husband; but Bertram refuses to be a trophy, he is a hunter and sexual predator (like Adonis, he's determined to hunt the boar in foreign warfare rather than be a kept man). He leaves her with a catch-22 riddle to solve: he'll accept her only if she gains the familial ring he'll never part with, and bears his baby without sleeping with him. The game is on. Helena accepts these rules, and in her calculating silence we can almost hear an echo of Shakespeare's other Helena, *"Run when you will, the story shall be changed. / Apollo flies, and Daphne holds the chase."* (MND II.i)

Bertram goes off to war, and Helena tracks him from France to Italy on the pretext of a religious pilgrimage. She's really on a hero quest to prove her worthiness, not *to* Bertram, but by gaining this guy, she wants to prove her worthiness to herself. Identifying a maiden Bertram is trying to seduce, Helena enlists her in a plot to demand Bertram's family ring as proof of honest intentions, then sets up a meeting in a darkened chamber. Helena stealthily substitutes herself for the maiden, thus gaining both the ring and the miraculous pregnancy Bertram demanded. But she's not quite done. Helena then fakes her own death, implicating Bertram as the killer, so that when she reveals herself, he's happy to see her.

For Helena, the symbolic underworld has a revolving door: she goes there to cure the king, to conceive a baby, and then makes one more journey to the realm of death so that she can rescue Bertram from ending up in the king's dungeon (never mind that she framed him for her own fake death—all's well that ends well). Her final line in the play lets Bertram know that if he should *"prove untrue, / Deadly divorce step between me and you!"* (AWTEW V.iii)

Shakespeare will repeat the blackout blind date in his next play, *Measure for Measure*, a nauseating dystopian nightmare in which lust is outlawed in the city of Venus. Isabella, a novice nun, descends into an underworld dungeon to see her brother who faces a death-sentence for premarital sex.[241] The unjust judge, a corrupt fundamentalist named Angelo, attempts to sexually blackmail Isabella: her brother's life can be redeemed through the sacrifice of her virginity. But a devious Duke disguised as a monk proposes a darkened bait-and-switch, substituting the judge's spurned ex-fiancée for Isabella, then forcing them to marry. The play ends on a dark note. In exchange for rescuing Isabella from the judge's sexual blackmail, the Duke demands Isabella yield her virginity to *him*. And blackout, before she can answer. Perhaps we're to assume that this virgin sacrifice will somehow cleanse the city, but the Duke is so sleazy, it's doubtful.

All's Well That Ends Well and *Measure for Measure* are "comedies" in that they end with conception, but they're not funny. Scholars sometimes classify these as "problem plays." They were followed by a run of great tragedies: *Othello, King Lear, Macbeth,* and *Antony and Cleopatra,* two of which contain unsuccessful journeys to the underworld (or perhaps three, if we count Desdemona's foiled journey to the bridal bed, which in the end becomes a mass grave stacked with cadavers).

The heroine's successful return from the underworld will resolve Shakespeare's final four plays. In *Pericles, Prince of Tyre,* the prince's wife Thaisa seemingly dies in childbirth at sea and is set adrift in a casket. Later, his daughter Marina is abducted into the underworld of a brothel but escapes through virtue and ingenuity. The family is at last be reunited: Marina rescues her father from living-death and together they find Thaisa in Diana's Temple. The Princess Imogen in *Cymbeline* is poisoned and buried in a cave, and then awakens to rescue her husband Posthumous.[242] *The Winter's Tale* begins with a queen being dragged down into a dungeon and concludes with her emergence from a cavernous chapel (this is very complex and will be examined in greater detail). Finally, *The Tempest* features Miranda, who has spent sixteen years on a purgatorial island fending off the Plutonian Caliban. She finally rises to become Queen of Naples, and her elevation restores Prospero to the dukedom of Milan.

These characters are not goddesses. But the goddess Diana plays a prominent role in several of these stories, and it's worth noting that Diana as a moon goddess is a symbol of resurrection: each month the moon is born anew, matures, ages, and dies, followed by a rebirth. Thaisa in *Pericles, Prince of Tyre,* becomes a priestess of Diana, and by extension the Abbess in *The Comedy of Errors* and Isabella in *Measure for Measure* could be seen as votaries of the virgin goddess. Hero in *Much Ado About Nothing* is restored after a hymn to Lunar Diana, and the moon has guarded Hermia and Helena in *A Midsummer Night's Dream* (it could be argued that the moon has also blocked Titania from descending into bestial infidelity with Bottom). Diana in her huntress aspect is clearly manifested in Helena in *All's Well That Ends Well,* who even temporarily assumes the name Diana to entrap Bertram in the dark. The absence of moonlight enables the bait-and-switch in *All's Well That Ends Well* and *Measure for Measure,* further circumstantial evidence of Diana's assistance. There is no explicit Classical myth of Diana rescuing someone from the realm of death, but she was Shakespeare's favorite deity. And in her lunar aspect, she is in a constant cycle of death and resurrection.

Flora & Proserpina

Spring Cleaning

William Shakespeare didn't give interviews or do commentaries, nor did he write authorial prefaces for his plays, so we're in the dark about how he saw each piece in relation to the full scope of his creative journey. Reading his last few scripts, it does seem fairly clear that he saw the end of his career coming. *Cymbeline* is a scramble to tie up loose ends on various career-long themes, and he tries to pack so much in that the whole thing falls flat: it's got everything except for the memorable characters that make his plays worth watching. He approached the issue from the opposite angle in *The Winter's Tale*, establishing dynamic characters first, then checking off the boxes of thematic unfinished business. Having accomplished it, he did a self-indulgent victory lap with *The Tempest*, and then co-wrote some pieces to launch his successor, John Fletcher.

At this late stage of his career, Shakespeare was haunted by three skeletons in his closet: the innocent victim in his poem *The Rape of Lucrece*, the abruptly hanged Cordelia in *King Lear*, and the unjustly punished Desdemona in *Othello*. So, in *Cymbeline*, he reincarnated all three tragic heroines in the princess Imogen. Her Lear-lite father castigated her for choosing her own mate, and her husband Posthumus (like Lucrece's husband) brought on calamity by bragging about her virtue and was then plagued with Othello-esque jealousy by the impish incubus Iachimo, a name that means "little Iago." Imogen is a great character, intelligent and resourceful, and she's the last of Shakespeare's cross-dressed heroines. But unfortunately, she's surrounded by male characters who are flat and forgettable.

So, Shakespeare went back to the drawing board, reincarnating Desdemona as Hermione and Cordelia as Perdita in *The Winter's Tale*, pairing them with memorable male characters. He succeeded, and *Cymbeline* has been pretty much forgiven and forgotten. *The Winter's Tale* contains a great deal of exploration of the divine feminine, touching on personified Nature as well as the Classical deities Flora and Proserpina. We'll also examine the story as a sort of "spring cleaning" in which Shakespeare delves into his mixed feelings about women.

Husbandry —or— Lock, Stock and Barrel
THE WINTER'S TALE

In the beginning was Nature. Shakespeare describes a childhood friendship between two young princes as a pure and perfect paradise. A servant uses the metaphor of two grafted trees, *"They were train'd together in their childhoods; and there rooted betwixt them then such an affection which cannot choose but branch now,"* (WT I.i) and Polixenes recalls *"We were as twinn'd lambs that did frisk i' th' sun / And bleat the one at th' other."* (WT I.ii)[243] Then these two natural shapeshifters attained adult humanity by becoming husbands and fathers (they don't marry each other, although their boyhood playmate memories sound a bit snuggly). They have also both grown up to be kings: Leontes of Sicilia and Polixenes of Bohemia; the two boys raised in Nature have been separated by culture.

But they still visit each other when they can. As Polixenes prepares to go home from a playdate, Leontes's wife Hermione entreats him to stay a bit longer. Tragically, Leontes failed to overhear that she brokered this by bargaining that Leontes could stay an extra week on his next trip. But Leontes was distracted by a daydream of godlike omniscience which convinced him that his very pregnant wife was having an affair. As he becomes certain that he can see all, he also imagines that he's being watched by a theatrical audience, whose deepest secrets he can sense:

> *"And many a man there is, even at this present,*
> *Now while I speak this, holds his wife by th' arm*
> *That little thinks she has been sluic'd in's absence,*

And his pond fish'd by his next neighbour, by
Sir Smile, his neighbour. Nay, there's comfort in't,
Whiles other men have gates and those gates open'd,
As mine, against their will. Should all despair
That hath revolted wives, the tenth of mankind
Would hang themselves. Physic for't there's none;
It is a bawdy planet." (WT I.i)

While exalting himself to godhood, he reduces his pregnant queen to a pond that's been fished or a piece of land that's yielded to invasion. Later his friend will comment that Leontes looks as if *"he had lost some province, and a region / Lov'd as he loves himself."* When Hermione tells him that she and Polixenes are going for a garden stroll he takes this for evidence that his wife and friend are off to tiptoe through the tulips. Never mind that she's in her third trimester; Leontes sees Hermione's invitation into the enclosed garden as a sexual penetration of his bride, and by extension, himself and his country.

Leontes's equation of his wife and a tract of land is, oddly, not a symptom of his madness but the standard mentality of his era. Among nobility and royalty, marriage was a means of sealing a real estate deal.[244] Even in modernity we still use the word "husband" which derives from "husbandry," managing plant and animal reproduction. Hermione equates herself with a tree when she refers to her son as the *"first fruits of my body,"* and his name Mamillius means breast-fed, an odd name to give a royal heir. Leontes-as-husband-and-king is determined to control Hermione-as-productive-land/livestock, but he fears that below her placid surface she's roiling up some natural disaster, a libidinous volcano or tidal wave that will destroy him.

In Shakespeare's writings, male "Jealousy" is not so much the fear of losing a beloved female partner but fear of losing one's own manhood. In marriage, Leontes has made Hermione co-owner of his masculinity as he is co-owner of her fertility, but he fears the part of her that he cannot control—her deep, primal nature (Similarly, Othello, unmoored with jealousy, mourns: *"O curse of marriage, / That we can call these delicate creatures ours, / And not their appetites!"* OTH III.iii) And Hermione's gravid pregnancy, symbol of her loyalty to Leontes, is distorted into a twisted vision of anarchic sexuality. Convinced that the fetus is a Bohemian spy, Leontes will attempt to foil an infiltration with a sentence of infanticide.

The baby is delivered in an underground dungeon, and Hermione's friend Paulina immediately brings the infant to Leontes as proof of his paternity: *"It is yours. And, might we lay th' old proverb to your charge, so like you 'tis the worse."* (The proverb is that the baby would be perfect but for the genes inherited from the father, an old joke that dads never tire of hearing). She commands that Leontes acknowledge how the *"good goddess Nature"* has truly copied his looks onto this baby girl. The mad king responds that Paulina is a witch who should be burned, and her husband should he hanged for his failure to shut her up. Paulina's husband rolls his eyes, *"Hang all the husbands that cannot do that feat, you'll leave yourself hardly one subject."* (WT II.iii) Fortunately, Antigonus will not be executed for antagonizing the king. Unfortunately, he'll soon be dismembered and devoured by a bear. One way or another, that man was destined to die with soiled pantaloons.

So begins *The Winter's Tale*, Shakespeare's great exploration of masculine folly in straining for totalitarian control over female Nature.

Apollo and Paulina
The Winter's Tale

"'The Pythia, with raving mouth, uttering her unlaughing, unadorned words, reaches us over a thousand years with her voice–through the inspiration of a god,' says Heraclitus."[245] Leontes's delusion of oracular grandeur satisfies him that persecuting Hermione is the right thing to do, for himself and for his imaginary audience of cheated theater patrons. But to calm the murmuring commoners, he sends emissaries to the oracle at Delphi so the Greek God Apollo himself can corroborate the accusation. The messengers' travel time unfortunately means Hermione spends twenty-three days in the dungeon, including delivery day, as they await news from Delphi.

Shakespeare is on shaky ground in his writing about the oracle, plagiarizing from someone who hadn't done his homework. Well, "plagiarism" is a strong word, since everybody knew he was adapting Robert Greene's popular 1588 novel, *Pandosto*. It's from Greene that Shakespeare got the misspelling "Delphos" and maybe some misconceptions about the shrine, as well.

Delphi, north of Athens, had long been known as Pytho, home of the immortal serpent Python and a priestess Pythia, who could enter an ecstatic trance state and reveal divine secrets to mortals. When patriarchal pirates overthrew the indigenous Mediterranean matriarchy, the temple was claimed in the name of Phoebus Apollo, and the sacking of this shrine (barbarians beating up some nuns) was mythologized into a story of the enlightened Apollo slaying a chthonic snake-monster. Although the site was renamed for Phoebus, its high priestess retained the title Pythia, and it was said that her visions came from inhaling the fumes of the decaying subterranean serpent. Modern archaeologists say there may have been a natural gas leak, and she might have just been getting high on the fumes. Archaeology is the antidote to poetry.

Leontes's emissaries describe a *"fertile isle, the temple much surpassing / the common praise it bears"* (Delphi is not an island; perhaps it was mixed up with Delos, but then again in this play, the Czech Republic is an island—who are we to argue with Shakespeare?) They comment on the priestly vestments and solemn sacrifices but were most struck by *"the burst / And the ear-deaf'ning voice o' th' oracle, / Kin to Jove's thunder."* (WT III.i) This all sounds a bit Wizard-of-Ozy, especially considering that the Oracle didn't say anything. The messengers didn't hear a message, they still don't know if Hermione has been declared guilty or innocent. They received a document, *"This seal'd-up oracle, by the hand deliver'd / Of great Apollo's priest [and] have not dar'd to break the holy seal / Nor read the secrets in't."* (WT III.ii)

In this play, the oracular message comes from a male priest of Apollo, not a priestess inhaling snake-smoke. So maybe they got mixed up and went to Delos after all, but more likely, Greene and Shakespeare had been careless in their research. Regardless, the words of the oracle, read aloud at Hermione's trial, are true: *"Hermione is chaste; Polixenes blameless;* [and] *Leontes a jealous tyrant; his innocent babe truly begotten; and the King shall live without an heir, if that which is lost be not found."* (WT III.ii) It's fascinating to note that the prophecy is dull legalistic prose in a scene otherwise comprised of poetic verse. The oracle is surprisingly officious, ironically coming from the god of poetry. Here again, this is meant to sound like Apollo the great attorney (Apollo got Orestes off the hook for murdering his own mother!). It sure doesn't sound like a hippie trippy psychedelic shamaness.

Leontes is a politician. When challenged by the oracle, he simply shrugs it off as fake news. It's comically ironic to say this now, since the oracle is indeed superstitious mumbo-jumbo, except in the world of Shakespeare, oracles and soothsayers and witches are always correct in their predictions. And when Leontes proceeds with his wife's trial, a messenger runs in with bad tidings: the young prince has suddenly died. Leontes concludes that his son has been killed by Apollo: *"Apollo's angry; and the heavens themselves / Do strike at my injustice."* As he says these words, Hermione drops too, and as she's being carried out he cries, *"Apollo, pardon / My great profaneness 'gainst thine oracle."* He vows to mend his ways and re-woo his wife (good luck with that).

Hermione's friend and attorney Paulina re-enters and tears Leontes down with the news of Hermione's death, shattering his illusion of godhood:

> *"I say she's dead; I'll swear't. If word nor oath*
> *Prevail not, go and see. If you can bring*
> *Tincture or lustre in her lip, her eye,*
> *Heat outwardly or breath within, I'll serve you*
> *As I would do the gods. But, O thou tyrant!*
> *Do not repent these things, for they are heavier*
> *Than all thy woes can stir; therefore betake thee*
> *To nothing but despair. A thousand knees*
> *Ten thousand years together, naked, fasting,*
> *Upon a barren mountain, and still winter*
> *In storm perpetual, could not move the gods*
> *To look that way thou wert."* (WT III.ii)

After the punctilious legalism of the Apollonian oracle, Paulina's curse is a breath of fresh (or foul) air—*this* is what a Shakespearean prophecy should sound like. And there's a fascinating connection between Paulina and Apollo: Paulina has three times called Leontes a tyrant, then the oracle echoes her by calling him a tyrant, and she uses the word again. Shakespeare seems to be establishing some correspondence between them, and as we'll see, Paulina will become the high priestess of a shrine in Sicilia.

Upon losing his wife and son, Leontes is crushed. His delusion of all-knowing grandeur is gone, the theatrical spectators he envisioned depart. The play itself abandons blighted Sicilia for the sunny shores and imaginary beach of Bohemia and will not return to Sicilia until what's been lost is found: the abandoned babe, the dead wife, and the old lovable Leontes.

Exit, Pursued by a Bear
–or– On Some Faraway Beach
THE WINTER'S TALE

The plot of *The Winter's Tale* requires that the baby born to Hermione and Leontes, whose name will be "the lost girl" Perdita, be as lost as possible. Finding her will break the winter spell, but first she must blossom into womanhood. The child must be abandoned, and Shakespeare must eliminate everyone who knows where she is.

Leontes does not specify a location, he only says to *"bear it to some remote and desert place, quite out of our dominions,"* and leave the baby to die or be adopted. Antigonus takes the infant and utters a quiet prayer that birds of prey might decide to nurse it, then muses, *"Wolves and bears, they say / Casting their savageness aside, have done / Like offices of pity."* (WT II.iii) He's referring to two myths of newborns left to die by exposure. Romulus and Remus, the legendary founders of Rome, were born to a Vestal Virgin who was assaulted by the war-god Mars. The infant twins were abandoned beside the Tiber river, adopted by a she-wolf, and later raised by shepherds. In Greek myth, the baby girl Atalanta was left out to die because her father wanted a son. She was adopted by a bear and later taken in by hunters. Growing up, she identified the bear as a manifestation of the huntress goddess Artemis and became a legendary hunter herself.

Perhaps the repetition of *"bear it"* and *"bears"* inspired Shakespeare's most memorable stage direction, when Antigonus leaves the baby on the beach amid the clamor of a sea storm, then sees a terrifying sight, and: *"Exit, pursued by a bear."* How this was originally staged we don't know. Perhaps it was a man in costume, like Snug the Joiner playing a lion in *"Pyramus and Thisbe."* There's some possibility that a tame bear was borrowed from a nearby bear-baiting arena. This was the English theater's major competition: pitting bears against packs of dogs (Macbeth, during the battle of Dunsinane, says *"They have tied me to a stake; I cannot fly,*

/ *But bear-like I must fight the course.*" MAC V.vii) Or perhaps it was a comical moment. King James had recently acquired a polar bear cub for his personal zoo, and records show he loaned it out for theatrical productions.

Symbolically, the tempest and bear are manifestations of Mother Nature's rage over this attempted infanticide. The Mariner has warned that *"the skies look grimly and threaten present blusters... The heavens...are angry and frown upon 's."* (WT III.iii) An eyewitness report of what follows will be an apocalyptic chaos, an undoing of creation. The *Metamorphoses* begins with a formless void, "The face of Nature in a vast expanse was naught but Chaos uniformly waste... But God, or kindly Nature, ended strife [and] cut the land from skies, the sea from land."[246] In *The Winter's Tale*, as a shepherd finds the baby on the beach, a frantic clown runs on and reports:

> *"I have seen two such sights, by sea and by land! But I am not to say it is a sea, for it is now the sky; betwixt the firmament and it you cannot thrust a bodkin's [needle's] point... How it chafes, how it rages, how it takes up the shore! But that's not to the point... And then for the land service—to see how the bear tore out his shoulder-bone; how he cried to me for help, and said his name was Antigonus, a nobleman! But to make an end of the ship—to see how the sea flap-dragon'd it; but first, how the poor souls roared, and the sea mock'd them; and how the poor gentleman roared, and the bear mock'd him, both roaring louder than the sea or weather."* (WT III.iii)

The sea swallowed the land and ship while a beast ate the man (who apparently thought that introducing himself as *"Antigonus, a nobleman"* might give the animal pause). This is a painful irony: Antigonus prayed for the baby to be adopted by a bear, and then found himself in the most dangerous place in nature—between a bear and its cub. Jeanne Addison Roberts wrote, "The bear seems actually to be the agent of female Nature, liberating the play world from some of the tyranny of male culture... The bear marks the change in the mode of the play from tragedy to comedy,"[247] from sterility to fertility. Michael Steffes proposes that this bear may be a manifestation of the huntress-goddess Diana.[248]

The second half of Antigonus's wish, that Perdita be shepherded by a wolf, will also come true in a roundabout way. Antigonus himself will be reincarnated as the shapeshifting wolf-man Autolycus (likely played by the same actor in the original production), who will introduce himself with a wink at the audience while faking an injury, *"I fear, sir, my shoulder blade is out,"* (WT IV.iii) reminding us of *"how the bear tore out [Antigonus's] shoulder-bone."* (WT III.iii)

The Triumph of Time
THE WINTER'S TALE | SONNETS

The novel on which Shakespeare based *The Winter's Tale* was called *Pandosto: The Triumph of Time.* This is odd because Time definitely does not heal all wounds in it: the queen dies, never to return, the king kills himself, and the ending implies that the princess perishes too.[249] Shakespeare changed the name of the story and all of its characters, he switched the locations, and altered the action and ending. But a bit of the subtitle survives in that Shakespeare stops the story halfway through and brings out a character called "Time" to explain the passage of sixteen years. Or it might be more precise to say that Shakespeare himself (the author and perhaps the actor) appears in the disguise of Time:

> *"TIME. I, that please some, try all, both joy and terror*
> *Of good and bad, that makes and unfolds error,*
> *Now take upon me, in the name of Time,*
> *To use my wings. Impute it not a crime*
> *To me or my swift passage that I slide*
> *O'er sixteen years, and leave the growth untried*
> *Of that wide gap, since it is in my pow'r*
> *To o'erthrow law, and in one self-born hour*
> *To plant and o'erwhelm custom... This allow,*
> *If ever you have spent time worse ere now;*
> *If never, yet that Time himself doth say*
> *He wishes earnestly you never may."* (WT IV.i)

Time here is a senile old fuddy-duddy. He acknowledges breaching the *"custom"* that a comedy play should take place in a single span, and not leap a generation. But then he reminds us that, as the inventor of days and years, he is not bound by theatrical conventions. Then, if I'm reading this correctly, he apologizes for draining our youth during the dull and dreary first three acts of this play.

The character of Time seems to come out of nowhere, but actually Shakespeare has written quite a bit about this character. At least thirteen of Shakespeare's Sonnets refer to personified Time (more could be argued, but these thirteen have Time clearly capitalized as a proper name).[250] While the Sonneteer entreats the beautiful boy and pursues the Dark Lady, Time is not just ticking away the moments that make up the dull day but stalking them with deadly intent. Time in the Sonnets is frequently called a tyrant and a thief. *"Time wastes life,"* we read in *Sonnet 100*, it devours all things *"and make[s] the earth devour her own sweet brood"* (*Sonnet 19*). It is a killer of flowers and ravager of youthful beauty.

Five of the Sonnets mention Time's scythe or sickle-blade, *"And nothing 'gainst Time's scythe can make defence."* (*Sonnet 12*) This is a curved blade on a stick, the one that the Titan Saturn used to castrate his father, more familiar to us from images of Time as the Grim Reaper. And in *The Winter's Tale* monologue, he also has wings, so apparently Time can fly.

In the fifth *Sonnet*, "Time" is not capitalized as a proper name but is clearly personified and described in terms related to *The Winter's Tale*:

> *"Those hours that with gentle work did frame*
> *The lovely gaze where every eye doth dwell*
> *Will play the tyrants to the very same,*
> *And that unfair which fairly doth excel:*
> *For never-resting time leads summer on*
> *To hideous winter and confounds him there,*
> *Sap checked with frost and lusty leaves quite gone,*
> *Beauty o'er-snowed and bareness every where."* (*Sonnet 5*)

The intrusion of Time onstage is generally regarded as a clumsy plot device, and this impression is supported by the clunky rhyming couplets that make his brief cameo so tedious. But the celebrity guest appearance of Father Time is significant in itself when we remember that personified Time was the Greek Titan Kronos, whom the Romans called Saturn. Just as Time devours all things, Saturn devoured his own children. This Titan feared that one of his offspring would overthrow him as king (perhaps he feared this because he overthrew his own father), so each time his wife bore a baby, he swallowed it: Neptune, Pluto, Juno, Ceres, and Vesta. When Rhea bore his last son, Jupiter, she wrapped a stone in swaddling clothes for Saturn to swallow and hid the baby in a cave. When Jupiter grew to adulthood he clobbered his father, forcing him to vomit up the other gods. Saturn parallels the story of Leontes as an insecure tyrant who attempts infanticide. In the Sonnets, Shakespeare calls him the *"bloody tyrant Time"* (*Sonnet 16*) and Leontes is called a tyrant by Paulina and Apollo.[251]

Saturn has further mythic significance in the story because he was a deity of the pre-hierarchical "Golden Age." His Roman festival, the Saturnalia, was celebrated with social inversions: the nobility were expected to treat the peasantry like royalty, and the merrymaking would be overseen by a temporary clown-king, a Lord of Misrule. Similarly, in *The Winter's Tale*, the carnival conman Autolycus briefly takes control of Bohemia while the king and prince go around disguised as commoners.

Easy Come, Easy Go, Any Way the Wind Blows
THE WINTER'S TALE

The personification of Time should also tell playgoers to buckle their seatbelts and keep hands and feet inside the theater, because while we time-travel we're also flying through space, from Sicilia to Bohemia. The first three acts have been a roller coaster, click-click-clicking up the first summit, and after this it'll get pretty fast and wild, with flashing lights, swirling dancers, and dizzying disguises.

A brief scene reintroduces Polixenes, the king of Bohemia, but he's too distracted to rule. His son, Prince Florizel, has been out galivanting with a shepherdess, and the king will go undercover to investigate. While he skulks around disguised as an anonymous old man, Bohemia will become a Neverland ruled by a Peter Pan con man, the shapeshifting trickster Autolycus. He emerges like a circus ringleader.

"When daffodils begin to peer,

With heigh! the doxy over the dale,
Why, then comes in the sweet o' the year,
For the red blood reigns in the winter's pale.
The white sheet bleaching on the hedge,
With heigh! the sweet birds, O, how they sing!
Doth set my pugging tooth on edge,
For a quart of ale is a dish for a king.
The lark, that tirra-lirra chants,
With heigh! with heigh! the thrush and the jay,
Are summer songs for me and my aunts,
While we lie tumbling in the hay." (WT IV.iii)

The carnival barker sings of the sweetness of spring, but it's too sweet, hurting his teeth. He prefers the late summer harvest season, when barley is brewed into beer and he can tumble in the hay.[252] Autolycus springs from the eleventh book of Ovid's *Metamorphoses*. Funny story (actually a horrible story). Apollo and Mercury fell in love with the same maiden, and she bore twin sons: a musician for Apollo, and a thief for Mercury, named Autolycus. He's described in Golding's translation, "And such a fellow as in theft and filching had no peer...he could mens' eyes so blear, as for to make the black things white, and white things black appear." He could shift his shape and create optical illusions around stolen goods.

After singing his song, *The Winter's Tale* trickster tells the audience, "*My father nam'd me Autolycus; who, being, I as am, litter'd under Mercury, was likewise a snapper-up of unconsidered trifles.*" (WT IV.iii)[253] And then we see him in action. Spotting a hapless hillbilly, the con man reports that he was robbed by a rogue named Autolycus, who turned to banditry after being fired by Prince Florizel. While sharing this sad tale, he picks the bumpkin's pocket so he can go buy goods to mark up and sell at the sheep-shearing festival.

Mercury is best known as the messenger god, but he was more importantly the god of in-between spaces: the guardian of travelers, nomadic shepherds, and scavenging thieves. He was worshiped in the wilderness at wayside shrines called Herms, stemming from his Greek name Hermes, from which we also get the word "hermit," a loner in the no-man's-land between kingdoms.[254] He was a trickster and transgressor of boundaries (a child born to Hermes and Aphrodite was named Hermaphrodite, a word still applied to persons on the border of gender). In *The Winter's Tale* his avatar Autolycus is a boundary-crossing shapeshifter, geographically and socially mobile, as Joanne Field Holland notes. "Autolycus is transient. He moves easily from court to country, from Bohemia to Sicilia. He is as much at home as anywhere at any of the social levels of the play."[255] The first three acts and the last act of the play take place in the Apollonian realm of Sicilia, but the fourth act is when the play really comes to life in Bohemia. Nietzsche might call this a Dionysian realm, but Shakespeare hadn't read Nietzsche, so it's a Mercurial realm.

As messenger, Autolycus will later bring the shepherd and clown to Sicilia bearing the evidence of Perdita's parentage. Of course, he does this for his own selfish reasons:

> *"If I had a mind to be honest, I see Fortune would not* [allow] *me: she drops booties in my mouth. I am courted now with a double occasion—gold, and a means to do the Prince my master good; which who knows how that may turn back to my advancement? I will bring these two moles, these blind ones, aboard him."* (WT IV.iv)

The Lost Girl
THE WINTER'S TALE

At last we meet Perdita, "the lost girl," daughter of Hermione and Leontes. We've known her since she was just a pillow strapped to a boy-actor's belly in the first act, then an inanimate object in the second and third acts, perhaps a wooden baby doll brandished by Paulina, abandoned by Antigonus and embraced by a shepherd, but finally we see her in the flesh as a teenager. Well, a twelve-year-old boy playing a sixteen-year-old girl. But all kidding aside, this adaptability is what makes Perdita such a hardy Shakespearean heroine. Perdita is a good shepherdess; a bystander jokingly refers to her as *"the queen of curds and cream"* (the joke's on him—this dairy queen will soon wear the crown). She's a generous hostess at the sheep-shearing festival, plays a goddess in the fertility pageant, travels disguised as a lad, then seamlessly assumes the role of princess. Perdita can fit in anywhere.

And whereas Shakespeare usually marries his great heroines to clods and gigolos like Claudio and Bassanio, Perdita meets her match in Florizel, a fairy tale prince "who does not concern himself with the mere appearance of outward trappings. Through infallible intuition and the highest integrity he pierces externals to discover the emotional truth of Perdita's real quality."[256] This is Shakespeare's great teen romance. Romeo and Juliet were a manic-depressive mess; one minute starry-eyed optimists, the next minute suicidal pessimists, tragically impetuous, and as a couple they couldn't communicate clearly. They would have been doomed even without the family feud. Perdita and Florizel are realistic about themselves and each other, and they work well as a team.

Shakespeare inherits this story from Greene's *Pandosto*, and from the Pastoral tradition in general. He'll alter Greene's story, particularly by mixing in elements of Classical Mythology. But it's worth a quick look at the plot conventions of the Pastoral genre, some of which will be familiar from fairy tales like *Sleeping Beauty*. Pastorals generally involved a princess, abandoned or kidnapped at birth and raised as a shepherdess, who then falls in love with a prince in a shepherd's disguise. Their love is challenged because of her low status, and then in the end, her royalty is revealed and they live happily ever after.

The Pastoral was a major entertainment trend in Shakespeare's time, when subsistence farmers and shepherds were losing lock, stock, and barrel to capitalist land barons and then being forced into crowded urban slums. Pastoral entertainment touched on sentimental memories, with a vague hint that the vices of the city could be cured by the virtues of the countryside. The Pastoral also contained a subtle political statement: that royals raised in palaces could not understand peasant life, and therefore could not govern conscientiously. The riches-to-rags-to-riches Pastoral genre offered the fantasy of people who'd lived among peasants assuming the thrones and ruling with empathy.

The Winter's Tale is an excellent example of the Pastoral as wish-fulfillment: Leontes and Polixenes were once like *"twinn'd lambs that did frisk i' th' sun,"* but then growing up in castles alienated them from Nature and reality. Leontes, like a modern fundamentalist, is so obsessed with persecuting a woman for getting pregnant (supposedly out of wedlock) that he's blinded to an oncoming environmental catastrophe.[257] Polixines can admire a young lady's nurturant abilities, yet he would sooner sever his own posterity than see a commoner rise above her social station. But the kingdoms will ultimately be saved by a shepherdess who turns out to be a full-blooded fairy tale princess.

Wildflowers
THE WINTER'S TALE

Hermione withered in stifling Sicilia, but Perdita blooms in Bohemia. This begins immediately. As a newborn in Sicilia, she was called *"the brat"* and *"the bastard,"* but then, just as Antigonus lays the baby on Bohemian soil, he calls her *"blossom."* In addition to growing up a shepherdess, she'll be an expert botanist, perhaps an inheritance from her mother who enjoyed walking in (and presumably cultivating) the royal gardens. Perdita is conversant in planting, has knowledge of herbal medicines, and has also studied Classical stories involving flowers.

Perdita and Prince Florizel's introductory scene is wrapped in numerous layers of disguise and mythical symbolism. Perdita is a princess as a shepherdess playing a deity, and Florizel is a prince dressed as a shepherd. But what's really remarkable here is that they're honest with each other. Perdita feels silly in her goddess costume, and Florizel is concerned that she'll misread his disguise as a sign of hidden intentions. And Shakespeare the chaperone blusters a bit to let us know that these two haven't been tumbling in the hay.

In the source story, Robert Greene's novel *Pandosto*, the heroine Fawnia appears "with a garland made of bows and flowers, which attire became her so gallantly, as she seemed to be the Goddess Flora herself for beauty."[258] Shakespeare puts this observation into the mind of Prince Florizel, as Perdita prepares to represent the goddess at a fertility pageant:

> *"FLORIZEL. These your unusual weeds to each part of you*
> *Do give a life - no shepherdess, but Flora*
> *Peering in April's front. This your sheep-shearing*
> *Is as a meeting of the petty gods,*
> *And you the Queen on't...*
> *PERDITA. Your high self,*
> *The gracious mark o' th' land, you have obscur'd*
> *With a swain's wearing; and me, poor lowly maid,*
> *Most goddess-like prank'd up. But that our feasts*
> *In every mess have folly, and the feeders*
> *Digest it with a custom, I should blush*

To see you so attir'd; swoon, I think,
To show myself a glass... Even now I tremble
To think your father, by some accident,
Should pass this way, as you did. O, the Fates!
FLORIZEL. ...Nothing but jollity. The gods themselves,
Humbling their deities to love, have taken
The shapes of beasts upon them: Jupiter
Became a bull and bellow'd; the green Neptune
A ram and bleated; and the fire-rob'd god,
Golden Apollo, a poor humble swain,
As I seem now. Their transformations
Were never for a piece of beauty rarer,
Nor in a way so chaste, since my desires
Run not before mine honour, nor my lusts
Burn hotter than my faith...
PERDITA. O Lady Fortune,
Stand you auspicious!" (WT IV.iv)

As a prince visiting the bottom of the social ladder, Florizel recalls gods who took animal forms to pursue maidens.[259] Perhaps the bull, ram, and swain spring to Florizel's mind because he's wooing a shepherdess; these are two herd animals and a shepherd, but in the myths all three have wolfish intent. He must quickly distinguish himself from these dastardly deities, reminding her (and the audience) that his honorable intentions are stronger than his libidinous impulses. He'll prove this a couple of scenes later by publicly proposing and abdicating his succession to the throne.

But Florizel unknowingly stumbles onto something deeper when he compares himself to Apollo. First, as Jonathan Bate points out, "His wooing of Perdita is part of the pattern that will eventually lead to the fulfillment of Apollo's oracle."[260] Second, his identification with Apollo reminds us of Apollo and Mercury siring twins, the poet Philammon and the trickster Autolycus. The poetic pairing of Florizel (flower) and Autolycus (wolf) diffuses any suspicion about the prince by contrasting him with a self-serving con man. We might suspect that someone who wears a disguise and deceives his own father will likewise lie to this shepherdess, but he's up front with her. And Autolycus himself tells the audience that he used to work for Florizel, but that the prince fired him, presumably for trying to lead him into schemes. By having Autolycus *"whipt out of the court,"* Florizel has symbolically banished his own impish id.

Although it is late summer, Florizel describes Perdita as *"Flora peering in April's front,"* like a flower goddess emerging in spring.[261] Shakespeare inherited the Flora comparison from Greene but may also have known her from the fifth book of Ovid's *Fasti.* Flora was a field-nymph pursued by the wind-spirit Zephyr, but her story stands out from Ovid's usual reports of sexual predation in that the spirit then married her and made her the queen of flowers, with a large garden as a dowry. She reports, "I enjoy perpetual spring; most buxom is the year ever...the Graces draw near, and twine garlands and wreaths to bind their heavenly hair. I was the first to scatter new seeds among the countless peoples; till then the earth had been of but one color."[262]

Perdita is a gardener. Leontes had commanded that the baby be abandoned with nothing, but Antigonus, guilted by a visit from Hermione's ghost, left her with some gold which her foster family used to buy a large estate. So, in a sense, Perdita has inherited gardening land from her mother. She and her adopted family are also expert shepherds. As the family with the most prosperous flocks, they get to sponsor the sheep-shearing festival. Perdita sends her brother to purchase dried fruits for pressed raisin cakes while she busies herself making corsages for the shearers.[263] The host family could then gain blessings of continued prosperity by showing generosity to strangers, and they get a great opportunity when two wandering vagabonds show up and, as so often happens in legend, the wandering beggars are a king and his aid in disguise. Perdita rushes to welcome them:

> *"PERDITA. Give me those flow'rs there, Dorcas. Reverend sirs,*
> *For you there's rosemary and rue; these keep*
> *Seeming and savour all the winter long.*
> *Grace and remembrance be to you both!*
> *And welcome to our shearing.*
> *POLIXENES. Shepherdess –*
> *A fair one are you – well you fit our ages*
> *With flow'rs of winter.*
> *PERDITA. Sir, the year growing ancient,*
> *Not yet on summer's death nor on the birth*
> *Of trembling winter, the fairest flow'rs o' th' season*

Are our carnations and streak'd gillyvors,
Which some call nature's bastards. Of that kind
Our rustic garden's barren; and I care not
To get slips of them.
POLIXENES. Wherefore, gentle maiden,
Do you neglect them?
PERDITA. For I have heard it said
There is an art which in their piedness shares
With great creating nature.
POLIXENES. Say there be;
Yet nature is made better by no mean
But nature makes that mean; so over that art
Which you say adds to nature, is an art
That nature makes. You see, sweet maid, we marry
A gentler scion to the wildest stock,
And make conceive a bark of baser kind
By bud of nobler race. This is an art
Which does mend nature – change it rather; but
The art itself is nature...
PERDITA. I'll not put
The dibble in earth to set one slip of them;
No more than were I painted I would wish
This youth should say 'twere well, and only therefore
Desire to breed by me. Here's flow'rs for you:
Hot lavender, mints, savory, marjoram;
The marigold, that goes to bed wi' th' sun,
And with him rises weeping; these are flow'rs
Of middle summer, and I think they are given
To men of middle age. Y'are very welcome." (WT IV.iv)

In this scene, we overhear a conversation between two floral enthusiasts, so as we flail in Shakespearean English, we're also mired in garden nerd-speak.

Let's start with beginner level symbolism. In poetry, mythology, and biology, a flower is never just a flower. Flowers are the primal symbol of sex and sexual development: budding virginity, blooming maturity, then barren withering, followed by death and resurrection. Blossoms are metamorphic shapeshifters and masters of disguise that can seduce pollinators (bees and botanists) to do their dirty work for them while fooling us into thinking we're in charge. Flowers dominate by feigning submission. They look nice, but they're not just decorative; without them there would be no bees, no fruit, and no people. Furthermore, a botanical debate between an old man and a young maiden is far more than just flower talk; the blossom is a universal symbol of human sexual reproduction, particularly the female apparatus, so a man patronizing a maiden about how to tend flowers should have us smirking from the start.

Like Ophelia in *Hamlet*, Perdita hands him rosemary for remembrance and rue for regret, herbal remedies for loss of memory and vision. The disguised king commends her medicinal knowledge but asks if she has something prettier. Perdita responds that the flashier flowers of the season are carnations and gillyflowers, but she considers these unnatural because they require grafting. The girl who was called a bastard by her father refuses to grow *"nature's bastards."*

This launches a debate about Nature and Art ("art" in the sense of artifice or artificiality). Polixenes argues that Nature benefits from human engineering, in this case the grafting of plants, which he explains in terms of an arranged marriage: *"We marry / A gentler scion to the wildest stock"* to produce a *"nobler race."* He goes on to say this *"art"* improves *"nature."* Perdita argues that *"great creating nature"* can do her own matchmaking without intrusive human husbandry. And she spurns artificial beauty with the metaphor of a wooer who falls in love with a maiden's makeup and can't see her natural looks.[264]

Then she silences further mansplaining by shoving more medicinal herbs at the old man: lavender to strengthen bowels and ease flatulence, mint to aid digestion, savory to dull aching joints, marjoram for memory loss, and marigolds for heart palpitations.[265] This list of prescriptions is an herbalist's inside joke, loosely translated: "Well you're an incontinent, senile, old fool." This scene would be the Elizabethan gardener's version of a freestyle rapper-battle (all on the same iambic beat), and this is when she would drop the mic. But for modern audiences, it's just a bunch of botany-babble.

The scene is also comically ironic, because the undercover king sees that his son has been slumming with this garden-variety shepherdess. Polixenes assumes the boy has been sowing wild oats and presses the topic of bastardy to feel her out on the subject of illegitimate offspring (and single motherhood). But then his inner nerd takes over, admitting that flowers are strengthened by grafting with hearty weeds. The eugenicist Edmund would agree: *"Now, gods, stand up for bastards!"* A moment later he'll snap back into king-mode: all is fair in art and nature, but when it comes to culture and social class, he forbids cross pollination.

Flowers in Mythology
THE WINTER'S TALE

Having silenced the old garden gnome with her encyclopedic knowledge of folk pharmacology, Perdita resumes her role as the goddess Flora. Turning to her fellow maidens and sweetest friend Florizel, she delivers a lyrical lecture on flowers in Classical Mythology. She begins with the story of Proserpina, daughter of the grain goddess Ceres, who was abducted by the underworld god Dis while out picking flowers (we may be more familiar with these deities by their Greek names, Persephone, Demeter, and Hades). She'll also refer to flowers associated with Juno and Cytherea/Venus, and maidens who die unmarried before midsummer, when the sun-god Phoebus reaches his zenith.[266]

> *"PERDITA. I would I had some flow'rs o' th' spring that might*
> *Become your time of day - and yours, and yours,*
> *That wear upon your virgin branches yet*
> *Your maidenheads growing. O Proserpina,*
> *From the flowers now that, frighted, thou let'st fall*
> *From Dis's waggon! - daffodils,*
> *That come before the swallow dares, and take*
> *The winds of March with beauty; violets, dim*
> *But sweeter than the lids of Juno's eyes*
> *Or Cytherea's breath; pale primroses,*
> *That die unmarried ere they can behold*
> *Bright Phoebus in his strength - a malady*
> *Most incident to maids; bold oxlips, and*
> *The crown-imperial; lilies of all kinds,*

The flow'r-de-luce being one. O, these I lack
To make you garlands of, and my sweet friend
To strew him o'er and o'er!
FLORIZEL. What, like a corse [corpse]*?*
PERDITA. No; like a bank for love to lie and play on;
Not like a corse; or if - not to be buried,
But quick, and in mine arms. Come, take your flow'rs." (WT IV.iv)

Perdita wishes she were indeed the goddess Flora, who could conjure the flowers of spring in any season, especially those that would express her verdant love for Florizel. Little does she suspect that the florid verse of her speech generates a stage-magic miracle, transforming the summer scene into springtime and invoking a powerful illusion of the flowers she describes. A. D. Nuttall observes, "The poetry dresses her in the flowers she says she lacks."[267]

The Persephone story, which Shakespeare would have known from the fifth book of Ovid's *Metamorphoses,* begins with Venus's attempt to overthrow the underworld by distracting Dis with thoughts of love. She sends her son Cupid to prick the death-god with desire, and points him at a budding maiden goddess whom she fears will spurn romance like Diana and Minerva.[268] Ovid's report of Persephone/Proserpine's abduction is a flurry of floral imagery: she's putting blossoms in her lap, and then loses them in this drive-by kidnapping:

"While in this garden Proserpine was taking her pastime,
In gathering either Violets blue, or Lillies white as lime, [limestone]
And while of Maidenly desire she filled her maund [basket] and lap,
Endeavoring to outgather her companions there, by hap
Dis spied her: loved her: caught her up: and all at once well near,
So hasty, hot, and swift a thing is Love as may appear.
The Lady with a wailing voice afright did often call
Her Mother and her waiting Maids, but Mother most of all.
And as she from the upper part her garment would have rent,
By chance she let her lap slip down, and out her flowers went.
And such a silly simpleness her childish age yet bears,
That ev'n the very loss of them did move her more to tears."
(Book V, Golding translation, updated)

The scene of this crime is Sicily, which may explain why Shakespeare switched the locations in the story: Perdita, like Proserpine, is the lost daughter of a Sicilian queen.[269] Venus's plot to gain a foothold in the underworld backfires. Proserpine's mother, the grain goddess Ceres, goes on strike, blasting the world with blight and barrenness that threaten to starve the human race (and the gods as well, who subsist on sacrifices). Jupiter brokers a deal in which the girl will spend half of each year with her mother on the surface, and the other half in hell with her husband. This story explains the cyclical seasons of winter sterility and spring fertility.[270]

The Proserpine story pops up numerous times during this period of Shakespeare's career. His daughter Susanna bore a baby named Elizabeth in 1608; William Shakespeare became a grandfather in same the year his mother Mary passed away. And he becomes fixated on floral symbols of birth, death, and resurrection.

In the second half of *Pericles, Prince of Tyre,* Marina is kidnapped while picking flowers and imprisoned in a hellish brothel from which she must escape (and at last be reunited with her long-presumed-dead mother). Then Shakespeare wrote *Cymbeline,* in which Imogen, who has been temporarily poisoned, awakens strewn with flowers in a subterranean cave.

Approaching *The Winter's Tale,* he flexes the story further with not one but two Persephones. Hermione descends from the floral garden to the underworld of Leontes's dungeon, briefly emerges, then dies and spends sixteen years in a crypt until she's finally restored and spring returns to Sicilia. Perdita was born in the dungeon underworld, then blossoms as a florist in Bohemia. But just as she reaches maturity, Hades (in the form of Polixenes), threatens to torture her to death, presumably underground: *"I will devise a death as cruel for thee / As thou art tender to't."*[271] She is then smuggled to Sicilia, a land cursed with deathly gloom until its lost princess is found. As in the Classical myth, the reunion of mother and daughter will restore fertility.

Happily Ever After
THE WINTER'S TALE

The Winter's Tale returns to Sicilia, blasted with sixteen years of barren winter. Courtiers murmur fearfully that if the aging Leontes should die without a legitimate heir, the kingdom will plunge into chaos or be devoured in an invasion. Leontes cannot rule Sicilia or himself, the king and kingdom are ruled by Hermione's friend, Paulina. Robert Ornstein wrote, "The erstwhile apostle of common sense seems to have become the high priestess of a cult devoted to the worship of the martyred Hermione—a cult that has a shrine, a sacred statue, and a royal flagellant."[272] True to his vow after the queen's death, Leontes has become a monk performing daily penitence, *"saint-like sorrow"* by his wife and son's grave.

But though Leontes's penance is described in Christian terms, he has actually become a devotee of Diana as manifested in Hermione, the ethereal virgin-mother, and the high priestess is the widow Paulina (whose husband was devoured by a bear). This manipulation might sound a bit sinister, especially since Paulina has numerous times been called a witch and accused of practicing dark arts. However, the play clearly situates her as a priestess of Diana, like the lost mothers in *The Comedy of Errors* and *Pericles, Prince of Tyre*, and the final scene will clearly establish that her actions have been benevolent.

When Perdita and Florizel arrive in Sicilia, Leontes immediately recognizes the prince as a faithful reprint of his *"father's image,"* but does not yet recognize his own daughter.[273] He does, however, seem to intuit that this maiden's arrival might somehow resolve Sicilia's climate catastrophe:

> *"And your fair princess—goddess! ...Welcome hither,*
> *As is the spring to th' earth... The blessed gods*
> *Purge all infection from our air whilst you*
> *Do climate here!"* (WT V.i)

He briefly wavers when a messenger reveals that Polixenes has arrived in hot pursuit of the runaway couple. But then Leontes decides to grant them sanctuary—a big step, since they look just like Polixenes and Hermione. The resolution scene with the big reveal, in which Perdita's parentage comes to light and the two kings decide to bless the marriage, is not shown onstage. We get the news secondhand in bits of chatter. Shakespeare is saving the big fireworks for the finale.

Paulina leads Leontes, Polixenes, Perdita, and Florizel into a chapel filled with statues described only as *"singularities"* (presumably the Greek gods and goddesses popular in the statuary of Shakespeare's age). And when at last they reach the statue of Hermione, Leontes is struck dumb. At Paulina's urging he speaks, noting that this statue looks sixteen years older than the wife he remembers, and Paulina credits this to the sculptor who presents her as she would look today. The king finally admits, *"I am asham'd. Does not the stone rebuke me / For being more stone than it?"* Perdita reveres the statue as a religious icon:

> *"PERDITA. And give me leave,*
> *And do not say 'tis superstition that*
> *I kneel, and then implore her blessing. Lady,*
> *Dear queen, that ended when I but began,*
> *Give me that hand of yours to kiss."* (WT V.iii)

Paulina must prevent both Perdita and Leontes from touching the statue—she claims the paint is not yet dry. But then Paulina says she can bring the statue to life on the condition that she not be burned for witchcraft. The spell will require music and incantation, but most of all Leontes must have faith.[274]

> *"PAULINA. For more amazement. If you can behold it,*
> *I'll make the statue move indeed, descend,*
> *And take you by the hand, but then you'll think–*
> *Which I protest against – I am assisted*
> *By wicked powers... It is requir'd*
> *You do awake your faith. Then all stand still...*
> *Music, awake her: strike. (Music)*
> *'Tis time; descend; be stone no more; approach;*
> *Strike all that look upon with marvel. Come;*
> *I'll fill your grave up. Stir; nay, come away.*
> *Bequeath to death your numbness, for from him*
> *Dear life redeems you. You perceive she stirs.*

(HERMIONE comes down from the pedestal)
Start not; her actions shall be holy as
You hear my spell is lawful. Do not shun her
Until you see her die again; for then
You kill her double." (WT V.iii)

Paulina's warning that Leontes's dumbfounded stillness could *"kill her double"* (cause her to die again) is a reference to the story of Orpheus and Eurydice. In the tenth book of Ovid's *Metamorphoses*, Orpheus descends to rescue his dead wife and meets the underworld king and queen Dis/Hades and Persephone. In this story, the former playful girl Proserpine is called by her Greek name Persephone, signifying death, and she has become a stern queen of the cold underworld. They tell Orpheus that he can lead his wife out of the realm of death, only on the condition that he not look at her. "The King and Queen of Death will yield to great love only if, in return, love will agree to behave like cold indifference."[275] Glancing back with concern, Orpheus fails, consigning his bride to a second, final death.

Shakespeare twists the story in *The Winter's Tale* finale: Leontes can lead his bride from the underworld gallery only if he shows his true love. The reunited king and queen embrace and Leontes agrees that Paulina has not performed any dark sorcery: *"If this be magic, let it be an art / Lawful as eating."* But there's also an unsettling undertone here. In these last lines of the play, Leontes speaks only to Paulina, never to Hermione, and Hermione does not speak to Leontes. These two are going to need some serious couples' counseling. Hermione's only line in the scene is a prayer: *"You gods, look down, / And from your sacred vials pour your graces / Upon my daughter's head!"*

Looking at this resolution, an optimist could say the tomb's half empty, but a pessimist would say the tomb's half full: Mamillius, the son of Leones and Hermione, is dead. But this lost son will be reincarnated as a future child of Perdita and Florizel, grandchild of Hermione, Leontes, and Polixenes. This might sound weird but at the end of the Shakespearean shell-game, Leontes and his wife *and* his boyhood friend will make a baby together.[276]

The happy ending of *The Winter's Tale* is so miraculous that Shakespeare twice acknowledges its implausibility. A bystander reporting the princess's farfetched reappearance warns listeners that *"This news, which is call'd true, is so like an old tale that the verity of it is in strong suspicion."* (WT V.ii) And when the statue of Hermione comes to life, Paulina admits that this phenomenon, *"were it but told you, should be hooted at / Like an old tale."* (WT V.iii) They're referring to "old wives' tales," what we now call fairy tales, stories about princesses and curses told by nannies and grannies. These bedtime stories tend to encode important information about transitional stages of life: sexual awakening, loss, death, and weddings. And yet, because these tales were traditionally told by women and tended to have happy-ever-after endings, they are considered kids' stuff.

The Winter's Tale contains many recognizable conventions of old wives' tales, and its female characters emerge from the classic roster of fairy tale archetypes: the princess bride Perdita, the long-lost virgin-mother Hermione (virginal in the sense that her chastity is restored by her exoneration and by sixteen years in an enchanted tomb), and the widow Paulina, who lives right on the border of witchery. To this list we could add the wicked stepmother/whore who exists in Leontes's mind. It's his Quixotic indignation at this delusional construct that summons the ice age. Finally, at the end, he matures to acknowledge that women can be both virtuous and sexual: he reunites with his wife Hermione and blesses the weddings of the virginal Perdita and the widow Paulina.

Leontes doesn't arrive at this realization on his own, however. The loss of his family caused a total breakdown and a reversion to childish helplessness. Paulina stepped in as foster mother and raised him for sixteen years, while apparently keeping Hermione alive. Then, at last, the arrival of the lost daughter sparks the big reveal. Or, in a poetic sense, the trinity of the maiden, wife, and widow had to be complete in order to reach its full, godlike power. By redeeming this one lost soul, the trinity saves the world.

Juno, Ceres, & Iris

Pageantry

THE TEMPEST

In *The Shakespearean Wild*, Jeanne Addison Roberts thoughtfully examines William Shakespeare's career-long exploration of the frontiers of forest and femaleness: the untamed wilderness and the woman who must be "husbanded," domesticated, and planted with seed.[277] In Shakespeare's early writings, Adonis shrivels in horror as Venus personifies the wild forest, Tamora in *Titus Andronicus* transforms the tranquil park into a man-eating, maiden-mangling thicket, the four wooers in *Love's Labour's Lost* stalk brazen bachelorettes in a private gaming reserve and are then emasculated and banished.

Shakespeare's forest and females become more benevolent in *A Midsummer Night's Dream* and *As You Like It*, in which maidens get to choose their mates and the wilderness heals the ills of the city. "The early plays deal with the mating of young lovers—the male foray into the mysterious female forest—the later plays focus on the problems generated by having incorporated Wild creatures uneasily into Culture. Once the male is enmeshed with the precariously 'domesticated' Wild, emphasis shifts toward fears of unbridled lust, infidelity, [and] entrapment."[278] The male fear of female "nature" (a projection of anarchic appetite) is snickered away in *The Merry Wives of Windsor* and *Much Ado About Nothing*, but then takes the reins in *Hamlet*, *Othello*, and *King Lear*, arguably Shakespeare's most misogynistic plays in which no woman can be left alive.[279] He seemed to be making some progress when he created his portrait of Cleopatra—female, foreign, fierce, and fertile. Then the death of Shakespeare's mother, Mary, launched him into a series of resurrection plays: *Pericles, Prince of Tyre, Cymbeline,* and *The Winter's Tale,* in which the wives survive but they're emotionally and psychologically scarred.

"The Wild landscape of the later plays is not the fertile forest but the sterile heath, the isolated island, the foreign outpost, the treacherous sea, or the rocky 'desert' place."[280] If we're on a quest for woman and wilderness in Shakespeare, our voyage really seems to run aground and strand us on a desert island in *The Tempest.* The nature-goddess had apparently been usurped by the witch-goddess a while ago, and now both are long dead. The fairies, including Ariel (arguably female, since male pronouns only appear in questionable stage directions), have become the secret police in Prospero's totalitarian dystopia. He has micromanaged his daughter Miranda the way he administrates everything else, raising her as a sort of rare bird in his zoo, which is nothing like a natural habitat. The forecast only gets darker when the shipwrecked nobles arrive, and we gradually learn that Miranda is only an ornate purse to contain Prospero's most precious natural resource: her maidenhead, which he intends to bargain with for a ticket off the island. It's tempting to say, "Abandon hope, ye who enter *the Tempest* in search of wild womanhood."

When the tourists wash ashore, Prospero gives a quick nod to *"Bountiful Fortune, / Now my dear lady"* who brought his enemies within range of his magic. He separates out prince Ferdinand and convinces him that his royal father is dead, so the king can't hamper the matchmaking. But having preemptively removed this obstacle, Prospero has made the maze too easy. Ferdinand and Miranda fall in love faster than expected and, having brought them together, he must struggle to keep these two teens from sneaking off. This is further complicated because he's multitasking, managing the whole island as a ghoulish amusement park, arranging haunted rides for numerous tourist parties while trying to block off the tunnel of love.

A story keeps popping into Prospero's head, a tragic romance from the fourth book of Virgil's *Aeneid.* Venus's son Aeneas, refugee from the fallen Troy, sought a place to fulfill his destiny and start a mighty nation. Juno used a tempest to blow the refugees off course from Italy and they landed in Northern Africa, where Juno enlisted Venus to set up Aeneas with Queen Dido. But the Carthaginian queen was too hasty in her affections, seduced him in a cave, then committed suicide when he abandoned her. Prospero notes that Ferdinand, like Aeneas, has been shipwrecked sailing from Carthage to Naples, and fears that Miranda will repeat Dido's tragic mistake.[281]

Prospero must keep Ferdinand busy and exhausted. Having earlier neutralized Caliban's libido by making him haul logs, Prospero assigns the job to the young prince. At last, Prospero blesses the engagement but warns the young pair that if they start coupling before their marriage has been officially notarized in Naples, they'll be forever cursed:

"PROSPERO. If thou dost break her virgin-knot before
All sanctimonious ceremonies may
With full and holy rite be minist'red,
No sweet aspersion shall the heavens let fall
To make this contract grow; but barren hate,
Sour-ey'd disdain, and discord, shall bestrew
The union of your bed with weeds so loathly
That you shall hate it both. Therefore take heed,
As Hymen's lamps shall light you." (TEM IV.i)

A wedding bed was traditionally strewn with flowers by a mother, but Prospero threatens that premarital sex will summon a trinity of demonic goddesses, personified hate, disdain, and discord, to pollute the mattress with allergenic weeds. Then he conjures another trinity of goddesses (perhaps casting fairies to act) for a phantom pageant celebrating the joys of premarital prudence.[282] Like the romance of Dido and Aeneas, this masque will feature Juno, the queen of Olympus, with her messenger Iris and the grain goddess Ceres. But significantly, this fertility pageant will omit the erotic goddess Venus, whose double cross sealed Dido's tragic fate. Prospero's ideal courtship is tepid and temperate, he doesn't want it tainted by any tropical temptation. The bridal shower he arranges is decidedly *un*-tempestuous.

She's a Rainbow
THE TEMPEST

Prospero's pageant begins with Iris, the divine messenger who rides on rainbows. The rainbow is significant here as a symbol of calm after a tempest. The gloomy darkness of rainfall gives way to sunshine and the full spectrum of color. The glowing bow, a weapon pointed away from the earth, is also a mythical sign of peace between the celestial deities and the inhabitants of the land. In the Biblical story of Noah, the first rainbow signals an armistice halting the apocalyptic destruction of the flood.

In Classical mythology, Iris is the messenger of Juno (queen of the gods, whom the Greeks called Hera, primary bride of Zeus/Jupiter). Iris was well known from contemporary court masques and her role in the doomed romance of Dido and Aeneas. Shakespeare would also have known Iris from the story of Romulus and Hersilia in the fourteenth book of Ovid's *Metamorphoses*. When Romulus, the legendary founder of Rome, was deified, his wife Hersilia mourned that they would someday be parted by her own mortality. "Hersilia for her fear as lost, of mourning made no end, until Queen Juno did command dame Iris to descend upon the Rainbow down,"[283] and grant immortality to Hersilia. The elevation of Hersilia to equality with her husband may relate to Miranda, daughter of a banished duke, ascending to the throne of Naples.

Iris summons the grain goddess Ceres (it's from this name we get the word "cereal"). Ceres is the Roman name of the Greek Demeter, overseer of crop growth and teacher of agriculture. As we read in the *Metamorphoses*:

> "Dame Ceres first to break the Earth with plough the manner found,
> She first made corn and stover soft to grow upon the ground,
> She first made laws: for all these things we are to Ceres bound."
> (Book V, Golding translation, updated, "corn" meaning grain and "stover" being secondary grains to feed cattle in winter)

In the *Tempest* masque, the powers of Ceres are greatly expanded. Not only does she produce diverse grains, but also grasses to feed livestock and grapes for wine. Shakespeare's Ceres has incorporated the roles of the wine-god Bacchus/Dionysus, the flower-goddess Flora, and the earth-goddess Rhea/Gaia, becoming a full fertility goddess.

As a rainbow, Iris can connect the celestial Juno with the terrestrial Ceres.

"*IRIS. Ceres, most bounteous lady, thy rich leas*
Of wheat, rye, barley, vetches, oats, and pease;
Thy turfy mountains, where live nibbling sheep,
And flat meads thatch'd with stover, them to keep;
Thy banks with pionèd and twillèd brims,
Which spongy April at thy hest betrims,
To make cold nymphs chaste crowns...[284] *Thy pole-clipt vineyard;*
And thy sea-marge, sterile and rocky hard,
Where thou thyself dost air – the Queen o' th' sky,
Whose wat'ry arch and messenger am I,
Bids thee leave these; and with her sovereign grace,
Here on this grass-plot, in this very place,
To come and sport. Her peacocks fly amain.
(JUNO descends in her car [chariot]*)*
Approach, rich Ceres, her to entertain.
CERES. Hail, many-coloured messenger, that ne'er
Dost disobey the wife of Jupiter;
Who, with thy saffron wings, upon my flow'rs
Diffusest honey drops, refreshing show'rs;
And with each end of thy blue bow dost crown
My bosky acres and my unshrubb'd down,
Rich scarf to my proud earth – why hath thy Queen
Summon'd me hither to this short-grass'd green?
IRIS. A contract of true love to celebrate,
And some donation freely to estate
On the blest lovers." (TEM IV.i)

Ceres asks why she has been summoned, then immediately wants to know if Venus will be present. These two have history. In Venus's attempt to overthrow the underworld, she sent her son Cupid to make Dis (the Greek Hades or Roman Pluto) fall in love. He abducted Ceres's daughter, and the enraged mother blighted the earth and then managed to negotiate her return for half of each year. Ceres threatens to boycott the ritual if queen Juno invites Venus or Cupid. Despite all their lofty grandeur, these goddesses are not above some Golden Girls-style backbiting.

> "CERES. *Tell me, heavenly bow,*
> *If Venus or her son, as thou dost know,*
> *Do now attend the Queen? Since they did plot*
> *The means that dusky Dis my daughter got,*
> *Her and her blind boy's scandal'd company*
> *I have forsworn.*
> *IRIS. Of her society*
> *Be not afraid. I met her Deity*
> *Cutting the clouds towards Paphos, and her son*
> *Dove-drawn with her. Here thought they to have done*
> *Some wanton charm upon this man and maid,*
> *Whose vows are that no bed-rite shall be paid*
> *Till Hymen's torch be lighted; but in vain.*
> *Mars's hot minion is return'd again;*
> *Her waspish-headed son has broke his arrows,*
> *Swears he will shoot no more, but play with sparrows,*
> *And be a boy right out. (JUNO alights)"* (TEM IV.i)

Iris assures Ceres that Venus has not been seen since departing for Paphos. Here we may recall the final couplet of Shakespeare's *Venus and Adonis*, where the heartbroken love goddess alights in her chariot drawn by doves: *"Holding their course to Paphos, where their queen / Means to immure herself and not be seen."* (V&A ln. 1193-1194) Now Shakespeare adds that Cupid followed her into self-exile. Apparently, they considered showing up to work some mischief (stinging Ferdinand and Miranda with premarital lust) but decided against it.

In modern times, Cupid is often depicted as a baby, symbolizing the byproduct of eroticism. But in Classical mythology he was a preteen sociopath and *"waspish"* prankster, his bow a weapon from his father the war-god Mars, and his arrows tipped with eros from his mother Venus. Armed Cupid didn't represent pure puppy-love, but "love" as predation and venomous temptation.

Shakespeare's characters often lament that Cupid is "blind," meaning physical attraction is irrational. William Shakespeare has never had nice things to say about Cupid, whom he calls a *"wicked bastard of Venus that was begot of thought, conceived of spleen, and born of madness, that blind rascally boy that abuses everyone's eyes because his own are out."* (AYL IV.i) And here, at the end of his writing career, he disarms the little hornet and strips him of his divine power. Cupid has broken his arrows and become an ordinary boy.

Cupid's opposite in Shakespeare's plays is Hymen, the god of wait-till-marriage.[285] Hymen physically showed up at the end of *As You Like It* to bless the quadruple wedding, and they sang:

> *"Wedding is great Juno's crown;*
> *O blessèd bond of board and bed!*
> *Tis Hymen peoples every town;*
> *High wedlock then be honourèd.*
> *Honour, high honour, and renown,*
> *To Hymen, god of every town!"* (AYL V.iv)

Prospero's references to Hymen's lamps signify a torch-lit procession toward the bridal bed. In the *Aeneid*, Juno herself deigns to oversee this wedding march, enlisting Venus's aid:

> "I will myself the bridal bed prepare,
> If you, to bless the nuptials, will be there:
> So shall their loves be crown'd with due delights,
> And Hymen shall be present at the rites."
> (Aeneid IV, Dryden trans. 1697)

When Dido and Aeneas go hunting, Juno sends a rainstorm so they'll seek shelter together in a cave. What happened next we may recall from Tamora's description in *Titus Andronicus:*

> *"The wand'ring prince and Dido once enjoyed,*
> *When with a happy storm they were surpris'd,*
> *And curtain'd with a counsel-keeping cave*
> *...each wreathèd in the other's arms."* (TA II.iii)[286]

But Juno's plan backfired when Dido (perhaps urged by Venus and .) impetuously mistook this for a wedding and went all the way with Aeneas. Any torches that may have been lit were doused in the storm, and Hymen arrived too late to validate the marriage rites. Prospero is determined that Classical history not be repeated.

The Queen of Olympus
The Tempest

Juno is named several times in Shakespeare's writings, primarily as the matron of matrimony. Ironic, since her own marriage to the adulterous Jupiter was always such a mess, and she was most famous in Classical mythology for her many attempts to kill his illegitimate children. Juno was named several times in *Coriolanus*, often in conjunction with the overbearing mother, Volumnia. And in *All's Well That Ends Well*, when Helena blames herself for alienating her husband, she writes, *"I, his despiteful Juno, sent him forth."* (AWTEW III.iv) There's a comical moment in *King Lear* when the king finds that Regan has put his servant in stocks. Lear can't believe that his daughter would disrespect him in this way. *"LEAR. By Jupiter, I swear no. / KENT. By Juno, I swear ay."* (KL II.iv) Kent wryly observes that patriarchalism has been overturned.

Ceres was concerned that Juno might have invited Venus to the celebrity gala, but she needn't have worried; Juno won't get out of her car until she knows Venus won't be on the red carpet. These two also have some history, going back to when Venus rigged a beauty pageant. Juno,

Venus, and Minerva got into an argument about who was the most beautiful and asked Jupiter to judge. In an uncharacteristic moment of wisdom, he declined to comment, so they brought in the Trojan Prince Paris. Then Venus bribed the judge (actually all three contestants offered bribes, but Venus promised him the most beautiful woman in the world, thus he kidnapped Helen and the Trojan War broke out). Then the love goddess double-crossed Juno in *The Aeneid*. Juno still wants nothing to do with Venus and her brat Cupid.

> "CERES. *Highest Queen of State,*
> *Great Juno, comes; I know her by her gait.*
> JUNO. *How does my bounteous sister? Go with me*
> *To bless this twain, that they may prosperous be,*
> *And honour'd in their issue.*
> *(Sings) Honour, riches, marriage-blessing,*
> *Long continuance, and increasing,*
> *Hourly joys be still upon you!*
> *Juno sings her blessings on you.*
> CERES. *Earth's increase, foison plenty,*
> *Barns and garners never empty;*
> *Vines with clust'ring bunches growing,*
> *Plants with goodly burden bowing;*
> *Spring come to you at the farthest,*
> *In the very end of harvest!*
> *Scarcity and want shall shun you,*
> *Ceres' blessing so is on you.*" (TEM IV.i)

For all the fanfare about Juno's arrival, the queen of Olympus only gives a brief blessing and a snippet of song. It's a quick bridal shower checklist of fertility, longevity, and wealth.

Ceres's song about springtime following the late summer harvest season caps off a recurring theme in Shakespeare's writing, that winter will be abolished. In Classical mythology, winter did not exist before the underworld god kidnapped the grain goddess's daughter, and medieval Christians considered winter to be a punishment upon the world for lust in Eden (in both scenarios, winter stems from a crime of passion).

So, Ceres's song about the abolition of winter represents a hope that an ancient crime can be undone. In the context of this engagement ceremony, Ceres is promising year-round natural bounty on the condition that Miranda and Ferdinand restrain their eroticism until the wedding has been officially sealed.

The masque concludes with a circle dance of springtime river-fairies and late summer grain farmers: a merger of female and male, water and wheat fields, nature and culture.

> "IRIS. You nymphs, call'd Naiads, of the wind'ring brooks,
> With your sedg'd crowns and ever harmless looks,
> Leave your crisp channels, and on this green land
> Answer your summons; Juno does command.
> Come, temperate nymphs, and help to celebrate
> A contract of true love; be not too late.
> (Enter certain NYMPHS)
> You sun-burnt sicklemen, of August weary,
> Come hither from the furrow, and be merry;
> Make holiday; your rye-straw hats put on,
> And these fresh nymphs encounter every one
> In country footing.
> (Enter certain REAPERS, properly habited; they join with the
> NYMPHS in a graceful dance.[287]) (TEM IV.i)

ꝙrospero's ꝙresent ꝼancies
THE TEMPEST

In a study of Shakespearean representations of the divine feminine, this pageant presents us with some obvious problems. Prospero himself says that these are *"Spirits, which by mine art / I have from their confines call'd to enact / My present fancies."* This is clearly not a *Deus ex Machina* appearance of the goddesses themselves on the stage. They are projections of the male mind—Prospero's and Shakespeare's—and their function in the plot is to safeguard legitimacy and patriarchy.

But there is some flexibility here in whether we consider them puppets strictly controlled by Prospero. He has enlisted fairies for this show, possibly including Ariel as Iris, and we've seen that Ariel is allowed to improvise within the broad strokes of Prospero's direction. Prospero himself, watching this show, gets so distracted that he momentarily forgets his whole revenge plot (lust has been banished from this pageant, but it's alive and well on the island, fueling a plan to overthrow the dictator). So, yes, these goddesses are projections of Prospero's *"present fancies,"* but the spirits may have some autonomy. If that's too ambiguous an ending for a study of Shakespeare's goddess, we should recall that the revels don't really end here. Venus and Diana will unite behind the scenes in *The Two Noble Kinsmen* a couple of years later.

Prospero abruptly ends the goddess pageant because he must run off and attend to his vindictive business. Miranda and Ferdinand are put to the test; they go off to hide unsupervised in a cave. With the chaperone away, will these two repeat the mistake of Dido and Aeneas? Returning to the cavern an hour or two later, we find them playing an innocent game of chess. Well, not *so* innocent–this game of wearing down a player's defenses and exposing their figurehead was a form of foreplay. Also, Miranda suspects that Ferdinand has cheated: *"Sweet lord, you play me false."* Perhaps a sign that he knows that she's smarter than he is, or at least a sign that she can keep a vigilant eye on him. Either way, the chess match gives us a sense that the future king and queen will both have ideas on how to rule. And the board game lets Prospero know that he's been successful in his pedantic nagging.

Personally, I think we want too much from Prospero. We hear he's got arcane knowledge, maybe we expect some great wisdom, but he doesn't tell us anything about ourselves and how to be human. There are no great quotations from Prospero. His years as a hermit have not led to enlightenment.[288] Ultimately, he's a crusty old misogynist obsessed with getting back at people who have slighted him and he wants his old job back (not that he cares about being Duke of Milan, he just doesn't want his *brother* to be duke). He's willing to pimp his daughter and fantasizes that Nature can be totally tamed and dominated. Prospero is a petty dictator, but there's another wise old man on the island; Gonzalo saved Prospero and Miranda's lives long ago, and even let the wizard sail with his beloved books.

While Prospero's enemies see the island as a barren, blasted wasteland, Gonzalo sees a primeval paradise. He fantasizes about a utopia where the evils of civilization have been abolished: no more unjust laws and loopholes and police, no more esoteric books, no more inherited wealth and hereditary poverty. Nature, instead of being ravaged and robbed, will freely feed humanity with nuts and berries. Men and women will be equal:

> "I' th' commonwealth I would by contraries
> Execute all things; for no kind of traffic
> Would I admit; no name of magistrate;
> Letters should not be known; riches, poverty,
> And use of service, none; contract, succession,
> Bourn, bound of land, tilth, vineyard, none;
> No use of metal, corn, or wine, or oil;
> No occupation; all men idle, all;
> And women too, but innocent and pure;
> No sovereignty...
> All things in common nature should produce
> Without sweat or endeavour. Treason, felony,
> Sword, pike, knife, gun, or need of any engine,
> Would I not have; but nature should bring forth,
> Of its own kind, all foison, all abundance,
> To feed my innocent people." (TEM II.i, "foison" meaning bounty)

Conclusion

Don't Try This at Home

"Love, first learnèd in a lady's eyes,
Lives not alone immurèd in the brain,
But with the motion of all elements...
And when Love speaks, the voice of all the gods
Make heaven drowsy with the harmony.
Never durst poet touch a pen to write
Until his ink were temp'red with Love's sighs;
O, then his lines would ravish savage ears,
And plant in tyrants mild humility.
From women's eyes this doctrine I derive.
They sparkle still the right Promethean fire;
They are the books, the arts, the academes,
That show, contain, and nourish, all the world." (LLL IV.iii)

In *Love's Labour's Lost,* four maidens at a slumber party giggle over clumsy sonnets and gifts from their foppish suitors.

"ROSALINE. Witness this.
Nay, I have verses too, I thank Berowne;
The numbers true, and, were the numb'ring too,
I were the fairest goddess on the ground.

I am compar'd to twenty thousand fairs.
O, he hath drawn my picture in his letter!
PRINCESS OF FRANCE. Anything like?
ROSALINE. Much in the letters; nothing in the praise." (LLL V.ii)

And they laugh their heads off.[289] William Shakespeare may be considered the greatest love poet of all time, but the female characters in his plays are totally unimpressed by Shakespearean poetry. And they hate being called goddesses. It's the great irony of writing a book called *Shakespeare's Goddess* that most of the quotes referring to the divine feminine are spoken by male characters. The heroines evade these epithets and dodge deification: they don't want to be idols or ideals or deities. They don't want an apostle, they want a partner.

Berowne must have felt blessed by the muses as he wrote, *"Celestial as thou art, O, pardon love this wrong, / That singes heaven's praise with such an earthly tongue."* (LLL IV.ii) But Rosaline would have preferred something earthier, and she rejects his proposal in the end. She tells him to spend a year cheering people in hospice. He needs to get his head out of the clouds.[290]

In *As You Like It*, Rosalind (in male disguise) runs into her hopeless wooer in the woods and says, *"There is a man haunts the forest that abuses our young plants with carving 'Rosalind' on their barks; hangs odes upon hawthorns and elegies on brambles; all, forsooth, deifying the name of Rosalind. If I could meet that fancy-monger, I would give him some good counsel."* (AYL III.ii) This costumed heroine must painstakingly rehabilitate the hopeless romantic; Rosalind does not want to be deified.

Romeo, we may recall, had the same problem with a young lady named Rosaline: *"She'll not be hit / With Cupid's arrow, she hath Dian's wit."* (R&J I.i) Romeo laments that she is as chaste as Diana, but chances are she's just not into a guy who compares her to a goddess. We never see Romeo's failed approach to Rosaline, but we get a sense of his strategy. As soon as he meets Juliet, he starts sputtering drivel about how she's a sacred monument:

> *"ROMEO. If I profane with my unworthiest hand*
> *This holy shrine, the gentle sin is this,*
> *My lips, two blushing pilgrims, ready stand*
> *To smooth that rough touch with a tender kiss.*

JULIET. Good pilgrim, you do wrong your hand too much,
Which mannerly devotion shows in this;
For saints have hands that pilgrims' hands do touch,
And palm to palm is holy palmers' kiss." (R&J I.v)

This poetry is very pretty, but when we translate it into modern English, he's doing the old "heaven must be missing an angel" pickup line and she's saying, "shut up with the corny adoration, I'm as human as you." Their love is already going to be hampered by a family feud; it doesn't need a human-divine division too.[291]

A similar scene plays out in *The Tempest*, when Ferdinand first sees Miranda. In this case, she wonders if he might be divine because he looks so unlike the crusty Prospero and the fish-monster Caliban, and he wonders if she is the musical goddess of the island:

"MIRANDA. I might call him
A thing divine; for nothing natural
I ever saw so noble....
FERDINAND. Most sure, the goddess
On whom these airs attend! ...My prime request,
Which I do last pronounce, is, O you wonder!
If you be maid or no?
MIRANDA. No wonder, sir;
But certainly a maid." (TEM I.ii)[292]

There are many more examples: Portia in *The Merchant of Venice* clearly objects to being objectified as the Golden Fleece; Diana in *All's Well That Ends Well* evades Bertram's comparison with her virgin-goddess namesake293; Perdita in *The Winter's Tale* feels silly *"prank'd up"* like Flora.[294]

When Antipholus of Syracuse meets the maiden Luciana in *The Comedy of Errors*, he asks, *"Are you a god? Would you create me new? / Transform me, then, and to your pow'r I'll yield."* (COE III.ii) We can kick this around as a corny pickup line, the worn-out cliché of the woman transfigured in a wooer's gaze, but we should take at least a moment to look at this from the suitor's perspective and see how it functions in the alchemical clockwork of the Shakespearean universe. Antipholus expects to be reborn in two ways: first, his world-weary embitterment can be scraped away, reverting him to the purity of an infant in the arms of a divine mother. Second, Shakespeare believed that a man could be reincarnated by siring a son in ritualistic intercourse ("ritualistic" in the sense that it had been preceded by the magical incantations of a wedding). In scientific terms, Shakespeare believed that a man could clone himself in a female crock-pot, but in order for this to work properly, the incubation machine had to be brand new. Well, none of that sounds particularly romantic, but that's the method to this madness.

On the topic of heroines alienated by adoration, Robert Ornstein observes, "For Orsino as for other votaries of passion in the comedies, love is a masculine sport and dedication. Women may be enshrined and adored by such romanticists, but they exist as objects of male desire, prompters of male pain, and projections of male fantasy. They are the justification for a hero's self-indulgent absorption in his own emotions."[295] Often, a Shakespearean hero will anxiously praise the heroine's looks and wit to make her a goddess, and simultaneously exaggerate her dependence on him to make her a pet. But he'll have trouble seeing her as a fellow human with strengths and needs—and seeing her as a sexual woman makes him feel threatened and inadequate. The comedies generally end with *"Jack shall have Jill,"* but this usually requires that Jack first tumble down the hill and spill his pail of romantic ideals about being Jill's savior and worshiper.

Shakespeare was arguably aware of this pattern in his work. He makes a joke about it in *A Midsummer Night's Dream*, when Helena, who idolizes Demetrius, abruptly finds her love requited:

> *"DEMETRIUS. (Awaking) O Helen, goddess, nymph, perfect, divine!*
> *To what, my love, shall I compare thine eyne?...*
> *HELENA. O spite! O hell! I see you all are bent*
> *To set against me for your merriment...*
> *If you were men, as men you are in show,*
> *You would not use a gentle lady so:*
> *To vow, and swear, and superpraise my parts,*
> *When I am sure you hate me with your hearts." (MND III.ii)*

Shakespeare also plays with the theme of heroines dodging deification in his transvestite comedies. Orsino in *Twelfth Night* compares Olivia to Diana and longs for *"her sweet perfections"* from a distance, but she takes no interest. Then the dismissive tone of his messenger (Viola in male disguise) gets Olivia's attention and, in the end, she marries Viola's twin brother Sebastian, whom she's barely met. This ending seems a bit far-fetched at first, but it does make sense. Orsino envisioned her as a goddess; Viola and Sebastian see her as a woman. Then Orsino marries Viola, whom he never objectified or deified. Thinking she was his wingman, he communicated candidly with her. In *As You Like It*, the shepherdess Phebe resists being worshiped by her suitor, Silvius. But when the saucy lackey Ganeymede (Rosalind in male disguise) tells her to take what she can get, Phebe is aroused by the youth's realism. A woman falling for a woman in male disguise is a good comedic device, but also carries the deeper subtext of female characters wanting to be treated like human beings.

Shakespeare's heroines duck and dodge comparison with Diana, and none of them want to be associated with the promiscuous Venus (even Venus herself, in *Venus and Adonis*, doesn't want to be treated like a goddess by the guy she's trying to seduce). In *Much Ado About Nothing*, Claudio throws a tearful temper tantrum when he suspects that Hero might not be the divine virgin he expected:

> *"You seem to me as Dian in her orb,*
> *As chaste as is the bud ere it be blown;*
> *But you are more intemperate in your blood*
> *Than Venus, or those pamper'd animals*
> *That rage in savage sensuality." (MAAN IV.i)*

This is overheard by the confirmed bachelor Benedick, who is wrangling with his own fear of marriage. He finds Beatrice demonic, and yet she's the only woman who excites him. Ironically, of all of Shakespeare's wooers, Benedick turns out to be the most realistic about what he would want in a life partner: *"Rich she shall be, that's certain; wise, or I'll none; virtuous, or I'll never cheapen her; fair, or I'll never look on her; mild, or come not near me; noble, or not I for an angel; of good discourse, an excellent musician, and her hair shall be of what colour it please God. Ha!"* (MAAN II.iii) He wants someone who will take care of him and be faithful, someone pretty (he's not particular about looks), but the quality he mentions twice is *"wise* [and] *of good discourse,"* intelligent and articulate. Being a chatty guy, he wants to marry someone he can hang out and talk with.

Shakespeare's wooers are full of bubbly love poetry about goddesses, and his intelligent heroines are generally unimpressed. They don't want to be monuments on pedestals, or *"beauty too rich for use, for earth too dear."* (R&J I.v) Objectification and deification are both dehumanizing, and both feed a divisive us-and-them mentality that can make romantic partnership difficult. In Chapter One I mentioned the song from *Kiss Me Kate,* "Brush Up Your Shakespeare," about clumsily using Shakespearean poetry as an aphrodisiac. I repeat my caution: quoting Orlando or Romeo won't necessarily melt a maiden's heart, and these bachelors' puffed-up poetry didn't do them much good either. If you want to impress someone with your knowledge of Shakespeare, instead of throwing sonnets at her, take her out to see one of these plays, and then ask her what she thinks about it.

A Book Called *Shakespeare's Goddess*

Should this book have been called *Shakespeare's Goddesses?* Maybe. I don't care for that title; it gives me the impression that William Shakespeare possessed a stable of female deities that he could collect and race and trade. To my ear, *Shakespeare's Goddess offers* a balance between the two topics of this book, and lets the reader decide which one's in charge.

Did Shakespeare believe in goddesses? We don't know. But it's clear he thought about them a lot. And it's clear that the original audiences of these works, from the gentry to the groundlings, didn't find it heretical or unbelievable for these characters to worship goddesses. There's a comical irony that, while the Protestant Reformation banished the goddess Mary (the Catholic Virgin as a stand-in for indigenous fertility goddesses) from Christian Ritual, English royalty banished the Father, Son, and Holy Ghost from the stage.[296] Theater companies could be fined for naming the Christian gods, and sometimes got around this by using Classical names like "Jove" which meant Jupiter, not Jehovah. The main "God" in Shakespeare's plays is arguably the top God of the Christian trinity, and yet in these scripts He's married (and a sexual being, both inside and outside of wedlock). More significant, the Shakespearean canon shows a remarkable balance between gendered deities.

If some alien anthropologist found a copy of *the Collected Works of William Shakespeare* and assumed it was our sacred text, what conclusions would be drawn about our theology? The whole Christian story and system would be represented by fragments scattered on the fringes; a diligent researcher might conclude that there was some minor idiosyncratic sect somewhere. They would have to assume that most people believed in Classical deities, primarily Diana and Venus, who would seem to be in some sort of eternal struggle for power. But they are really two sides of one power: the world must be peopled, but peopling must be governed by some self-discipline or "people" are just talkative beasts. In this theology, male gods would be ambiguous, secondary figures. Jupiter is at one moment the distinguished judge, at the next a sex-crazed maniac. He's Mercurial, almost Dionysian. Only the goddess remains constant.

In Shakespeare's writings we encounter many manifestations of the divine feminine, which goes by many names: Venus, Diana, Juno, Ceres, Fortune, Hecate, Flora, Revenge, Iris, Proserpine, and others. The one name we never see is Gaia, the self-created grandmother of the Classical pantheon. And yet this primal earth-goddess is a major player on the Shakespearean stage as personified Nature. Or perhaps it would be more accurate to say she *is* the Shakespearean stage, and the Globe, and the world.

Nature is the most powerful goddess in Shakespeare's cosmology, the matrix of relation between the human and the many manifestations of the divine. In biology, the "Gaia hypothesis" is a term for the interrelation of all natural phenomena, a web of life that binds all living things in ways that are still mysterious to humanity ("mysterious" in the sense that, unlike the gods and saviors of Western religions, Nature does not favor humanity over toadstools and gnats and bacteria).

As eco-critics are finding, William Shakespeare is often remarkably modern in his ideas about nature's ways. His personification of maternal Nature, encompassing a spectrum of good, bad, ugly, and beautiful, deserves attention as perhaps his most nuanced character study. As we begin to discover Shakespeare's generative and tempestuous, multifaceted characterization of Nature, it becomes clearer that the named goddesses in his works are all avatars of this mysterious divine feminine presence.

Notes

Preface and Prologue

1   Kakkonen (2015) p. 19

2   If you realize that what you were really looking for was a concordance of classical deities in Shakespeare, Virginia Mason Vaughan's *Shakespeare and the Gods* is a very useful guidebook, and Robert Root's *Classical Mythology in Shakespeare* is the classic.

3   The British henges seem to have originally been built of wood and used for parties (archaeologists find broken pottery and bones from the time of the wooden structures) but when the wooden posts were replaced with stone pillars, we don't find party garbage anymore. One theory is that the stone henges were abandoned by the living to be used by the spirits of the dead.

4   Hutton (2014) p. 235-247

5   Hughes (1992) p. 9

6   As a seminary graduate, it bothers me to continue this slander against Mary of Magdala. None of the Gospels say she was a prostitute. This goes back to a misunderstanding about the woman who anointed Jesus. She is nameless in the Gospels of Mark and Matthew, the Gospel of Luke calls the anonymous woman a "sinner," and the Gospel of John says Jesus was baptized by Mary of Bethany, who was Jesus' friend and clearly not a sex worker. None of the Marys in the Gospels were called a whore until the year 591 when Pope Gregory the Great jumbled three different female characters from three different Gospels to create this contorted composite of Mary the whore (not a harmless misunderstanding: the first person to preach the resurrection was a woman, and this myth drags her through filth). The real mystery here is not who Mary was, but how Gregory got to be Pope without having read the Gospels. Anyway, the Christian divine feminine needed a Venus-like representative of erotic desire, and this way her name is easy to remember.

7   Hughes (1992) p. 56. Hughes also points out a fascinating parallel between Shakespeare's time and the golden age of Greek Tragedy, arguably the two most celebrated eras in theatrical history: "In both the Greek world and

Shakespeare's the archaic reign of the Great Goddess was being put down, finally and decisively, by a pragmatic, skeptical, moralizing, desacralizing spirit: in Greece by the spirit of Socrates, and in England by the spirit of the ascendant, Puritan God of the individual conscience, the Age of Reason cloaked in the Reformation." (Hughes, 1992 p. 85) In both cases, when religion tries to shut the door on the goddess, she comes flying through the window of the theater.

8   Barber (1972) p. 121

9   On the topic of distinguishing Titania from Queen Elizabeth, Jonathan Bate wrote, "Shakespeare cannot afford to license the interpretation of this as an image of the Queen in a perverse encounter which upsets both the natural and the social order; if such an interpretation were at all prominent, the Master of Revels would not have licensed the play." (Bate, 1993 p. 141) "Master of Revels" is as Orwellian as it sounds; it meant the chief bureaucrat of the theatrical Thought Police.

10   Paster (1999) p. 233

11   Bloom (1998) p. 159

12   Elizabeth Truax brings up a fascinating parallel between the virgin Queen Elizabeth and the Princess of France in *Love's Labour's Lost*: she arrives on a diplomatic mission but becomes embroiled in a royal courtship. Yet she skillfully evades engagement and, in the end, when her father dies, she becomes sole ruler of a kingdom. This is Shakespeare's only comedy that doesn't end with wedding and bedding. (Truax, 1992 p. 87).

13   Vaughan (2020) p. 131

14   Raleigh, Sir Walter, "The Shepherd's Praise of his Sacred Diana" from *The Phoenix Nest* (1593)

15   Gascoigne, George, excerpt from *Princelie Pleasures at Kenelworth Castle* (1587) quoted in Vaughan (2020) p. 133.

16   Vaughan (2020) p. 140

17   There is a possibility that Shakespeare co-wrote *Henry VIII* with his protégé (co-author of *The Two Noble Kinsmen* and the lost *Cardenio*). In their collaborations they would take turns writing sections, with Fletcher handling subplots and in-between scenes. The climactic monologue about Elizabeth does appear to be Shakespeare's work.

18   From the diary of John Manningham, 1603, quoted in Hart (2003) p. 360, English updated.

19   Geoffrey of Monmouth's *De Gestis Britonum* or *Historia Regum Britanniae*: History of the Kings of Britain (circa 1136).

20   Anthony Munday, *Triumphs of Re-united Britania* (1605) quoted in Woodbridge (1994) p. 75.

21   There is some scholarly contention about categorizing Shakespeare's plays by genre. For the purpose of simplification, I have combined the "comedies" with the "romances." Also, a list of Shakespearean plays with classical settings should really include *Cymbeline*, as it takes place in Britain as a Roman colony.

Shakespeare and the Metamorphoses

23   Although Venus does not watch Adonis bathe in *Venus and Adonis*, this scene is contained in the sixth sonnet of *The Passionate Pilgrim*, a book published under Shakespeare's name (some of the sonnets were by other authors). Whether this sixth sonnet was Shakespeare's or not is debatable, but his reference to it in *The Taming of the Shrew* suggests it may have been his: *"Under an osier growing by a brook, / A brook where Adon used to cool his spleen: / Hot was the day; she hotter that did look / For his approach, that often there had been. / Anon he comes, and throws his mantle by, / And stood stark naked on the brook's green brim: / The sun look'd on the world with glorious eye, / Yet not so wistly as this queen on him. / He, spying her, bounced in, whereas he stood: / 'O Jove,' quoth she, 'why was not I a flood!'"* (Passionate Pilgrim, Sonnet VI) Or Shakespeare's reference to Venus watching Adonis bathe might have been inspired by Spenser's *The Fairie Queene*.

24   Shakespeare will revisit and reverse the image of Apollo stalking Daphne in *A Midsummer Night's Dream*, when the spurned Helena pursues Demetrius through the forest, saying: *"Run when you will; the story shall be chang'd: / Apollo flies, and Daphne holds the chase."* (MND II.i)

25   Shakespeare will return to "Wanton Pictures" toward the end of his career in *Cymbeline*, when a crafty con man narrates a verbal travelogue, describing a princess's bedroom: *"IACHIMO. Her bedchamber...was hang'd / With tapestry of silk and silver; the story, / Proud Cleopatra when she met her Roman / And Cydnus swell'd above the banks, or for / The press of boats or pride. A piece of work / So bravely done, so rich, that it did strive / In workmanship and value; which I wonder'd / Could be so rarely and exactly wrought, / Since the true life on't was... The chimneypiece / Chaste Dian bathing. Never saw I figures / So likely to report themselves. The cutter / Was as another nature, dumb; outwent her, / Motion and breath left out."* (CYM II.iv).

26   Books by authors other than Ovid do appear onstage in Shakespeare's plays, but their titles and authors are not given, as far as my research reveals. There's room for conjecture, and I'm quite fond of Catherine Belsey's circumstantial evidence that Hamlet possesses an advance copy of Erasmus's *In Praise of Folly* (Belsey, 2007 p. 113).

27   Bate in Nims (2000) p. xlii

28   Starks-Estes (2014) p. 9. In her book, *Violence, Trauma, and Virtus in Shakespeare's Roman Poems and Plays: Transforming Ovid*, Lisa Starks-Estes explores Ovid's reports of sexual violence in great detail, and writes, "Some critics see Ovid's poetry, especially in his treatment of rape, as misogynistic. I, however, argue the opposite... Ovid's verse centers to a large extent on female suffering as well as strength, on the victim's pain and humiliation when violated, on feminine outrage at masculine aggression, and on the subversive power of the female voice—even when it cannot be heard." (Starks-Estes, 2014 p. 93).

29   In *As You Like It*, the fool Touchstone compares his experience among

the goats with Ovid's exile among the Goths. Goats and Goths sound good together, although Jonathan Bate notes that "Goths" may have been a Renaissance misreading of the Getes. "But whichever they were it was agreed that they would have been incapable of appreciating the poet's witty writings." (Bate, 1993 p. 159).

30   In exploring Biblical stories that resemble Ovid's *Metamorphoses*, I assume the virgin birth is no mystery. The other two Biblical references might be more obscure. In Genesis 6:4 we read, "There were giants in the earth in those days; and also after that, when the sons of God came in unto the daughters of men, and they bare children to them, the same became mighty men which were of old, men of renown." (KJV, I covered this in my book *Genesis and the Rise of Civilization*). And the talking donkey is in the twenty-second chapter of the Book of Numbers: "And when the ass saw the angel of the Lord...the Lord opened the mouth of the ass, and she said unto Balaam, What have I done unto thee, that thou hast smitten me these three times? ...Am not I thine ass, upon which thou hast ridden ever since I was thine unto this day? was I ever wont to do so unto thee? and he said, Nay." (Numbers 22:27-30, KJV, and I love it that he answers the ass in its own language). I guess I could have brought up the talking snake in Genesis 3, but this is more fun. Also, there's a fascinating intertextuality here with *Comedy of Errors*, where the manservant Dromio compares himself to an ass who's been unjustly beaten by Antipholus.

31   John Frederick Nims comments that Golding's unabridged translation of the Metamorphoses was, "An odd collaboration, that between [Ovid] the sophisticated darling of a dissolute society, the author of a scandalous handbook of seduction, and [Golding] the respectable country gentleman and convinced Puritan who spent much of his life translating the sermons and commentaries of John Calvin. Hardly less striking than the metamorphoses the work dealt with." Arthur Golding became a celebrity, but the translation also seems to have cursed him. From 1575 "until the end of his life he was harassed by a series of lawsuits over mortgaged property. For all his famous friends and wealthy relatives, he spent a year or two in debtor's prison; when he died in 1606, he left debts so large that only a man once rich could have accumulated them." (Nims, 2000 p. xiv, xvi) It's hard not to see a parallel with Ovid's death in exile. Come to think of it, Shakespeare, who so loved Ovid and Golding's translation, also died in exile. Maybe we should be careful about messing with the *Metamorphoses*.

32   Keilen (2014) p. 239

33   Bate (2019) p. 29

34   Bate (1993) p. 208

35   Truax (1992) p. 61

36   Ovid, *Ars Amatoria* 3.19 quoted in James (2004) p. 73.

37   James (2004) p. 70

38   Maslen in Taylor (2000) p. 16

39   Nims, ed. (2000) p. 427, English updated, "his hew" changed to "this hue."

40   Jonathan Bate writes that the characters in *Titus* are like university

students, competitive in their use/misuse of Ovid and other classical texts: "The language of the schoolroom suffuses the play–characters keep coming up with remarks like 'Handle not the theme', 'I'll teach thee', 'I was their tutor to instruct them', and 'well hast thou lessoned us'." (Bate, 1993 p. 104).

41   Laroque (1993) p. 275

42   Barkan (1990) p. 244

43   Ovid related the story of Cephalus and Procris in *Ars Amatoria* (Art of Love) and also in *Metamorphoses*. In *Metamorphoses* book 7, Cephalus decides to test his wife's fidelity by disguising himself as another man and trying to seduce her. She hesitates a moment before refusal, causing him to call her unfaithful, and Procris runs away and devotes herself to Diana (symbol of chastity) but then returns. However, she also becomes jealous after hearing that Cephalus was overheard calling another woman named Aura to him while out hunting. Procris hides in a thicket and does indeed see Cephalus lie down and call for Aura, but then she realizes he's only summoning a breeze to cool himself. Relieved, Procris leaps out of her hiding place to embrace him, but he thinks an animal is attacking and shoots her with his bow. William Carroll observes a fascinating additional pattern in Pyramus and Thisbe's favorite love stories: "All these allusions, indeed the story of Pyramus and Thisby itself, are spectacularly violent and presumably inappropriate for a pre-consummation play. Each lover mentioned (except Cephalus) dies, by accident or suicide. Each pair of lovers, moreover, represents a different stage of sexual completion: Pyramus and Thisby never sexually unite, but 'die' together; Hero and Leander...die after their union; and Cephalus and Procris were married, but jealousy destroyed them. Thus the three pairs of lovers represent courtship, seduction, marriage, and jealousy. The only thing left is death, and they find that as well." Carroll (1985) p. 164

44   After the botched bedtime stories in *Pyramus and Thisbe*, Shakespeare would reprise the joke of jumbled Classical allusions the following year in *The Merchant of Venice*: as two bird-brained lovebirds pledge their eternal devotion, they take turns comparing their love to legends from ancient Greece. *"LORENZO. The moon shines bright. In such a night as this... / Troilus methinks mounted the Troyan walls, / And sigh'd his soul toward the Grecian tents, / Where Cressid lay that night. / JESSICA. In such a night / Did Thisbe fearfully o'ertrip the dew, / And saw the lion's shadow ere himself, / And ran dismayed away. / LORENZO. In such a night / Stood Dido with a willow in her hand / Upon the wild sea-banks, and waft her love / To come again to Carthage. / JESSICA. In such a night / Medea gathered the enchanted herbs / That did renew old Aeson."* (MV V.i) The simplest modern equivalent would be a love scene in which someone said, "And we'll live happily ever after, like Romeo and Juliet." All of these star-crossed love stories will end badly. Troilus was climbing-up-the-walls insane with jealousy because his beloved Cressida had been bartered into sexual slavery to the Greek army encampment and would eventually die of leprosy (Chaucer's horrible Trojan War tragedy of human trafficking would become the subject of Shakespeare's own *Troilus and Cressida*, a script so

rancid that it was withheld from the stage). In the fourth book of the *Aeneid*, the Carthaginian queen Dido was abandoned by Aeneas, and commanded that everything he'd left behind be piled up and burned. But just before the pyre was lit, she leapt on his sword and went up in flames. Ovid wrote a farewell letter from Dido to Aeneas in *Heroides*. Medea may be familiar to us from Euripides's play, but Shakespeare knew her story from Ovid (it was perhaps Ovid's favorite story, appearing in his *Heroides, Metamorphoses, Tristia*, and he even wrote a play called *Medea*, unfortunately lost). The young princess of Colchis betrayed her father to run away with Jason, then used enchanted herbs to restore her aging father-in-law's health. But Jason ditched her for a younger woman, and she murdered their children.

Diana of Ephesus

45   Frazer (1996) p. 163. Since Cybele's son/lover was killed by a boar, it's possible that the Ephesian Diana statue (really a Cybele statue) is many-breasted as a sign that the nature goddess is also a sow. Pigs have been known to eat their young. Just throwing that out there, since I think everyone's entitled to their own theory about the Ephesian statue.

46   In her essay "Great is Diana of Shakespeare's Ephesus," Elizabeth Hart writes that Ephesian "Diana" was a synthesis of many ancient goddesses including Inanna and Ishtar of Babylon, Isis of Egypt, Astarte of Israel and Syria, and Rhea, Aphrodite and Demeter of Greece, but particularly Cybele of Anatolia, goddess of moon worship, agriculture, and fertility. "Cybele remained bound to the pagan practices of the East, with that region's emphasis on live sacrifice, ritualized sexual intercourse, the self-castration of male priests, and the orgiastic devotions of female cult celebrants." (Hart, 2003 p. 348).

47   In his Biblical letter to the Ephesians, Paul writes that the small congregation is in recovery from "lusts of our flesh, fulfilling the desires of the flesh and of the mind... Having the understanding darkened, being alienated from the life of God through the ignorance that is in them, because of the blindness of their heart: Who being past feeling have given themselves over unto lasciviousness, to work all uncleanness with greediness." (Ephesians 2:3, 3:18-19).

48   Adding to the confusion about Dromios in *Comedy of Errors*, I keep watching the 1983 BBC TV movie, where Dromio is played by Roger Daltrey of The Who, and it seems at any moment he might burst out into "The Seeker," "Who Are You?" or "Won't Get Fooled Again."

49   In *Comedy of Errors*, pigs are spit-roasted and Antipholus's wife Adriana worries that their pork supper might be overcooked—if dinner gestates too long it'll be stillborn. Perhaps underneath this anxiety we hear the ticking of Adriana's biological clock—she and her husband have been delaying reproduction, and she's begun to worry that her *"wit"* (meaning both charm and sexuality) may be *"barren."* (COE II.i)

50   Dromio refers to a *"curtal dog"* meaning a dog with a docked tail. These

could not be used for hunting, so were sometimes put into large hamster-wheels in kitchens, connected to pulley systems to rotate spit-roasting meat.

51 "Lucina" was an epithet the Romans applied to the virginal lunar goddess Diana (sometimes the queen/mother goddess Juno) in her role as divine midwife.

52 Having called Luciana a mermaid, Antipholus continues on the theme, saying if she's a siren he'd happily be lured to his death: "*And as a bed I'll take them, and there he; / And in that glorious supposition think / He gains by death that hath such means to die. / Let Love, being light, be drowned if she sink.*" Later he'll decide to follow Ulysses's example and "*stop mine ears against the mermaid's song*" but then he'll change his mind again and marry her. Shakespeare also mentions mermaids in *Henry VI:3*, *The Rape of Lucrece*, *A Midsummer Night's Dream*, *Hamlet*, *Antony and Cleopatra* and *The Tempest*. In some of these they're just fairies of the water, and in others they represent the perilous lure of the unattainable (and particularly how a man can lose himself in the primordial female chaos). The Elizabethan moralization of Ulysses's mermaid/siren encounter is represented in Geoffrey Whitney's 1585 *Choice of Emblems*: "With pleasant tunes, the Sirens did allure / Ulysses wise, to listen their song: / But nothing could his manly heart procure, / He sailed away, escaped their charming strong, / The face, he liked: the nether part, did loathe: / For woman's shape, and fish's had they both. / Which shows to us, when Beauty seeks to snare / The careless man, who doth no danger dread, / That he should fly, and should in time beware, / And not on looks, his fickle fancy feed: / Such Mermaids live, that promise only joys: / But he that yields, at length himself destroys." (Truax, 1993 p. 39, English Updated)

53 Adriana's speech about matrimony shows that she has clearly been reading Paul's Biblical Epistle to the Ephesians: "Husbands, love your wives, even as Christ also loved the church... That he might present it to himself a glorious church, not having spot, or wrinkle, or any such thing; but that it should be holy and without blemish. So ought men to love their wives as their own bodies. He that loveth his wife loveth himself." (Ephesians 5:25-28)

54 "Good Lovin (Makes it Right)" (1971) written by Billy Sherrill, recorded by Tammy Wynette.

55 Shakespeare got the basic plot of *Comedy of Errors* from Plautus's *Menaechmi*. Elizabeth Truax observes that Shakespeare also mixed in elements of Plautus' *Amphitruo*, where the god Jupiter takes the form of Amphitryon to seduce the absent soldier's wife Alcmena while his servant Mercury stands guard (and she notes how Shakespeare changed the character names from *Menaechmi* to Antipholus, like Amphitryon, and Adriana, like Alcmena). It was from Zeus's union with Alcmena that Hercules was born. (Truax, 1992 p. 29)

56 Bate (2019) p. 67. Jonathan Bate notes that *Comedy of Errors* is the only Shakespearean play with "comedy" in the title, and none of his other "comedies" so closely adheres to the rules of a single setting, single day, and single plot. Shakespeare likely had not read Aristotle's *Poetics*, but had probably learned the formal conventions of Comedy and Tragedy from Aelius Donatus's essays on the

plays of Terence. From these, Elizabethan schoolboys learned "a rigid division of genres: comedies are concerned with private citizens and lowlife characters; tragedies with monarchs, rulers, and heroes. Comedies end in reversals for the better: recognition of children, happy marriages. Tragedies end in reversal for the worse: a mighty fall, a mournful death." (Bate 2019 p. 69)

57　　Luciana is a feminist's nightmare, seeing the world as a hierarchy in which males have a godlike dominance over animals and women: *"Man, more divine, the master of all these, / Lord of the wide world and wild wat'ry seas, / Indu'd with intellectual sense and souls, / Of more pre-eminence than fish and fowls, / Are masters to their females, [as] their lords."* (COE II.i) Like her sister, Luciana has been reading Paul's Epistle to the Ephesians: "Wives, submit yourselves unto your own husbands, as unto the Lord. For the husband is the head of the wife, even as Christ is the head of the church: and he is the savior of the body. Therefore as the church is subject unto Christ, so let the wives be to their own husbands in everything." (Ephesians 5:22-24).

58　　Roberts (1994) p. 142

59　　Jeanne Addison Roberts points out a pattern that *Comedy of Errors, All's Well* and *The Winter's Tale* were all based on pre-existing plots from other authors, but in all three of these plays, Shakespeare adds an older woman to aid in resolving the plot (and round out a trinity). (Roberts, 1994 p. 148).

60　　Roberts (1994) p. 14

Diana

61　　In the first scene of *A Midsummer Night's Dream,* Hermia must challenge a powerful patriarchy. Shakespeare amps up the patriarchalism further by giving Hermia's father Egeus the same name as Theseus's father Aegeus (who committed suicide due to a misunderstanding, leaping into the sea they then named after him: the Aegean).

62　　In the late Middle Ages, Christian convents had offered women (particularly women who were not inclined toward husbandry and domestic drudgery) opportunities otherwise reserved for men: "Within the religious community, women could be landowners, managers, and scholars," but during the Reformation, "the profession of nun had been abolished with the dissolution of the monasteries between 1536 and 1539." (Paster, 1999 p. 221).

63　　Dictynna (or Britomartis) was a Cretan huntress-goddess associated with moon worship, a parallel to the Greek Artemis and Roman Diana. It seems the over-educated teacher Holofernes in *Love's Labour's Lost* is crowing about his own esoteric elitism by referring to Diana by a more obscure and complicated name.

64　　Shakespeare adapted his description of Old Man Winter from Golding's translation of Ovid (and referred back to the Latin original to replace Golding's "Winter" with Ovid's "Hiem"): "And lastly quaking for the cold, stood Winter [Hiem] all forlorn, / With rugged head as white as Dove, and garments all to torn, / Forladen with the Icicles that dangled up and down / Upon his gray and hoary beard and snowy frozen crown." (Ovid's *Metamorphoses*, Book II, Golding Translation Updated). And thanks to Robert Root for pointing out that, *"Hiem's thin and icy crown"* was originally *"Hiem's chin and icy crown."* This makes a lot more sense (Root, 1965 p. 75) However, in following Golding, Shakespeare repeats the error of presenting Hiem as male, whereas in Ovid Hiem is female.

65   Paster (1999) p. 267

66   In Pre-Christian Britain, ornamental weapons would be forged and sacrificed (sunk in wells and lakes) to symbolize an armistice at the end of a war (a native parallel to the Iroquois tradition of "burying the hatchet" as a sign of peace). We may be familiar with this from Arthurian legends in which the sword Excalibur was thrown into a lake (sacrificed to a peace goddess, the Lady of the Lake). The *"silver bow"* Hippolyta refers to here may be related to this tradition, as her marriage to Theseus will bring peace between the Amazons and Athenians.

67   Theseus and Hippolyta are minor characters in *A Midsummer Night's Dream* and yet Shakespeare subtly provides us with enough moments to see a clear development in their relationship. When Theseus first judges the case of Hermia's disobedience to her father, Hippolyta stands by silently, and yet Theseus's question to her, *"What cheer, my love?"* is the Elizabethan equivalent of a husband asking, "What did I do wrong *this* time?" She doesn't answer, but apparently he works it out on his own. Later, when the four young lovers are found near the forest, Theseus grants Hermia's wish to marry Lysander, bypassing her father and the laws of Athens. The next time we see Theseus and Hippolyta together, they have been listening to the testimony of the four lovers. Theseus, like the Duke in *Comedy of Errors*, thinks they've all gone mad, but Hippolyta, like Mother Superior in *The Comedy of Errors*, has carefully listened to each independent report and deduces from the correspondences that something real must have happened. Theseus wisely backs out of the debate, and finally we see affectionate moments between them as these two great warriors join forces to lambaste some poor theatrical players.

68   Titania and Oberon's past relationships with Theseus and Hippolyta are described thusly: *"TITANIA. But that, forsooth, the bouncing Amazon, / Your buskin'd mistress and your warrior love, / To Theseus must be wedded, and you come / To give their bed joy and prosperity? / OBERON. How canst thou thus, for shame, Titania, / Glance at my credit with Hippolyta, / Knowing I know thy love to Theseus? / Didst not thou lead him through the glimmering night / From Perigouna, whom he ravished? / And make him with fair Aegles break his faith, / With Ariadne and Antiopa?"* (MND II.i) And here Oberon lists several of Theseus's former lovers, including Hippolyta's sister Antiope.

69   Bottom becomes a mythical chimera, a sort of half-assed mini-Minotaur except, unlike that bloodthirsty beast, he's totally harmless. Whether Shakespeare had the Minotaur in mind or not is debatable, but the inclusion of the Minotaur-slayer Theseus in the play suggests that we should at least take a glance at possible

parallels. The bestial union from which the Minotaur was born was a prank by Poseidon, causing the Cretan queen Pasiphae to fall madly in love with a bull (as Titania will be pranked into falling in love with the monstrous Bottom). The Athenian teenagers in *A Midsummer Night's Dream* enter a labyrinthine forest, like the sacrificial Athenian teenagers in the Minotaur story. And when Theseus chooses 'Pyramus and Thisbe' as wedding entertainment, he symbolically enters Bottom's labyrinth (and although Bottom has by this point been restored to his human appearance, he's still essentially the same jackass). The two are onstage together only briefly but note that Bottom challenges Theseus's authority by correcting him during the performance. Then Theseus defeats Bottom by silencing him when the actor offers a monologue at the end of the show. Cobbled together, that makes a pretty slim case for a Minotaur sub-theme, but it's not entirely insignificant when we consider that Theseus and Bottom have both been romantically linked to Titania, so there is a bit of rivalry there, even though neither character is aware of it.

70   Taylor in Martindale (2004) p. 54

71   Helena and Hermia both use lunar goddess imagery to describe the inconstancy of a young man's affection. Hermia, awakening abandoned and confused, babbles *"The sun was not so true unto the day / As he to me. Would he have stolen away / From sleeping Hermia? I'll believe as soon / This whole earth may be bor'd* [drilled through], *and that the moon / May through the centre creep and so displease / Her brother's noontide with th' Antipodès."* (MND III.ii) The "Antipodes" were mythical people who walked upside down on the underside of the earth. And Helena, who has demanded to follow Demetrius like a dog, is totally befuddled when he worships her as a goddess. She suspects that Hermia has enlisted him in a cruel practical joke: *"HELENA. Have you not set Lysander, as in scorn, / To follow me and praise my eyes and face? / And made your other love, Demetrius, / Who even but now did spurn me with his foot, / To call me goddess, nymph, divine, and rare, / Precious, celestial? Wherefore speaks he this / To her he hates?"* (MND III.ii)

72   Like Hades/Pluto, Oberon seems to live underground, and Puck once calls him *"king of shadows"* (although "shadows" in this script can mean fairies or actors but does not mean "shades" in the Greek sense of ghosts).

73   As Jonathan Bate points out, the menu of options for Theseus and Hippolyta's wedding entertainment in *A Midsummer Night's Dream* is "a choice of Ovidian performances: before 'Pyramus and Thisbe' is selected, 'The battle with the Centaurs' from Book Twelve of the *Metamorphoses* is rejected, as is a dramatization of 'The riot of the tipsy bacchanals / Tearing the Thracian singer in their rage', the final stage of the Orpheus myth from Book Eleven… Everybody in Athens seems to have been rehearsing the matter of the *Metamorphoses* in preparation for the wedding festivities of Theseus and Hippolyta, themselves characters from ancient myth." (Bate, 1993 p. 130) Adding to the irony, the *Metamorphoses* would not be written until 1,500 years after Theseus died.

74   The Elizabethan belief that the (female) moon was patrolled by a man

with a dog and a bush is also mentioned in *The Tempest*, when Caliban first encounters the shipwrecked Stephano and thinks that he is the magical moon-man his mother (the witch Sycorax) told him about: *"CALIBAN. Hast thou not dropp'd from heaven? / STEPHANO. Out o' th' moon, I do assure thee; I was the Man I' th' Moon, when time was. / CALIBAN. I have seen thee in her, and I do adore thee. My mistress show'd me thee, and thy dog and thy bush."* (TEM II.ii)

75 Nosworthy (1982) p. 98

76 A little sidenote for fans of Euripides: *"Triple Hecate's team"* and Puck's earlier reference to *"night's swift dragons"* (MND III.ii) refer to Hecate's dragon-drawn flying chariot–the one she sent to rescue Medea after the murder of the children (Root, 1965 p. 56). Shakespeare hadn't read Eurpides' *Medea* but knew the story from Ovid.

77 Roberts in Woodbridge (1992) p. 138

78 Ovid's *Metamorphoses* Book three (Translated by Brookes More, 1949). In Shakespeare's time, people would have read this in Ovid's original Latin or in Golding's verse translation. But to orient modern readers on the basic plot, this Brookes More translation is much easier to follow.

79 The mythic motif of the male god stalking the mortal woman with violent intent is a rebellion against the older pattern in which the female hunted the male. Greek mythology retains many of these: Diana hunting Actaeon, the goddess-as-boar goring Adonis, the Bacchanals dismembering Pentheus and Orpheus, etc. Then the matriarchal cultures of Crete and Greece were overthrown in a male mutiny (the myth of Orestes being absolved of matricide and rescued from the Furies signifies this change). And from that time on, Greek and Roman mythology became more focused on male deities as sexual predators.

80 Batman, Stephen (1577) quoted in Vaughan (2020) p. 129

81 Wagner (2004) p. 137-141. People ask me how I manage to memorize so many names and stories for writing these books of Biblical, Mythological and Shakespearean commentary. It's because I grew up reading comic books! And memorizing the names of characters and writers and artists.

82 Bate (1993) p. 162

83 In *Titus Andronicus*, Tamora's sons have been instructed by Aaron: *"My lords, a solemn hunting is in hand... / The forest walks are wide and spacious, / And many unfrequented plots there are / Fitted by kind for rape and villainy. / Single you thither then this dainty doe, / And strike her home by force if not by words."* (TA II.i) Aaron verbally transforms Lavinia to a *"doe"* (a deer, a female deer), like the Actaeon myth, and the forest as a place of violence is a recurring theme in Ovid's *Metamorphoses*.

84 The story of Malvolio in *Twelfth Night* will contain aspects of the myth of Diana and Actaeon. Receiving a forged letter, the servant fantasizes about marrying the countess Olivia, entering her bedroom like Actaeon penetrating the goddess's inner sanctum. But as he gives his speech in the garden he's being watched, stalked by the merry pranksters Toby, Maria, and Andrew, who are

hunting him for sport. Malvolio will be symbolically torn apart by these dogs, and when the prank is revealed, he'll storm off, comparing them to a pack of hounds, *"I'll be reveng'd on the whole pack of you."* (TN V.i) (Bate, 1993 p. 147)

85   Shakespeare's *Julius Caesar* contains no reference to Diana, but numerous poetic allusions to Caesar as a stag torn apart by hounds. The conspirators are frequently compared to dogs baying and baiting. Caesar calls his opponent a *"spaniel"* and a *"cur,"* Antony speaks of the conspirators as *"hounds"* and his avenging army as *"dogs of war."* Planning Caesar's assassination, Brutus specifies: *"Let's carve him as a dish fit for the gods, / Not hew him as a carcass fit for hounds."* But Antony, arriving too late and standing over the cadaver, nonetheless speaks of Caesar as a stag torn by baying dogs: *"Pardon me, Julius! Here wast thou bay'd, brave hart; / Here didst thou fall; and here thy hunters stand, / Sign'd in thy spoil, and crimson'd in thy lethe. / O world, thou wast the forest to this hart; / And this indeed, O world, the heart of thee. / How like a deer strucken by many princes, / Dost thou here lie!"* (JC III.i, note the distinct spellings of heart and hart/stag) Shakespeare knew from Plutarch that Caesar suffered twenty-three wounds, and from Ovid that Actaeon was torn apart by thirty-three hounds. Whether consciously or unconsciously, Shakespeare gives Caesar *"three and thirty wounds."* But the numerous references to dogs and Actaeon throughout Shakespeare's work suggest this was intentional. (Wood, 1973 p. 87)

86   Miriam Kammer wrote, *"Love's Labour's Lost* is a comedy that flows from the absurd proposition that culture and nature, the domestic and the wild, can be clearly delineated and kept separate in a world demanding interaction." The men set a boundary the women cannot cross, but the men keep crossing it. This at first seems like male entitlement to cross boundaries and enter female space, but the play also subverts the idea of women trapped at home and men venturing forth into the wild world. "That is the great irony in Love's Labour's Lost—while the men believe that they are getting the upper hand in their pursuit of the women by relegating them to the outdoors, they are actually empowering them, for through their own independent and forceful actions the women will go on to mark the territory as a feminine space of their own." (Kammer, 2018 p. 471-472)

87   *All's Well* may be nobody's favorite Shakespeare play, but it might be the author's most autobiographical piece—Bertram's abandonment of Helena bears a certain resemblance to Shakespeare's own marriage to Anne Hathaway, whom he kept in the countryside while he pursued fame (and sex) in the city.

88   The Robin Hood legend is linked to the "Major Oak" that still stands in Sherwood Forest, Nottinghamshire, England. This may have been the inspiration for Herne's Oak, since there has been no definite identification of a specific tree by that name in Windsor Forest (although there have been a couple of contenders). In Shakespeare's time, some early forest conservationists proposed naming local trees and attaching legends to them as a way of protecting them from being cut down.

89   Excerpt from Michael Drayton's "Poly-Olbion" (1612)

90   Quoted in Steadman (1963) p. 233

91   The Garter Knights' motto, *Honi soit qui mal y pense*, "evil be to him who thinks evil," was printed on early editions of Golding's translation of Ovid's *Metamorphoses*. The inscription was wrapped around the image of a bear chained to a stake (awaiting a canine onslaught in a bear-baiting arena). This cover illustration and cautionary inscription echoes Golding's concern that reading the lewd stories could turn men into beasts, resulting in troubles akin to the punishment of Actaeon.

92   Bloom (1998) p. 603

93   The narrator of *Pericles* describes Marina's goddess-like abilities to sing, dance, and tutor young maidens in embroidery (and the lengthy description of her lively sewing, which seems to bring thread to life as fruits and berries, shows an almost divine creativity): *"Marina thus the brothel 'scapes, and chances / Into an honest house, our story says. / She sings like one immortal, and she dances / As goddess-like to her admired lays; / Deep clerks she dumbs; and with her nee'le composes / Nature's own shape, of bud, bird, branch, or berry, / That even her art sisters the natural roses; / Her inkle, silk, twin with the rubied cherry: / That pupils lacks she none..."* (PER V.i)

94   When Pericles says he will offer *"Oblations"* to the goddess Diana, it means that he will pour either milk or bull-blood or wine over a statue of her.

Venus

95   Bate (2019) p. 1

96   Shakespeare (as Hamlet) sadly describes how a script about Dido and Aeneas was rejected by the general public: *"It was never acted, or if it was, not above once, for the play, I remember, pleased not the million, 'twas caviare to the general* [public]. *But it was—as I received it, and others, whose judgments in such matters cried in the top of mine—an excellent play, well digested in the scenes, set down with as much modesty as cunning. I remember one said there were no sallets* [shallots?] *in the lines to make the matter savoury, nor no matter in the phrase that might indite the author of affectation, but called it an honest method, as wholesome as sweet, and by very much more handsome than fine."* (HAM II.ii) Then two monologues from the script are performed.

97   There's some scholarly controversy surrounding Shakespeare's involvement in a supposed *Cardenio* script. But reading through a synopsis of the Cervantes subplot, I can certainly see why this would have interested Shakespeare—it's got forbidden love, misunderstandings, escapes into the wilderness, some of his favorite themes (anybody with scissors, paste, and a copy of Shakespeare's Collected Works could create a *Cardenio* script without having to change anything but the names of the characters).

98   Venus says she's *"hemm'd"* (enclosed) Adonis *"within the circuit of this ivory pale"* meaning she's confined him in her white arms. But there may also be a pun here on the circuit of the pale moon, Diana.

99   Because Shakespeare was not writing for the stage (upon which Venus

would be played by a boy), he could present Venus as the painters did, fully nude. *The Passionate Pilgrim* (a publication attributed to Shakespeare in 1599, although several of its sonnets were not by him) contains four sonnets about Venus and Adonis, two of which contain references to Venus undressing. In one sonnet she does a striptease, "'Even thus,' quoth she, 'the warlike god [Mars] unlaced me,'" (PP 11) and in another sonnet, Venus lifts her skirt to urge Adonis into a game of I'll-show-you-mine-if-you-show-me-yours: "'Once,' quoth she, 'did I see a fair sweet youth / Here in these brakes deep-wounded with a boar, / Deep in the thigh, a spectacle of ruth! / See, in my thigh,' quoth she, 'here was the sore.' / She showèd hers: he saw more wounds than one, / And blushing fled, and left her all alone." (PP 9) It's not printed in italics here because it's probably not by Shakespeare. On the other hand, the four Venus/Adonis sonnets in *The Passionate Pilgrim* could conceivably have been Shakespeare's warm-ups for the epic poem, in which case this would represent an early planning stage in which Venus was clothed.

100   Venus does once get on top of Adonis, early on in the poem, *"and lo I lie between that sun and thee,"* (V&A ln 194) but this doesn't work; he plays possum.

101   Kiernan in Taylor (2000) p. 92

102   Roe in Taylor (2000) p. 44

103   The sun (the titan Hyperion) jealously watches Venus' unsuccessful seduction of Adonis: *"By this the love-sick queen began to sweat, / For where they lay the shadow had forsook them, / And Titan, tired in the midday heat, / With burning eye did hotly overlook them, / Wishing Adonis had his team to guide, / So he were like him and by Venus' side."* (V&A ln 175-180)

104   Roe (2014) p. 11

105   *Venus and Adonis* is 1,194 lines. Venus speaks 537, Adonis speaks 89, the Narrator has 568. To get a sense of length in relation to his plays, the shortest are *Comedy of Errors* with 1,786 lines and *Midsummer Night's Dream* with 2,165. Most of the scripts are in the 2,500-3,500 range, with *Hamlet* running the longest, 4,024 lines. In terms of performance time, an ensemble could speak about a thousand lines per hour.

106   Shakespeare, like others in his time, did not believe that an ovum contained any DNA, he saw it as a blank slate to be imprinted with male characteristics. In *A Midsummer Night's Dream*, the duke tells Hermia: *"To you your father should be as a god; / One that compos'd your beauties; yea, and one / To whom you are but as a form in wax, / By him imprinted."* (MND I.i) Similarly, Leontes in *Winter's Tale* tells a young man, *"Your mother was most true to wedlock, Prince; / For she did print your royal father off, / Conceiving you [in] Your father's image."* (WT V.i)

107   The tale of Adonis's incestuous conception, in the tenth book of the *Metamorphoses*, was so scandalous that even Ovid warns the reader not to read it: "Of wicked and most cursèd things to speak I now commence. / Ye daughters and ye parents all go get ye far from hence... / To hate one's father is a crime as heinous as may be, / But yet more wicked is this love of [hers] than any hate." (Book 10, Golding translation updated) It is worth noting here that Myrrha was possessed

with lust for her father through some divine manipulation, but Ovid insists that Venus and Cupid were innocent of this.

108   Shakespeare may have read Plato's *Symposium* in translation, or might have picked up the core elements from commentators. His use of the word *"banquet"* in line 445 is a reference to the banquet setting of this Platonic dialogue.

109   Kiernan in Taylor (2000) p. 93

110   Vision is the most selective of the senses. We can choose to focus on one detail or person and let all else blur in the background. Vision is also the only sense we can turn on and off at will, by closing our eyes. In this way, vision can be subjected to self-discipline (and censorship) in ways other senses cannot. Vision can be bargained with and reasoned with, interpreted, and intentionally "rose-tinted," but there's no arguing with your nose and other senses. I suppose this must be what's meant by Plato elevating vision as the loftiest of the senses. But as I understand it, vision is the youngest of the senses on earth, the most recent innovation in evolutionary sensory development. It's the last sense to activate in human life (newborns are pretty much blind, but they can smell, taste, hear, and feel) and the first sense to fade at the end of life. In a natural death, the last sensation is scent, which was also the first sense to activate.

111   Paglia (1991) p. 50

112   If the topic of the "Male Gaze" is totally unfamiliar, Wikipedia has a lengthy page on the concept with a history and bibliography of scholarly debate about it.

113   The line "the tender nibbler would not touch the bait" comes from another of the sonnets contained in *The Passionate Pilgrim*, published under Shakespeare's name, although the authorship is in doubt. "She told him stories to delight his ear; / She show'd him favours to allure his eye; / To win his heart, she touch'd him here and there: / Touches so soft still conquer chastity. / But whether unripe years did want conceit, / Or he refus'd to take her figur'd proffer, / The tender nibbler would not touch the bait, / But smile and jest at every gentle offer: / Then fell she on her back, fair queen, and toward; / He rose and ran away; ah, fool too forward!" (Passionate Pilgrim, Sonnet II)

114   Belsey (1995) p. 262

115   Kott (1974) p. 176

116   Adonis's line *"love to heaven is fled"* is not a reference to the Christian heaven—he's using "heaven" as a word for the sky, and referring to a line in the first book of Ovid's *Metamorphoses,* in which the virgin goddess Astraea (Justice) is so horrified by human cruelty that she abandons the earth.

117   In choosing violence over sex, Adonis also resembles Bertram from *All's Well That Ends Well*, rejecting the offered love of Helena (and the advice of his own mother) and going off to war.

118   I understand Leonard Cohen has become something of a one-hit-wonder with the younger crowd and that's fine, "Hallelujah" is a great song. But I'm thinking here of the fifth verse of "Democracy," and the lyrics to "So Long,

Marianne" and "I'm Your Man."

119   Asimov (1978:1) p. 11

120   *Venus and Adonis* begins with the personified Sun: *"Even as the sun with purple-coloured face / had tane his last leave of the weeping morn."* (V&A ln 1-2) It sounds as though some act of Ovidian sexual violence has just taken place, but Lisa Starks-Estes reads the *"weeping morn"* as the dawn-goddess "Aurora, a forceful goddess who attempts to ravish her male beloved in Ovid's Cephalus and Procris...and elsewhere grieves for the loss of her son Memnon." (Starks-Estes, 2014 p. 71) In this reading, 'sun' is a pun on 'son', symbolizing how Adonis will disappoint Venus. The Sun will appear later in *Venus and Adonis* (called "Titan," suggesting that this is Hyperion and not Apollo), flying his chariot overhead, *"Wishing Adonis had his team to guide, / So he were like him and by Venus' side."* (V&A ln 179-180) The narrator can see him (obviously, he's the sun), and can also read his mind. Venus does not talk to/at/about him as she does the other gods.

121   Roe (2006) p. 125

122   Venus' relation to Jupiter can get a bit confusing, and it's difficult to explain in text because this is a Mediterranean story, so hand gestures are as important as words. Venus is the half-sister of Jupiter's father Saturn. When Saturn castrated his father Uranus and flung his testicles into the ocean, Venus emerged from the foam (so she's Uranus's daughter). Then Uranus's children Saturn and Rhea bore several Olympian gods, the youngest being Jupiter. So Venus is approximately Jupiter's aunt.

123   In her threat of global destruction, Venus is referring to the primordial chaos in the first book of the *Metamorphoses*: "For where was earth, was sea and air, so was the earth unstable. / The air all dark, the sea likewise to bear a ship unable / No kind of thing had proper shape, but each confounded other. / For in one selfsame body strove the hot and cold together, / The moist with dry, the soft with hard, the light with things of weight. / This strife did God and Nature break, and set in order straight." (Book 1, Golding Translation updated)

124   In the mechanics' production of "Pyramus and Thisbe," Tom splits two fingers to represent the hole in the wall, and Bottom encourages Jove/Jupiter to look away from this lewd gesture (In Britain, a V-sign is still a vulgar gesture, somewhat akin to the middle finger).

125   A lengthier excerpt from Jupiter's speech in *Cymbeline* about rescuing Posthumus Leonatus from imprisonment: *"JUPITER. No more, you petty spirits of region low, / Offend our hearing; hush! How dare you ghosts / Accuse the Thunderer whose bolt, you know, / Sky-planted, batters all rebelling coasts? / Poor shadows of Elysium, hence and rest / Upon your never-withering banks of flow'rs. / Be not with mortal accidents opprest: / No care of yours it is; you know 'tis ours. / Whom best I love I cross; to make my gift, / The more delay'd, delighted. Be content; / Your low-laid son our godhead will uplift; / His comforts thrive, his trials well are spent."* (CYM V.iv)

126   In *Shakespeare and the Goddess of Complete Being*, Ted Hughes describes the boar as the "most impressive, dangerous, fascinating and human of the animals

that are both domesticated and hunted... Her combination of gross whiskery nakedness and riotous carnality is seized by the mythic imagination, evidently, as a sort of uterus on the loose–upholstered with breasts, not so much many-breasted as a mobile tub entirely made of female sexual parts, a woman-sized, multiple udder on trotters...famous for gobbling her piglets, magnified and shameless, exuberantly omnivorous and insatiable." (Hughes, 1992 p. 11, see also p. 7 and 67)

127   Venus acknowledges the boar as a sexual being–maybe it didn't even mean to hurt him: *"And nuzzling in his flank, the loving swine / Sheath'd unaware the tusk in his soft groin. / Had I been tooth'd like him, I must confess, / With kissing him I should have kill'd him first."* (V&N ln 1115-1118)

128   Belsey (1995) p. 260

129   Ted Hughes, in *Shakespeare and the Goddess of Complete Being*, proposes that *Venus and Adonis* and its companion poem *The Rape of Lucrece* (in which Adonis symbolically becomes the bloodthirsty boar) are the skeleton key to a profound mystery at the heart of Shakespeare's canon. He writes that Shakespeare's Venus stands in for the vibrant, colorful Roman Mass and the Catholic relationship with the divine mother (combining the virgin Mary and Mary the whore), and that Adonis is an allegory for cold, grim Puritanism. Religious fundamentalists in Shakespeare's time were smashing colorful stained-glass windows, whitewashing murals on church walls, and demoting Mary the maternal intercessor, claiming these were all distractions from a personal relationship with the male trinity. Behind a thin veneer of Venus, the divine mother sneers at her rejection and indicts the zealots' jealous God. "So how could Shakespeare write this poem without triggering a seismic response in the suppressed Catholicism and indeed in the suppressed Puritanism of the Elizabethan nightmare? ...Those pagan names, Venus and Adonis, would insulate the archaic myth from any short circuit with the deadly serious, explosive religious feelings of their own times." (Hughes, 1992 p. 56) Shakespeare escaped censure by hiding behind fanciful deities and playful eroticism–the last place anybody would look for a theological/ecumenical treatise. Then the theaters reopened, a safe haven where the outlawed, multicolored, polyphonic pageantry of the Catholic Mass could hide in plain sight.

130   Starks-Estes (2014) p. 82

131   The flower in *A Midsummer's Night Dream* is similar to the one born of Adonis's death, but actually links with Ovid's story of Pyramus and Thisbe, whose blood also discolors a flower. Shakespeare doesn't mention this in his *"tedious brief scene of young Pyramus And his love Thisbe."* Instead, he makes Love-in-idleness the result of Cupid's misfire.

132   *The Two Noble Kinsmen* opens with three widowed queens alerting Theseus that their husbands have died in a siege of Thebes, and the cruel king Creon has decreed that their bodies must be left to rot without proper burial. Readers familiar with Greek tragedy will recognize this siege from Aeschylus' *Seven Against Thebes*, Sophocles' *Antigone* and Euripides' *The Suppliants*. I've written commentaries on these in my book *Welcome to Tragedy: A Beginner's Guide*

to Greek Drama.

133   As a prisoner of war, Arcite curses Lady Fortune (then thanks her for at least letting him suffer with a good friend) *"And in their Songs, curse ever-blinded Fortune, / Till she for shame see what a wrong she has done / To youth and nature... Yet, Cousin, / Even from the bottom of these miseries, / From all that Fortune can inflict upon us, / I see two comforts rising, two mere blessings, / If the gods please: to hold here a brave patience, / And the enjoying of our griefs together. / Whilst Palamon is with me, let me perish / If I think this our prison."* (II.ii Fletcher) Later, loaned out as Emilia's servant in an inmate labor program, he'll change his tune, asking Lady Fortune if he's on a winning streak: *"Tell me, O Lady Fortune, / Next after Emily my sovereign [master], how far / I may be proud."* (TNK III.i Shakespeare)

Venus & Diana

134   Oh, I see. So that's what it takes to get you to flip back into these Notes. Welcome. And while you're here, take a look around—there's a lot of cool material in this part of the book! Anyway, here are the steamy details you were looking for. *"Once with a time when I enjoyed a playfellow; / You were at wars when she the grave enriched, / Who made too proud the bed; took leave o' th' moon, / Which then looked pale at parting, when our count / Was each eleven... But I, / And she I sigh and spoke of, were things innocent, / Loved for we did, and like the elements / That know not what nor why, yet do effect / Rare issues by their operance, our souls / Did so to one another. What she liked / Was then of me approved, what not, condemned, / No more arraignment. The flower that I would pluck / And put between my breasts—O, then but beginning / To swell about the blossom—she would long / Till she had such another, and commit it / To the like innocent cradle, where, Phoenix-like, / They died in perfume. [and] This rehearsal— / Which fury-innocent wots well comes in / Like old importment's bastard—has this end, / That the true love 'tween maid and maid may be / More than in sex dividual."* (TNK I.iii, Shakespeare) This bears a similarity to Helena's recollection of her childhood friendship *"like to a double cherry"* with Hermia in *A Midsummer Night's Dream.* (MND III.ii) and Polixenes' happy memories of when he and Leontes grew up like *"twinn'd lambs that did frisk i' th' sun / And bleat the one at th' other. What we chang'd / Was innocence for innocence"* (WT I.ii) in *The Winter's Tale.* The Two Noble Kinsmen also contains some homoeroticism between Arcite and Palamon, imprisoned together: "We are one another's wife, ever begetting / New births of love" (TNK II.ii, Fletcher)

135   While Theseus is off attacking Thebes, Emilia vows to make blood sacrifices to the war-goddess Bellona for his safe return: *"Remember me / To our all-royal brother [in law], for whose speed / The great Bellona I'll solicit; and / Since in our terrene [earthly] state petitions are not / Without gifts understood, I'll offer to her / What I shall be advised she likes."* (TNK I.iii Shakespere) Earlier in his career, Shakespeare had referred to Macbeth as *"Bellona's bridegroom, lapp'd in proof."* (MAC I.ii, *"Lapp'd in proof"* meaning doused in blood) Later, when Emilia learns that Arcite and Palamon will fight to win her hand in marriage. She bitterly accuses Diana

of embroiling her in human sacrifice: *"What sins have I committed, chaste Diana, / That my unspotted youth must now be soiled / With blood of princes, and my chastity / Be made the altar where the lives of lovers— / Two greater and two better never yet / Made mothers joy—must be the sacrifice / To my unhappy beauty?" (TNK IV.ii, Fletcher)*

136   In Emilia's monologue, Shakespeare refers to an Amazon as a "knight." He will also call Hero a *"virgin knight"* in *Much Ado About Nothing*, and Helena will call herself a knight in *All's Well That Ends Well*. Shakespeare refers to male soldiers as knights as well. But in the case of these women, he seems to mean "knight" as a devotee of the virginal goddess Diana.

137   As Palamon and Arcite fight offstage, Emilia says a further prayer: *"Were they metamorphosed / Both into one!" (TNK V.iii, Shakespeare) and in a sense they are, by the death of Arcite.*

ᚠortune & ᚱature

138   In classical art, Fortuna was often depicted holding a ship's rudder, and in *Cymbeline*, a servant says, *"Fortune brings in some boats that are not steer'd."* (CYM IV.iii) But it's doubtful Celia means the *"housewife"* Fortuna is spinning the steering wheel of a boat.

139   *"'Good morrow, fool,' quoth I; 'No, sir,' quoth he, / 'Call me not fool till heaven hath sent me fortune,'"* (AYL II.vii) a bitter reference to the Latin proverb 'Fortuna favet fatuis,' Fortune favors fools.

140   In *As You Like It*, Shakespeare gives a third of his name to Jaques, and half of his name to William, the inarticulate bumpkin who's courting the country lass, Audrey. Touchstone will bully William out of the competition. So, both avatars of the author will be steamrolled by Touchstone, perhaps a playful expression of Shakespeare's doubt of ever living up to his hero, Ovid. (A second Jaques, middle brother of Oliver and Orlando, is away at university, and makes a brief cameo at the end. Ted Hughes gives a complex excursus on the two Jakes in *Shakespeare and the Goddess of Complete Being*.

141   Touchstone refers to Ovid's exile while courting a lovely goatherd: *"I am here with thee and thy goats, as the most capricious poet, honest Ovid, was among the Goths... When a man's verses cannot be understood, nor a man's good wit seconded with the forward child understanding, it strikes a man more dead than a great reckoning in a little room."* (AYL III.iii)

142   As evidence of love's follies, Touchstone tells what is perhaps the strangest love story in all of Shakespeare' works: *"I remember, when I was in love, I broke my sword upon a stone, and bid him take that for coming a-night to Jane Smile; and I remember the kissing of her batler* [washing-board], *and the cow's dugs that her pretty chopt hands had milk'd; and I remember the wooing of peascod* [pea-plant] *instead of her; from whom I took two cods, and giving her them again, said with weeping tears 'Wear these for my sake.' We that are true lovers run into strange capers; but as all is mortal in nature, so is all nature in love mortal in folly."* (AYL II.iv) It's worth noting

here that he uses the word "caper," which can mean a dance or a crime, but it's the Latin word for "goat." In the next act, he'll describe himself as being like the "capricious" (goat-like) poet Ovid.

143   Rosalind, familiar with Ovid's *Metamorphoses*, threatens to transform Touchstone into a tree: *"ROSALIND. Peace, you dull fool! I found them* [Orlando's poems] *on a tree. / TOUCHSTONE. Truly, the tree yields bad fruit. / ROSALIND. I'll graff* [graft] *it with you, and then I shall graff it with a medlar. Then it will be the earliest fruit i' th' country; for you'll be rotten ere you be half ripe, and that's the right virtue of the medlar."* (AYL III.ii)

144   Since Rosalind has been playing Cupid throughout *As You Like It*, Cupid's rival Hymen must show up and sort out the mess: *"HYMEN. Peace, ho! I bar confusion; / 'Tis I must make conclusion / Of these most strange events. / Here's eight that must take hands / To join in Hymen's bands, / If truth holds true contents. / [to Rosalind and Orlando] You and you no cross shall part; / [to Celia and Oliver] You and you are heart in heart; / [to Phebe and Silvius] You to his love must accord, / Or have a woman to your lord; / [to Audrey and Touchstone] You and you are sure together, / As the winter to foul weather. / Whiles a wedlock-hymn we sing, / Feed yourselves with questioning, / That reason wonder may diminish, / How thus we met, and these things finish."* (AYL V.iv)

145   When *As You Like It* concludes, pretty much everyone's a winner—except the melancholy philosopher Jaques, standing at the sidelines, saying *"So, to your pleasures: / I am for other than dancing measures."* (AYL V.iv) Ted Hughes pauses on this ominous moment: Shakespeare's own representative slinking off sullenly. Shakespeare was about to enter the darkest phase of his career, writing *Hamlet*, *Othello*, and *Macbeth*. Even the comedies he wrote after this would be bitter and rancid: *All's Well That Ends Well*, *Troilus and Cressida*, and *Measure for Measure*. Hughes (1992) p. 115

Nature

146   Archer (2012) p. 542, cf. Archer (2015) p. 15

147   Belsey (2007) p. 59

148   Furious that Cordelia will not become his foster mother, Lear lumps her in with barbarians who eat their own babies: *"Or he that makes his generation messes / To gorge his appetite, shall to my bosom / Be as well neighbour'd, pitied, and reliev'd, / As thou my sometime daughter."* (KL I.i, "messes" meaning food, as in a military "mess hall") Ironic coming from a man who wishes to be nursed by his own daughters.

149   Thanks for this great pun! Lawson, Mark, "Are These the 10 Best Shakespeare Screen Adaptations?" *The Guardian* (9 October 2015)

150   Gruber (2015) p. 108

151   Gabriel Egan in *Green Shakespeare* (2006, p. 141) identifies "germens" as ovum. The word can apparently mean egg or seed, and considering Shakespeare's idea of the human ova as a blank, wax-like mold to be imprinted with a father's traits, I would argue that "germens" here means sperm.

152   In his misogynistic tirades, Lear even goes so far as to dehumanize his daughters as mythical monsters: *"Down from the waist they are centaurs, though women all above. But to the girdle do the gods inherit, beneath is all the fiend's; there's hell, there's darkness, there is the sulphurous pit; burning, scalding, stench, consumption."* (KL IV.vi, "girdle" meaning waist) Presumably, Queen Lear would have shut him up by now, or maybe this kind of talk is why she's gone.

153   Gloucester recalls Edmund's conception: *"His breeding, sir, hath been at my charge: I have so often blush'd to acknowledge him that now I am braz'd to't."* (KL I.i, "Braz'd" meaning lit up like a furnace)

154   Shakespeare will return to the theme of Nature as a goddess who bestows nobility on the noble-born in *Cymbeline* (in which many elements of *Lear* are reprised). Two sons of King Cymbeline have been kidnapped as babies, and yet the man who raised them keeps noticing that they are princely by nature despite their lowly upbringing: *"How hard it is to hide the sparks of nature! / These boys know little they are sons to th' King... / They think they are mine; and* [yet] *nature prompts them / In simple and low things to prince it much / Beyond the trick of others."* (CYM III.iii) *"O noble strain! / O worthiness of nature! breed of greatness! / Cowards father cowards and base things sire base. / Nature hath meal and bran, contempt and grace... O thou goddess, / Thou divine Nature, thou thyself thou blazon'st / In these two princely boys!"* (CYM IV.ii)

155   Kott (1974) p. 147, 149

156   Appignanesi and Ilya (2009) p. 178. Part of what makes Cordelia's death so unsettling is that she's been gone for the whole play. And knowing she's important, directors and performers have no choice but to cram three hours' worth of love and sincerity into ten minutes of stage time, and she becomes too sweet. Hearing Cordelia in performance sets my teeth on edge worse than all the liars in this play. Keeping her onstage as the Fool would take this pressure off. Furthermore, Shakespeare's *King Lear* has strong thematic ties to *As You Like It* and *Cymbeline; King Lear* feels like the middle piece of a continuum. And both of these other plays feature a noble daughter in male disguise.

157   I'm dedicating this book to Terry Gilliam because I personally find him to be the modern storyteller most akin to the spirit of Shakespeare's creativity, particularly in the way he blends genres and interweaves imaginative magic and reality. The poetic arc of Gilliam's career helps me understand the various stages of Shakespeare's creative trajectory.

158   Archer (2012) p. 529. "The Autumn King: Remembering the Land in *King Lear*" catalogues the components of the crown in far greater detail. And while most of these are autumn flowers, cuckoo-flowers bloomed in spring, so in a sense Nature has brought springtime and harvest time together in this gift for Lear (for spring to arrive right after the harvest season, skipping winter, was symbolic of paradise in Shakespeare, as we see in *The Tempest: "Spring come to you at the farthest. In the very end of harvest."* IV.i)

159   Shakespeare twice refers to Nature by the Latin proper name *"Tellus,"*

(HAM III.ii and PER IV.i) but for the purpose of this book, it makes more sense to call her what he usually calls her: Nature.

160   In *Titus Andronicus*, a general speaks of how the land drinks to renew and revitalize herself. He offers to water her with a constant flow of tears (in the hope that the land will not drink the blood of his children): *"Let my tears stanch the earth's dry appetite; / My sons' sweet blood will make it shame and blush. / O earth, I will befriend thee more with rain / That shall distil from these two ancient urns, / Than youthful April shall with all his show'rs. / In summer's drought I'll drop upon thee still; / In winter with warm tears I'll melt the snow / And keep eternal spring-time on thy face, / So thou refuse to drink my dear sons' blood." (TA III.i, in saying "these two ancient urns" he compares his eyes to water-vessels.)*

161   The Archbishop in *Henry V*, describing a bee colony as a model for human utopia, goes on to describe its system of taxation and law-enforcement: *"The civil citizens lading up the honey, / The poor mechanic porters crowding in / Their heavy burdens at his narrow gate, / The sad-ey'd justice, with his surly hum, / Delivering o'er to executors pale / The lazy yawning drone. I this infer, / That many things, having full reference / To one consent, may work contrariously." (H5 I.ii).*

162   Egan (2006) p. 71

163   Shakespeare presents England as an Edenic paradise. We see the opposite in a description of France being invaded by Henry V, as a French Duke mourns that the war-torn land is becoming barren because all the farmers have been drafted into military service: *"Why that the naked, poor, and mangled Peace, / Dear nurse of arts, plenties, and joyful births, / Should not in this best garden of the world, / Our fertile France, put up her lovely visage? / Alas, she hath from France too long been chas'd! / And all her husbandry doth lie on heaps, / Corrupting in its own fertility. / Her vine, the merry cheerer of the heart, / Unprunèd dies; her hedges even-pleach'd, / Like prisoners wildly overgrown with hair, / Put forth disorder'd twigs; her fallow [fields] / The darnel, hemlock, and rank fumitory, / Doth root upon, while that the [ploughshare] rusts / That should deracinate such savagery." (H5 V.ii)*

164   Diamond (2017) p. 79

165   Barber (1972) p. 146

166   Day (2016) p. 95

167   Day (2016) p. 94. Gary Day notes a parallel between Titania and Hermia (who is threatened with death or nunnery for defying her father's command to marry Demetrius). Both of these women are commanded to make a sacrifice "as a sign of their submission to male power." Oberon threatens the end of natural fertility. Hermia's father threatens the destruction of his own genes–if his only daughter dies or becomes a nun, his family line comes to a bitter end.

168   Does Titania get it on with Bottom? Ultimately, considering the scrawny actresses they always cast in the role–who cares? If a twig does a tumble in the forest, is there a sound? When do we get to see the titan version of Titania? Ditto with Hippolyta–the script promised us a *"bouncing Amazon,"* not a bony anorexic. Now that women can play female roles, I don't understand casting actresses that

are built like twelve-year-old boys.

169   Swann (2000) p. 457

170   Shakespeare's first forest comedy seems to have been *Two Gentlemen of Verona*, in which the exiled nobleman Valentine becomes leader of a bandit gang and his first commandment is that they cease any sexual predation: *"No outrages on silly women."* (TGV IV.i) But then his friend Proteus shows up and attempts to sexually assault Silvia in the woods.

171   In *Titus Andronicus,* Aaron describes a monster called "Fame." Shakespeare will later bring this ill *"Fame"* to life on the stage, as the personified Rumour (described in a stage direction *"painted full of tongues"*) who appears like a Greek chorus introducing *2 Henry IV* with a false report. Shakespeare gets this horrific image from Vergil's *Aeneid*, in which Fame is: "A monstrous phantom, horrible and vast. / As many plumes as raise her lofty flight, / So many piercing eyes inlarge her sight; / Millions of opening mouths to Fame belong, / And ev'ry mouth is furnish'd with a tongue, / And round with list'ning ears the flying plague is hung." (Aeneid IV, Dryden trans. 1697)

172   I'm thinking of *The Rubaiyat of Omar Khayyam*, a supposed collection of Persian poetry translated (or forged) by Edmund FitzGerald. The most famous stanza, as I recall it: "Here with a loaf of bread beneath a bough / A flask of wine, a book of verse, and thou / Beside me singing in the wilderness / And wilderness is paradise enow." ["enow" meaning enough]

173   Tobias, Scott, "Titus," The A.V. Club (26 December 1999), describing Alan Cumming's performance in Julie Taymor's 1999 film *Titus.*

174   Semiramis was a legendary Assyrian queen (or perhaps a goddess like Ishtar who was humanized by historians). Both Aaron and Lavinia compare Tamora to her as a symbol of someone who is exotic and dangerous. In Ovid's *Metamorphoses*, a group of storytelling princesses consider telling her story to pass the time while weaving, but decide not to. Shakespeare may have heard of her from Boccaccio, who reported that she was a femme fatale who seduced men and then murdered them (this must be a remnant of a *Golden Bough*-type priestess whose virginity was annually renewed through human sacrifice). Lisa Starks-Estes suggests that Shakespeare may have been familiar with an obscure legend that Semiramis, abandoned to die in a rocky place, was adopted by doves and then transformed into one (when Tamora's corpse is cast out to rot, Lucius says, *"Let birds on her take pity."* TA V.iii) (Starks-Estes, 2014 p. 87-88)

175   Kahn (1997) p. 55

176   Like the mother in Hitchcock's *Psycho*, Titus wouldn't hurt a fly. When he sees his son has killed one, he says *"How if that fly had a father and mother? / How would he hang his slender gilded wings / And buzz lamenting doings in the air! / Poor harmless fly, / That with his pretty buzzing melody / Came here to make us merry! / And thou hast kill'd him."* (TA III.ii) Then, when the boy compares the fly to 's lover Aaron, Titus commends him for the kill.

177   Starhawk (1989) p. 94

178   Starhawk (1989) p. 22

179   Lavinia in *Titus Andronicus* was named after a heroine from the *Aeneid*, a king's daughter who loved one man but was ordered to marry another, as Lavinia was ordered to marry Saturninus. (Starks-Estes, 2014 p. 88).

180   Silvia in *Two Gentlemen of Verona* is rescued from attempted rape, but she does not speak again in the play.

181   Ovid's story of the rape victim Philomel involves multimedia communication: the rapist cuts out her tongue so she implicates him by weaving a tapestry, then transforms into a nightingale and sings. Lavinia also loses her speech, plus the ability to sew, and so must open a copy of Ovid's *Metamorphoses* with her stumps and then write her attackers' name in sand (as Io, another Ovidian victim transformed into a cow, revealed her true identity by scratching a line and circle in the dirt). Titus gradually learns to "read" and translate Lavinia's sign language, and the book she used to solve the mystery becomes a manual of revenge.

182   Kahn (1997) p. 156

183   Shaughnessy (2011) p. 225

184   Shaughnessy (2011) p. 260. "Womanish" according to the Norton and Oxford editors, some editions have "wolvish."

185   The romance between Coriolanus and Aufudius sparks some of Shakespeare's most florid love poetry: "*AUFIDIUS. O Marcius, Marcius! ...Marcius. Let me twine / Mine arms about that body, where against / My grainèd ash an hundred times hath broke / And scarr'd the moon with splinters; here I clip / The anvil of my sword, and do contest / As hotly and as nobly with thy love / As ever in ambitious strength I did / Contend against thy valour. Know thou first, / I lov'd the maid I married; never man / Sigh'd truer breath; but that I see thee here, / Thou noble thing, more dances my rapt heart / Than when I first my wedded mistress saw / Bestride my threshold.*" (COR IV.v).

186   Kahn (1997) p. 158

187   McCarthy in Barnet (1963) p. 234. Lady Macbeth hears that witches have made predictions about her husband, but she's not superstitious. For Lady Macbeth there is no fate but what we make for ourselves. During the grim finale, Lady Macbeth will be pronounced "*fiend-like,*" meaning possessed by an evil spirit, but the script is remarkably sympathetic toward her. If she were a devil she wouldn't have been driven to madness and suicide by guilt.

188   In his speeches about innocent sleep and bloody hands, Macbeth will paraphrase passages from Seneca's Roman play *Hercules Furens* (The Madness of Hercules) about the Greek hero, driven mad by his stepmother the goddess Juno, murdering his own children. (Martindale, 1994 p. 16, 18).

189   Kerridge in Bruckner (2016) p. 210. Apparently, Julius Caesar was not born by C-section (and there are no medical records from Classical antiquity of any mother surviving a surgical birth).

190   The uprising of Birnam forest in *Macbeth* can be seen as Nature triumphantly overthrowing a tyrant. At least that's more cheerful than saying

the next king, Duncan's son, has mass-murdered the trees and forced them on a zombie march.

191   Samuel Johnson, 1745 quoted in Barnet (1963) p. 158-159

Hecate, Circe, & Medea

192   Shakespeare makes a fool of Joan onstage, but also gives us a glimpse of her from the French perspective, in which she is a goddess, prophetess, and saint, as spoken by Charles the Dauphin (heir apparent to the throne) of France: *"CHARLES. Divinest creature, Astraea's [Justice's] daughter, / How shall I honour thee for this success? / Thy promises are like Adonis' gardens, / That one day bloom'd and fruitful were the next. / France, triumph in thy glorious prophetess... / And all the priests and friars in my realm / Shall in procession sing her endless praise... / No longer on Saint Denis will we cry, / But Joan la Pucelle shall be France's saint."* (1H6 I.vi)

193   Macbeth's two references to Hecate in context: *"Now o'er the one half-world / Nature seems dead, and wicked dreams abuse / The curtain'd sleep; witchcraft celebrates / Pale Hecate's offerings; and wither'd Murther, / Alarum'd by his sentinel, the wolf, / Whose howl's his watch, thus with his stealthy pace, / With Tarquin's* [the rapists's] *ravishing strides, towards his design / Moves like a ghost."* (MAC II.i) *"Ere the bat hath flown / His cloister'd flight, ere to black Hecate's summons / The shard-borne beetle with his drowsy hums / Hath rung night's yawning peal, there shall be done / A deed of dreadful note."* (MAC III.ii) Actually it could be argued neither of these quotes seem to use "Hecate" as a proper name. In the first, Hecate means moon, and in the second, Hecate means night. So, Macbeth does not seem to be talking to/about a deity, and he will never see the character named Hecate.

194   In my research for *Supernatural Shakespeare*, I read and accepted the theory that the Hecate scenes in *Macbeth* may have been copied in from Thomas Middleton's 1610 play *The Witch*. But having spent more time with this, I am less convinced. The meter and rhyme scheme of the Hecate scenes match the Weird Sisters' cadence, and Shakespeare has so many references to Hecate in his writing. The songs "Come Away" and "Black Spirits" in *Macbeth* appear to have been copied in from Middleton's musical, but the Hecate scenes do look like Shakespeare.

195   *Metamorphoses* Book VII (Golding Translation, updated)

196   The legend goes that Absyrtus accompanied Medea and Jason in their escape, but when her father pursued, she hacked her brother into pieces and scattered them on the road, so that the king would have to stop and gather them before resuming the chase.

197   After her famous escape in the flying chariot, the *Metamorphoses* follows Medea's adventures further: she married Theseus' father Aegeus and attempted to poison young Theseus. When this plot was foiled, she jumped into her chariot and escaped again. Although Shakespeare features Theseus in two plays (*A Midsummer Night's Dream* and *The Two Noble Kinsmen*), he does not make this connection.

198   Portia requests a song be played while Bassanio chooses between the three caskets made of gold, silver and lead. The particular song she chooses begins with three lines rhyming with lead: *"Tell me where is fancy bred, / Or in the heart or in the head, / How begot, how nourishèd?"* and then, in case he's missed the hint, the song ends with lines about ringing a leaden bell: *"Let us all ring fancy's knell: / I'll begin it – Ding, dong, bell."* (MOV III.ii).

199   Bassanio gave the ring to the lawyer for saving Antonio's life, and the play contains a clear theme of Antonio's homoerotic attachment to Bassanio. So having betrayed his wife to save his bosom buddy, Bassanio must then stand by as Antonio offers to sacrifice himself to make up for the loss of the ring: *"I once did lend my body for his wealth... / I dare be bound again, / my soul upon the forfeit, that your lord / will never more break faith advisedly."* (MOV V.i) Antonio swears to get out of Portia's way. And thank you Elizabeth Truax for numerous parallels between Portia and Medea (Truax, 1993 p. 187-192).

200   Bate (1993) p. 200

201   Bate (1993) p. 250

202   Ovid's Medea referred to "gods" of the hills, but Golding substituted English elves, and Shakespeare followed. But later, when Golding mentions unspecified "trees," Shakespeare refers back to the Latin original to restore the specific oak. (Bate in Nims, 2000 p. xlii).

203   Lyne in Taylor (2006) p. 159

204   Hughes (1992) p. 434. There is a theory that Sycorax's "strange name may be derived from one of the epithets for Medea, 'Scythian raven' ('Sy-', as prefix, 'korax' meaning raven, a bird with which Sycorax is associated in Caliban's first speech)." (Bate, 1993 p. 254).

Egypt

205   Plutarch, *Life of Marcus Antonius* (XXVI), Thomas North's 1579 Translation

206   Dave Gahan hasn't played Antony onstage, except to the extent that so many Depeche Mode songs would be perfect for an *Antony and Cleopatra* musical. Obviously "In Your Room" and "The Sweetest Condition" and "In Chains," the list goes on. James Purefoy was such an amazing Antony in HBO's *Rome* series, and he looks so much like Dave Gahan that I kept expecting him to sing "Rush." (All songs listed here were written by Martin L. Gore)

207   Shakespeare does not seem to have taken the Egyptian goddess Isis very seriously. She is named eight times in the script, five of which are Cleopatra's servant Charmian saying catty things about people she doesn't like (and a sixth reference is Charmian's fellow servant Iras agreeing with her) (A&C I.ii, III.iii). Cleopatra only uses the goddess' name once when swearing by Isis that she will bloody Charmian's teeth, so she might just be playing on her friend's faith (A&C III.iii, Cleopatra twice names the Roman goddess Juno, III.xi and IV.xv). And Caesar dismissively says that Cleopatra hosted a political rally dressed as Isis (A&C III.vi). Elements of Cleopatra's grand

barge entrance could be linked with Isis imagery, particularly from *The Metamorphoses of Apuleius* (but here we should note again that this was written by a Roman, not an Egyptian). Likewise, elements of Cleopatra's death tableau could perhaps be linked with representations of Isis, but it doesn't really seem as though Shakespeare had done any research on the Egyptian goddess. Furthermore, if Shakespeare had been familiar with Egyptian texts about Isis, he would presumably have poetically presented Antony as Osiris, her lover, who was dismembered and reassembled. Instead, the play contains metaphors of Antony melting and evaporating.

208   Apuleius, translated by William Adlington 1566, spelling somewhat modernized.

209   Paglia (1990) p. 223

210   Bloom (1998) p. 560

211   Paglia (1990) p. 213

212   Frye (1986) p. 123

213   Kott (1974) p. 171

214   Kott (1974) p. 172-173

215   Imperial propaganda celebrating the greatness of deified Caesar Augustus would take many forms, including a genre of text (speeches and poems) called "Gospel," meaning the "Good News." And the elevated vocabulary of Gospels written for Augustus would then be appropriated by early Christianity and applied to one of Rome's victims, Jesus. In this sense, Caesar's deification as world-savior after the Battle of Actium prepared the way of the Word in Christianity. This topic is explored in my book *Words (Between the Lines of Age)*.

216   Cleopatra is always accompanied by two maidservants (and usually by a eunuch as well) so we get the sense that even her "private" performances have some exhibitionism about them.

217   Nims (2000) p. 17, English updated.

218   In Antony's speech about Egyptian farming and crocodiles, Shakespeare refers to the first and last books of Ovid's *Metamorphoses*, the alpha and omega, so to speak. Ovid himself was about twelve years old when Augustus beat Antony at Actium, the *Metamorphoses* would not come out until about forty years later. But it's interesting to consider what young Ovid might have thought about the Cleopatra soap opera that ran through his formative years and if it might have influenced his idea of Egypt as a place of spontaneous generation.

219   Shaughnessy (2011) p. 261

220   Julius Caesar's fellow Triumvir Marcus Licinius Crassus apparently died this way: his lust for gold was so great that the Parthians poured molten gold into his mouth (and his name "Crassus" apparently survived in the word "crass," meaning unrefined)

221   Caesar's misty-eyed recollection of Antony's wartime diet is one of the play's great comical moments. "*CAESAR. Antony, / Leave thy lascivious wassails* [drinking parties]. *When thou once / Was beaten from Modena, where thou slew'st / Hirtius and Pansa, consuls, at thy heel / Did famine follow; whom thou fought'st*

against, / Though daintily brought up, with patience more / Than savages could suffer. Thou didst drink / The stale of horses and the gilded puddle / Which beasts would cough at. Thy palate then did deign / The roughest berry on the rudest hedge; / Yea, like the stag when snow the pasture sheets, / The barks of trees thou brows'd. On the Alps / It is reported thou didst eat strange flesh, / Which some did die to look on. And all this- / It wounds thine honour that I speak it now- / Was borne so like a soldier that thy cheek / So much as lank'd not." (A&C I.iv)

222   On the topic of Antony and Cleopatra swapping costumes, there is some speculation that the first scene contains a reference to Antony metaphorically castrating himself by dressing in drag: *"PHILO. Sir, sometimes, when he is not Antony, / He comes too short of that great property / Which still should go with Antony."* (A&C I.i)

223   Hughes (1992) p. 316

ℜisen Heroines

224   Bloom (1998) p. 549

225   In the middle of ., Caesar will establish a brotherly bond by giving Antony his sister Octavia in marriage, creating a momentary illusion that she could play referee between them (it doesn't play out that way). And Antony will challenge Caesar to a drinking contest, but Caesar wisely declines to meet his rival in this particular arena.

226   In his rivalry with Caesar, Antony fears that Cleopatra has made a separate peace, stacking the deck, *"Pack'd cards with Caesar, and false-play'd my glory / Unto an enemy's triumph."* But a servant enters with news of her suicide: *"No, Antony; my mistress lov'd thee, and her fortunes mingled with thine entirely."* (A&C IV.xiv) Of course, this report of her death is greatly exaggerated, Cleopatra has dispatched this news to send Antony on a guilt trip, from which she fully expects him to return refreshed. Like Juliet she hides in a tomb, and like Romeo, he kills himself. But unlike Romeo, Antony is too tough to die, and spends a few scenes bleeding out.

227   Antony enlists his lackey to assist with his suicide. But good help is hard to find, and Antony's intern Eros evades by stabbing himself, *"Thus do I escape the sorrow / of Antony's death."* Cue the kazoo music and slapstick comedy of Antony's zany final hours.

228   There's a fascinating inversion of a Mesopotamian myth: As Inanna/Ishtar descended into the underworld she passed through seven gates, and at each one she had to remove an article of jewelry or clothing (symbolic of authority), and as Cleopatra prepares for her suicide she gets dressed up in adornments of authority.

229   Frye (1986) p. 128

230   Kahn (1997) p. 138

231   Hughes (1992) p. 320

232   Kott (1974) p. 177

233   Bloom (1998) p. 547, 556

234   The name "Bergomask" comes from the Northern Italian town of

Bergamo, but this is probably just a foreign name given to an English folkdance, like relating the Morris Dance to the Spanish *Morisco*. Both dances were known to be silly and sexy, and naming them after exotic locations seems to have been a means of easing stiff English inhibitions.

235   In *Much Ado About Nothing*, Claudio accuses Hero, not only of being promiscuous, but of being a shapeshifter: *"You seem to me as Dian in her orb, / As chaste as is the bud ere it be blown; / But you are more intemperate in your blood / Than Venus, or those pamper'd animals / That rage in savage sensuality."* (MAAN IV.i) He accused her of being a whore disguised as a virgin, and even an old crone, a *"rotten orange"* (while his poetry transforms her from a blossom to a beast). Claudio and Don Pedro conduct their accusation of Hero like an Inquisition, they will accept no testimony or evidence that disagrees with their suit, and they justify this public abuse with the rationale that they're doing it for the defense of public morality. (Ornstein, 1986 p. 132, 134)

236   The Friar (Francis) in *Much Ado About Nothing* is not really the same Friar (Lawrence) from *Romeo and Juliet*. But it doesn't seem a coincidence that both of these friars come up with the same plan, especially when we recall that the Friar in *Measure for Measure* also fakes someone's death to solve a problem (actually, the Duke disguised as a Friar, and in this case he fakes the death of a male character named Claudio). Shakespeare's repeated use of the benevolent yet devious Friar is additionally interesting because the Franciscan monks had been chased out of England (*Romeo* and *Much Ado* take place in Italy, *Measure* is set in Austria). But in Shakespeare's time there were still folk festival traditions in which a local drunk dressed as a friar could help young people to escape from arranged marriages. The custom of the festival Friar or "Friar Tuck" is explored in the companion volume to this book, *Supernatural Shakespeare*.

237   It could be argued that Hero's (feigned) resurrection rescues Claudio from an annual journey to the underworld (he vows to sing to the tomb each year). Then, in *Measure for Measure*, Isabella descends into the dungeon underworld to visit her brother Claudio, who will be rescued in the end. The recurrence of the name does not seem to be a coincidence. Shakespeare's other famous Claude was Claudius in *Hamlet*, whose descent into the underworld (praying in the crypt) temporarily saves him from Hamlet. Chronologically placing *Hamlet* between *Much Ado About Nothing* and *Measure for Measure* is slightly complicated by Harold Bloom's convincing theory that Shakespeare wrote *Hamlet* early in his career, then significantly rewrote it in his middle period. There's also room for debate about adding Cloten from *Cymbeline* to the list of Claudes—he dies wearing Posthumus Leonatus' clothing, gets buried (his decapitated cadaver convinces Imogen that her husband Posthumus is dead) and then Posthumus is released from a subterranean dungeon and reunites with Imogen. That's a bit tangled, but there's a possible connection. On the topic of recurring male names associated with underworld journeys, it's also worth noting the multiple variations on the name Leon. In *Much Ado About Nothing*, Hero's father Leonato joins in her humiliation, then

assists with the plan of her restoration. An assassin named Leonine will agree to murder Marina in *Pericles* but will then stand by as she is kidnapped by pirates and sold into a brothel underworld; Leonine is a minor role. Leonato will return in *Cymbeline* as Posthumus Leonatus, who also accepts a false report about the fidelity of his bride Imogen (he gets imprisoned, she gets buried, in the end they're reunited), and then king Leontes in *The Winter's Tale* will jealously send his wife to a dungeon, she'll be reported dead, and will then arise sixteen years later. The repeated use of the name "Leon" might have been inspired by the lion, so-called king of the forest, but notoriously jealous and insecure (an alpha lion as the pack's sole sire must constantly be on guard against the lionesses being impregnated by his usurping brothers. Ironically there's something very Shakespearean about the social organization of a lion pack). Shakespeare also created three connected characters named Antonio: the titular merchant in *Merchant of Venice* whose wealth is (supposedly) lost at sea, resulting in his imprisonment. The pirate in *Twelfth Night* who is temporarily imprisoned. And Prospero's brother Antonio in *The Tempest*, who gets shipwrecked and detained in Prospero's island penal colony. My personal theory is that William Shakespeare may have played these three Antonios himself, since these were the sort of minor roles he could play onstage. The first two bear a certain resemblance to the voice of the Sonnets (homoerotically connected to a youth, Bassiano/Sebastian) and the third mirrors Prospero (and in a sense gets absorbed into Prospero at the end of the play). Of course, Shakespeare's most famous Antonio was the hero of *Julius Caesar* and *Antony and Cleopatra*. I don't include him in this pattern because obviously Shakespeare didn't get to make up a name for him (although he does fit in with the others–he loses a major battle at sea and descends into a tomb to be reunited with Cleopatra before his death. Perhaps he inspired Shakespeare's repeated use of the name Antony).

238   Bloom (1998) p. 196

239   Ornstein (1986) p. 176

240   In *All's Well That Ends Well*, after castigating the goddesses, Helena will later mutter a prayer to Diana and Cupid, when she claims Bertram as her prize for healing the king: *"Now, Dian, from thy altar do I fly, / And to imperial Love, that god most high, / Do my sighs stream."* (AWTEW II.iii) But she is premature in abjuring the virgin goddess Diana: Bertram will rabbit away from their wedding night, and Helena will become like the virgin huntress Diana in pursuit of him.

241   In *Measure for Measure*, while awaiting execution, Isabella's brother Claudio describes the horrors of the Shakespearean afterlife: *"Death is a fearful thing... / Ay, but to die, and go we know not where; / To lie in cold obstruction, and to rot; / This sensible warm motion to become / A kneaded clod; and the delighted spirit / To bathe in fiery floods or to reside / In thrilling region of thick-ribbèd ice; / To be imprison'd in the viewless winds, / And blown with restless violence round about / The pendent world; or to be worse than worst / Of those that lawless and incertain thought / Imagine howling - 'tis too horrible. / The weariest and most loathed worldly life / That age, ache, penury, and imprisonment, / Can lay on nature is a paradise / To what we*

fear of death." (MFM III.ii)

242   Shakespeare's *Cymbeline* contains numerous twists on the theme of a descent into a tomb. The heroine Imogen is so chaste that her banished husband *"spake of her as* [if] *Dian had hot dreams / And she alone were cold."* So, a traveler lures him into a bet that this paragon can easily be seduced. The tourist is appropriately named Iachimo, essentially "mini-Iago," and after failing to seduce Imogen he plays an impish trick, hiding in a trunk in her bedroom and emerging while she sleeps. Iachimo observes that she is in a deathlike slumber, and her bedchamber is like a tomb: *"O Sleep, thou* [copy] *of death, lie dull upon her* [like] *a monument / Thus in a chapel lying."* He doesn't hurt Imogen, but rather gathers enough circumstantial evidence to prove that he has entered her bedchamber and seen her nakedness. Shakespeare will link this voyeurism to the myth of Diana and Actaeon with Iachimo's report that the chimney is decorated with an image of *"chaste Dian bathing."* (CYM II.iv) Iachimo also takes note of the open copy of Ovid's *Metamorphoses* on her bedside table: *"She hath been reading late / The tale of Tereus; here the leaf's turn'd down / Where Philomel gave up."* (CYM II.ii) We may recall that, early in Shakespeare's career, the muted heroine Lavinia used Ovid's tale of Tereus raping Philomel to reveal a sex crime in *Titus Andronicus*. Tereus silenced Philomel by cutting out her tongue, and by spying on Imogen in her sleep, Iachimo will deprive her of the ability to argue her innocence. Ironically, Imogen has been reading Ovid's *Metamorphoses* for advice on how to avoid sexual violence, and Iachimo has been reading Ovid's *Fasti* (or Shakespeare's own poem *The Rape of Lucrece*) for advice on how to obtain carnal knowledge without punishment. Iachimo returns to successfully slander Imogen, launching her jealous husband into an *Othello*-esque rage. As the play goes on, Imogen will descend to the underworld again (having been lightly poisoned and buried, she'll awaken and emerge) and will assist in getting her husband released from an underground prison. Finally, she will assist in getting a public confession from Iachimo.

Flora & Proserpina

243   Munroe in Bruckner (2016) p. 145

244   The royal marriage of Leontes and Hermione was part of a deal between Sicily and Russia. This doesn't make much sense, because Shakespeare changed the kingdoms. In the source story, Leontes was Pandosto, king of Bohemia (part of the present day Czech Republic), and married the princess of nearby Russia, then accused her of having an affair with the king of Sicily. But Shakespeare makes Leontes the king of Sicily and Polixenes the king of Bohemia, which creates the comic error of giving landlocked Bohemia a seacoast.

245   Hughes (1992) p. 373

246   Ovid's *Metamorphoses* Book 1 (Translated by Brookes More, 1949).

247   Roberts (1991) p. 83. Jonathan Bate points out that the onstage bear in *Winter's Tale* would also have reminded educated audience members of Callisto, whose story was told in the second book of Ovid's *Metamorphoses*. Callisto was

one of Diana's virgin huntresses, who had the misfortune of being noticed by Jupiter. So, he disguised himself as Diana and raped her. Then, as Diana bathed with her acolytes, she noticed the bulge of Callisto's pregnancy and banished her. Callisto bears a son, Arcas, and then Jupiter's jealous wife, Juno (goddess of blaming-the-victim) transforms Callisto into a bear, and her son is adopted by a huntress, becoming a great hunter himself. Sixteen years later he encounters his mother the bear, and just as he is to about kill her, Jupiter transforms them both into constellations: Ursa Major and Ursa Minor. This is how Callisto winds up on the cover of a Third Eye Blind album. Jonathan Bate writes, "For Shakespeare and those members of his audience who knew their Ovid, a bear would have been more than just a bear–it would have brought with it a narrative that is characterized by destructive sexuality, disguise, abuse of an innocent woman, wrongful accusation, jealousy, and revenge." (Bate, 1993 p. 227) *Like The Winter's Tale.*

248   Though eternally virginal, Artemis/Diana was known to be the overseer of childbirth and guardian of new mothers, and her Greek name "Artemis" may have been linguistically linked with "arktos," the Greek word for bear. (Steffes, 2003 p. 38) No pun on childbearing is necessary here. At an ancient Greek initiation ritual at Brauron, Athenian girls would dance dressed as bears for Artemis, the bear an apparent symbol of "wild" femaleness that must be tamed in the transition to maturity and matrimony.

249   Holland (1970) p. 34

250   "Time" is a capitalized proper name in Sonnets 12, 15, 16, 19, 60, 63, 64, 65, 77, 100, 116, 123, and 126, but is also personified in others. Jan Kott wrote "*The Sonnets* can be interpreted as a drama. They have action and heroes. The action consists of lyrical sequences which slowly mount to a tragedy. There are three characters: a man, a youth, and a woman. This trio exhausts all forms of love and goes through all its stages. The three exhaust all variants and forms of faithlessness, all kinds of relationships, including love, friendship, jealousy. They go through the heaven and hell of love. [Although] another epithet would be more apt here: the characters go through Eden and through Sodom. The fourth character of the drama is Time. Time which destroys and devours everything. Greedy Time which has been compared to gaping jaws. It devours the fruits of human labour and man himself." (Kott, 1974 p. 238)

251   It's worth noting (or at least footnoting) here that Shakespeare in the *Sonnets* has such great anxiety about Time draining away a person's youth and vigor. But in the *Winter's Tale* finale, when Leontes sees the statue of Hermione (made sixteen years after her death) he is comforted to see that the sculptor has not endowed her with eternal youth, but adjusted her appearance to show what she would have looked like in middle age. Perhaps the softened, senile demeanor of Time in the middle of the play is indicative of an acceptance of natural aging.

252   Autolycus sings of a roll in the hay with his "aunts," probably not his parents' sisters, more likely some looser sense of the word, meaning mature maidens. On the other hand, if we read Autolycus as a son of Mercury, his mythical aunts would include the Muses, the Fates, and the Nymphs. It's fascinating that the satyr-like Autolycus does not participate in the Dance of Satyrs. He is offstage at the time, and he's not

a herder, so doesn't fit into any of the categories listed: *"There is three carters, three shepherds, three neat-herds, three swineherds, that have made themselves all men of hair; they call themselves Saltiers, and they have dance which the wenches say is a gallimaufry of gambols, because they are not in't; but they themselves are o' th' mind, if it be not too rough for some that know little but bowling, it will please plentifully."* (WT IV.iv) The women are indignant at not being allowed to participate. If we were going to speculate that Autolycus' "aunts" were supernatural, they would probably be the Nymphs, forest-dwelling acolytes of Diana, who were generally associated with spring, but appear dancing with autumn reapers in *The Tempest* (IV.i), symbolic of the abolition of winter.

253   Autolycus has quite a résumé: *"I know this man well; he hath been since an ape-bearer; then a process-server, a bailiff; then he compass'd a motion of the Prodigal Son, and married a tinker's wife within a mile where my land and living lies; and, having flown over many knavish professions, he settled only in rogue. Some call him Autolycus... He haunts wakes, fairs, and bear-baitings."* (WT IV.iii) We'll next see him as a salesman, and by the end of the play he'll be a courtier again.

254   Although Mercury (whom the Greeks called Hermes) is important in *The Winter's Tale*, it appears to be a coincidence that Hermione is named after him. The name Hermione can mean "messenger" or apparently "stone" (like the roadside Herm-stones at which Hermes was worshiped). Shakespeare may have chosen the name because Hermione will turn to stone and back again. Or he may have named her after the daughter of Menelaus and Helen of Sparta, to remind us of the famous scandal that sparked the Trojan War. There are even some very obscure myths in which Helen turned out to be innocent of the affair with Paris of Troy (myths which formed the basis of Euripides's play, *Helen*), but it's unlikely Shakespeare would have heard of this.

255   Holland (1970) p. 36

256   Bryant (1963) p. 396

257   Jerry Bryant wrote: "Leontes betrays the obligations of a good king. He becomes cruel and peremptory. He refuses the counsel of his nobles. He commits himself, without moderation, to his own passion. The results of this are serious... A ruler who treats the truth as something of his own making must eventually unhinge his state. The repercussions of his irresponsible suspicions, so firm in his mind that they create a world in which he actually sees and feels, are potentially cataclysmic. An apprehension of what is and what should be are principle requirements for the good ruler; Leontes attempts to shape reality to his own fantasies." (Bryant, 1963 p. 395) This quote from sixty years ago is eerily oracular in this age of mad kings, fake news, and climate crisis.

258   Quoted in Bate (1993) p. 229, English updated.

259   Florizel's constellation of disguised divinities comes from the sixth book of Ovid's *Metamorphoses*, in which Arachne the weaver created a tabloid tapestry of shapeshifting rapists. The image was so satirical and pornographic that the goddess Minerva destroyed it and then transformed Arachne into a spider.

260   Bate (1993) p. 230. In comparing Florizel to Apollo, Shakespeare also (perhaps unknowingly) stumbles onto something: Apollo's stint as a shepherd

comes up in Euripides' play *Alcestis*, in which a good wife dies, her husband declares he'll have a lifelike statue of her installed in his bed, and then she comes back to life. This will bear a certain resemblance to the last scene in *The Winter's Tale*.

261   With *"Flora peering in April's front"* Shakespeare makes an inside reference to *Sonnet 102*, about a love that was chirpy at the start (in its springtime) and has grown quieter since (in its summer) but is no less alive. *"As Philomel* [the nightingale] *in summer's front doth sing, / And stops her pipe in growth of riper days."* In addition to likening Perdita to the goddess Flora, Florizel is saying that his love for her has not dimmed since they met in spring.

262   Ovid's *Fasti*, Book V (Translated by Sir James G. Frazer, 1931). In Ovid's writings, the victims of sexual violence are usually traumatized into silence, or transformed into animals, minerals, or vegetables (and gods don't generally marry their victims). So, Flora is remarkable as an Ovidian survivor who is talkative and well adjusted, at least by Ovid's report. And apparently Flora's Roman holiday festival the *Floralia* (celebrated from late April to early May) was quite wild and licentious, celebrated with wine, human pollination, and nude prostitutes performing mock gladiatorial combat.

263   Perdita's foster brother, the Clown, reads off his shopping list in Act IV, Scene iii, including currants, prunes, raisins, nutmeg and ginger. Cakes of pressed dried fruits have long been associated with goddess worship. They were mentioned by the Biblical prophet . as a symbol of Israel's infidelity to God: "The Lord said to me again, 'Go, love a woman who has a lover and is an adulteress, just as the Lord loves the people of Israel, though they turn to other gods and love raisin cakes.'" (Hosea 3:1, NRSV) Hosea lived nearly three thousand years ago, and he's referring to older traditions of dying-rising fertility goddesses and their consorts (raisin cakes also seem to have been associated with the Babylonian goddess Ishtar). Shakespeare inherits this raisin-cake thing from Greene and from his own knowledge of rural tradition, and it's doubtful he was thinking about the goddess associations. But it's nonetheless an interesting connection with goddesses and resurrection.

264   The topic of Art vs. Nature will be reprised in the final scene, when Leontes and Perdita are invited to see a lifelike statue of Hermione. When Leontes sees that the statue looks sixteen years older than Hermione did at the time of her (supposed) death, he will realize that an artist's ability to freeze time in statuary is inferior to beauty of the natural aging process. Meanwhile his attempts to touch the statue (which would reveal that she is natural and alive) will be blocked by a warning that the paint on the statue is not yet dry: "art" will get in the way of reunion with "nature." But finally, Hermione the work of art will reveal herself to be a work of nature.

265   Snodgrass, from *Supernatural Shakespeare*, indebted to Sharon A. Kelley.

266   Phoebus is another name for Apollo, god of poetry and the sun. But Apollo is named thirteen times in this play, and figures significantly in its

action, whereas this single reference to "Phoebus" only means the sun. In all of Shakespeare's references to Phoebus, I don't see any that indicate Shakespeare considered this an alternate name for Apollo (except one reference to "Phoebus' lute" in Sonnet 6 of *The Passionate Pilgrim*, which seems to be by another author). So, this name-drop seems unconnected to the Apollonian theme of the play. With that said, bright Phoebus in this speech makes a good contrast to Dis, god of the dark underworld. Later, the fulfillment of the Apollonian oracle will rescue Perdita from dying disfigured and unwed in the underworld of Polixenes's dungeon. So, an Apollo reference would have been appropriate here.

267   Nuttall in Taylor (2006) p. 136, see also Bate (1993) p. 231

268   Minerva was the Roman name for the Greek Athena, goddess of wisdom and war. She is only named twice in Shakespeare's works: once as a symbol of how physical beauty is an indication of wisdom (TOS I.i) and once as the *"straight-pight Minerva"* (meaning upright in posture, CYM V.v). Shakespeare also wrote a nameless reference to the *"fire-eyed maid of smoky war,"* (1H4 IV.i) and Minerva was known to have smoke-gray eyes, but this is more likely a reference to the war-goddess Bellona, whom Shakespeare named in *Macbeth* and *The Two Noble Kinsmen* (it seems Shakespeare was familiar with Minerva as a goddess of wisdom, but not of warfare).

269   Vaughan (2020) p. 199, Bate (1993) p. 232

270   Shakespeare considered winter to be unnatural, a curse upon humanity for the crime of lust in Eden, and the Persephone myth also blames winter on a crime of passion. Perdita's wish that she could hand out the flowers of spring in midsummer is a wish that the primal crime could be forgiven and winter abolished. The desire for summer to be followed by spring is also expressed by Cleopatra (*"For his bounty, / There was no winter in't; an autumn 'twas / That grew the more by reaping."* A&C V.ii) and during the goddess pageant in *The Tempest* (*"Spring come to you at the farthest. / In the very end of harvest."* TEM IV.i, and we may note that this blessing is conditional on Miranda and Ferdinand overcoming premarital lust.)

271   To an exploration of Shakespeare's latter-year pursuit of Persephone we should add Proserpina as Prospero in *The Tempest*, exiled to a hellish island, and how he uses his daughter's virginity to get rescued and restored as Duke of Milan. Miranda herself narrowly escapes abduction by Caliban, and her engagement to Ferdinand is celebrated with a phantasm pageant featuring Proserpina's mother Ceres. Or a darker reading of *the Tempest* would cast Prospero himself in the role of Hades, dragging Miranda-as-Persephone into the underworld, and then she re-emerges through springtime love for Ferdinand.

272   Ornstein (1986) p. 231. The fifth act of *The Winter's Tale* opens with a summary of Leontes' last sixteen years, filled with language of Christian penance: *"CLEOMENES. Sir, you have done enough, and have perform'd / A saint-like sorrow. No fault could you make / Which you have not redeem'd; indeed, paid down / More penitence than done trespass. At the last, / Do as the heavens have done: forget your evil;*

/ With them forgive yourself." (WT V.i)

273　Shakespeare spares Perdita the further peril of the source novel *Pandosto,* where the king attempts to rape his unknown daughter, then kills himself. Leontes takes one incestuous glance and Paulina blocks him.

274　Seeing a statue come to life onstage may call to mind the myth of Pygmalion, who fell in love with a statue he'd carved, and then Venus brought it to life. Shakespeare would have known this story from the tenth book of Ovid's *Metamorphoses.* But the Pygmalion story shares only a few superficial details with this scene, and not much that will deepen our thematic understanding of it.

275　Nuttall in Taylor (2006) p. 137

276　Shakespeare distracts us from the many dizzying plot-twists at the end of *Winter's Tale* with something that seems totally willy-nilly. As icing on the wedding cake, Leontes declares that Paulina (widow of the bear-brunch Antigonus) will be married to his on-again-off-again henchman Camillo. And the curtain falls before anyone can ask why. Freed from wedlock, the widowed Paulina has attained great power and authority as a priestess of the virgin-mother and assumed a maternal influence over the immature king. Leontes has reverted to childhood, but now regains his manhood and will re-marry his wife, so he must sever the connection with his foster mother. Her high priestess power is dissolved and she is re-integrated into the patriarchal world, as Shakespeare had previously done with the Abbess in *Comedy of Errors* and the priestess of Diana in *Pericles.*

Juno, Ceres, & Iris

277　Shakespeare approached women and wilderness with neurotic anxiety, in both his plays and his business dealings. Remember, he was a country boy whose marriage was clouded by some scandal (he married an older woman who gave birth six months after the wedding), and he abandoned the country to seek his fortune in the city. But then he invested his theatrical earnings as a land baron, consolidating lands to grow grain, driving up prices through unscrupulous swindles (which repeatedly landed him in court; he would pay a fine and then do it again). It seems his long-con goal was to buy his way into the gentry, passing the Shakespeare name and lands to sons. But neither his son nor his grandsons survived. Meanwhile, we can see Shakespeare's obvious anxiety about marrying off his daughters in the way he frets about premarital chastity and legitimacy throughout his career.

278　Roberts (1991) p. 18

279　*Hamlet, Othello,* and *King Lear* are Shakespeare's most *famous* misogynist plays. But *Troilus and Cressida* is absolutely rancid, and his masterpiece of misogyny must be *Timon of Athens,* which contains no females at all except for a chorus-line of dancers dressed as Amazons (fearsome, powerful women reduced to paid erotic dancers) and a single brief scene with a pair of prostitutes, whom Timon encourages to infect all Athens with syphilis. Linda Woodbridge wrote of Shakespeare's "campaign to leave no women alive onstage at a tragedy's end."

Except in some Roman plays, Shakespeare kills off every woman prominent enough to have appeared in a tragedy's last scene: Lavinia, Tamora, Portia [in *Julius Caesar*], Ophelia, Gertrude, Desdemona, Emilia, Ladies Macbeth and Macduff, all three daughters in *Lear* (a play with no other women). Most of these deaths are ill-prepared for and thinly explained. Shakespeare identifies women with fertility (one reason their roles are central in comedy); his destroying them in tragedy stresses the triumph of sterility." (Woodbridge, 1994 p. 177)

280   Roberts (1991) p. 18

281   There are many perspectives on Dido in *The Tempest*. No sooner has the king's party landed than a debate breaks out about Aeneas and Dido (the name Dido is used six times in a single scene, TEM II.i). The cynical Sebastian and Antonio know the familiar story from the *Aeneid* in which Dido was seduced and abandoned by Aeneas and then committed suicide in shame. The wise Gonzalo calls her the *"widow Dido,"* referring to another mythic tradition in which the widowed Dido remained faithful to her first husband and committed suicide to evade remarriage to a local Carthaginian king. In this version of the story, it is argued that Dido was slandered in the *Aeneid*, and never slept with Aeneas.

282   Prospero's goddess pageant will follow the basic structure of a court masque. The court masque was one of King James' favorite entertainments, a skit in which chaotic pairs of opposites progress from discord to harmony under the wise supervision of royalty. The King's Men (the troupe in which Shakespeare was involved) had participated in several of these, some written by Ben Jonson, featuring Juno the queen of Olympus and her messenger Iris.

283   Ovid's *Metamorphoses* Book 14, Golding Translation in Nims, ed. (2000) p. 376 (English Updated)

284   Nymphs wearing *"chaste crowns"* is a reference to floral wreathes that maidens would wear as crowns at spring and summer festivals. Ophelia in *Hamlet* wears one, and Perdita in *The Winter's Tale* probably wears one too when she plays Flora in the sheepshearing festival. The wreath as a symbol of chastity may explain the mysterious lines that follow: *"and thy broom groves, / Whose shadow the dismissèd bachelor loves, / Being lass-lorn"* (TEM IV.i). This may mean that the maidens' chastity frustrates young suitors who go sulking off into the weeds.

285   Shakespeare mentioned Hymen in eight plays: *Titus Andronicus; Much Ado About Nothing; As You Like It* (including a physical appearance); *Hamlet; Timon of Athens; Pericles, Prince of Tyre; The Tempest;* and *The Two Noble Kinsmen* (including another brief cameo appearance)

286   Dido's seduction of Aeneas is narrated in the *Aeneid:* "The queen and prince, as love or fortune guides, One common cavern in her bosom hides. Then first the trembling earth the signal gave, And flashing fires enlighten all the cave; Hell from below, and Juno from above, And howling nymphs, were conscious of their love. From this ill-omen'd hour in time arose Debate and death, and all succeeding woes. The queen, whom sense of honor could not move, No longer made a secret of her love, But call'd it marriage, by that specious name To veil the

crime and sanctify the shame." (Aeneid IV, Dryden trans. 1697)

287   *(Enter certain REAPERS, properly habited; they join with the NYMPHS in a graceful dance; towards the end whereof PROSPERO starts suddenly, and speaks, after which, to a strange, hollow, and noise, they heavily vanish.)* (TEM IV.i) The masque is interrupted when Prospero remembers that Caliban, who once attempted to rape Miranda, has entered into a plot with the drunken butler Stephano to murder Prospero in his sleep and then sexually assault his daughter. In Prospero's fantasy puppet show, lust (in the forms of Venus and Cupid) has been banished from the world, but the wizard then remembers it still exists on the island and must be punished.

288   Robert Ornstein observes that Prospero's "quirks of personality—an irritability and readiness to hector those about him—are understandable in one who is growing old without the company of men and women his own age." (Ornstein, 1986 p. 238) Instead of attaining enlightenment, Prospero is developmentally stunted. When this poor guy returns to Milan, he'll be surrounded by people who have evolved and developed during his ten-year absence, and they will no doubt wonder why he's so stuck in his ways. No wonder he predicts that he'll long for death.

Conclusion

289   Women laugh at Berowne's worship in Love's Labour's Lost. Really Berowne should know better. He's already been mocking his friends for idolizing women: *"LONGAVILLE. A woman I forswore; but I will prove, / Thou being a goddess, I forswore not thee: / My vow was earthly, thou a heavenly love; / Thy grace being gain'd cures all disgrace in me... / BEROWNE. This is the liver-vein, which makes flesh a deity, a green goose a goddess - pure, pure idolatry. God amend us, God amend! / ...DUMAIN. O most divine Kate!...By heaven, the wonder in a mortal eye! / BEROWNE. By earth, she is not, corporal: there you lie." (LLL IV.iii)*

290   As noted earlier, *Love's Labour's Lost* is Shakespeare's only comedy that does not end in weddings: for the crime of deifying these maidens, the suitors are banished to live like monks for a year. There is an irony here that they will thus become monastic votaries of these maidens-as-goddesses. It's hard to imagine that a year of stewing in their own fantasy-construct juices will cure them of unrealistic idealization.

291   Romeo's come-on line is a bit corny, but we've got to hand it to Shakespeare: Romeo's first words to Juliet describe their final scene in the holy shrine (tomb) when she has been (temporarily) transformed into a stone-cold statue of herself, and his lips *"seal with a righteous kiss"* before he dies. (R&J V.iii)

292   During the *Tempest* reunion finale, when king Alonso is reunited with his son Ferdinand, he asks if Miranda is the goddess of the island. But Ferdinand affirms that she is human. *"ALONSO. What is this maid? ...Is she the goddess that hath sever'd us, / And brought us thus together? / FERDINAND. Sir, she is mortal; / But by immortal Providence she's mine." (TEM V.i)*

293   In *All's Well That Ends Well*, Bertram compares the maiden Diana to both a goddess and a monument. But Diana sees through this pickup line (which combines cheap, sleazy, and cheesy). *"BERTRAM. They told me that your name was Fontibell. / DIANA. No, my good lord, Diana. / BERTRAM. Titled goddess; / And worth it, with addition! But, fair soul, / In your fine frame hath love no quality? / If the quick fire of youth light not your mind, / You are no maiden, but a monument; / When you are dead, you should be such a one / As you are now, for you are cold and stern; / And now you should be as your mother was / When your sweet self was got... / DIANA. Ay, so you serve us / Till we serve you; but when you have our roses / You barely leave our thorns to prick ourselves."* *(AWTEW IV.ii)*

294   Cleopatra may seem like an obvious exception to this pattern of Shakespearean women rejecting deification, but she rejects all kinds of classification. She's a heroine but not a maiden, and she's comfortable with adoration because in Egypt she's considered a living divinity.

295   Ornstein (1986) p. 18

296   While the names of God were being banished from the English stage, gloomy Protestant and Puritan Christianities were whitewashing over colorful murals, smashing stained-glass windows, and slamming the doors on flamboyant men who would have become Catholic clergy, but instead found themselves working in the theaters. And they're still here.

References

Appignanesi, Richard and Ilya. *Manga Shakespeare: King Lear*. London, 2009.

Archer, Jayne Elisabeth, Richard Marggraf Turley, and Howard Thomas. "The Autumn King: Remembering the Land in *King Lear.*" *Shakespeare Quarterly* 63, no. 4 (2012): 518-543.

Archer, Jayne Elisabeth, Howard Thomas, and Richard Marggraf Turley. "Reading Shakespeare with the Grain: Sustainability and the Hunger Business." *Green Letters: Studies in Ecocriticism* 19, no. 1 (2015): 8-20.

Asimov, Isaac. *Asimov's Guide to Shakespeare*. Vol 1 and 2. New York: Avanel Books, 1970.

Barber, C. L. *Shakespeare's Festive Comedy: A Study of Dramatic Form and its Relation to Social Custom*. Princeton, NJ: Princeton University Press, 1972.

Barnet, Sylvan, ed. *William Shakespeare: The Tragedy of Macbeth*. New York: Signet Classic, 1963.

Bate, Jonathan. *Shakespeare and Ovid*. Oxford: Clarendon Press, 1993.

Bate, Jonathan. "Shakespeare's Ovid" in *Ovid's Metamorphoses: The Arthur Golding Translation 1567*. Philadelphia: Paul Dry Books, 2000.

Bate, Jonathan. *How the Classics Made Shakespeare*. Princeton: Princeton University Press, 2019.

Barkan, Leonard. *The Gods Made Flesh: Metamorphosis & the Pursuit of Paganism*. New Haven, CT: Yale University Press, 1990.

Belsey, Catherine. "Love as Tromp-l'oeil: Taxonomies of Desire in Venus and Adonis." *Shakespeare Quarterly* 46, no. 3 (Autumn, 1995): 257-276.

Belsey, Catherine. *Why Shakespeare?* New York: Palgrave Macmillan, 2007.

Bloom, Harold. *Shakespeare: The Invention of the Human.* New York: Riverhead Books, 1998.

Braden, Gordon "Ovid's Witchcraft," in *Reception and the Classics: An Interdisciplinary Approach to the Classical Tradition.* Cambridge: Cambridge University Press, 2012.

Bruckner, Lynne and Dan Brayton, eds. *Ecocritical Shakespeare.* London: Routledge, 2016.

Bryant, Jerry T. "*The Winter's Tale* and the Pastoral Tradition." *Shakespeare Quarterly*, 14, no. 4 (Autumn, 1963): 387-398

Carroll, William C. *The Metamorphoses of Shakespearean Comedy.* Princeton, CT: Princeton University Press, 1985.

Day, Gary. *The Story of Drama: Tragedy, Comedy and Sacrifice from the Greeks to the Present.* London: Bloomsbury, 2016.

Diamond, Catherine. "Four Women in the Woods: An Ecofeminist Look at the Forest as Home." *Comparative Drama* 51, no. 1 (2017): 71-100.

Egan, Gabriel. *Green Shakespeare: From Ecopolitics to Ecocriticism.* London: Routledge, 2006.

Eisler, Riane. *The Chalice and the Blade: Our History, Our Future.* San Francisco: Harper Collins, 1994.

Frazer, Sir James George. *The Golden Bough.* New York: Touchstone Press, 1996.

Frye, Northrop. *Northrop Frye on Shakespeare.* New Haven, CT: Yale University Press, 1986.

Gesner, Carol. *Shakespeare & the Greek Romance: A Study of Origins.* Lexington, KY: University Press of Kentucky, 1970.

Gruber, Elizabeth D. "Nature on the Verge: Confronting 'Bare Life' in *Arden of Faversham* and *King Lear.*" *Interdisciplinary Studies in Literature and Environment* 22, no. 1 (Winter 2015): 98-114.

Hart, F. Elizabeth. "'Great is Diana' of Shakespeare's Ephesus." *Studies in English Literature 1500-1900*, 43, no. 2, Tudor and Stuart Drama (Spring 2003): 347-374.

Holland, Joanne Field. "The Gods of '*The Winter's Tale*'." *Pacific Coast Philology* 5 (April 1970): 34-38.

Hughes, Ted. *Shakespeare and the Goddess of Complete Being.* New York: Farrar Straus Giroux, 1992.

Hutton, Ronald. *Pagan Britain.* New Haven, CT: Yale University Press, 2014.

James, Heather. "Shakspeare's Learned Heroines in Ovid's Schoolroom" in *Shakespeare and the Classics.* Cambridge: Cambridge University Press, 2004.

Kahn, Coppélia. *Roman Shakespeare: Warriors, Wounds, and Women.* London: Routledge, 1997.

Kakkonen, Gordana Galić and Ana Penjak. "The Nature of Gender. Are Juliet, Desdemona and Cordelia to their Fathers as Natureis to Culture?" *Critical Survey* 27, no. 1 (Mar 2015): 18-35.

Kammer, Miriam. "Breaking the Bounds of Domesticity: Ecofeminism and Nature Space in *Love's Labour's Lost." Shakespeare Bulletin* 36, no. 3 (Fall 2018): 467-481.

Keilen, Sean. "Shakespeare and Ovid" in *A Handbook to the Reception of Ovid.* New York: John Wiley & Sons, 2014.

Kott, Jan. *Shakespeare our Contemporary.* Translated by Boleslaw Taborski. New York: W. W. Norton & Company, 1974.

Lafont, Agnès. "Introduction, Interacting with Eros: Ovid and Shakespeare" in *Shakespeare's Erotic Mythology and Ovidian Renaissance Culture.* London: Routledge, 2013.

Laroque, François. *Shakespeare's Festive World: Elizabethan Season Entertainment and the Professional Stage.* Translated by Janet Lord. Cambridge: Cambridge University Press, 1993.

Laroque, François "Erotic Fancy/Fantasy in *Venus and Adonis, A Midsummer Night's Dream* and *Antony and Cleopatra* in *Shakespeare's Erotic Mythology and Ovidian Renaissance Culture.* London: Routledge, 2013.

Martindale, Charles and Michelle. *Shakespeare and the Uses of Antiquity.* London: Routledge, 1994.

Nims, John Frederick, ed. *Ovid's Metamorphoses: The Arthur Golding Translation 1567.* Philadelphia, PA: Paul Dry Books, 2000.

Nosworthy, J. M. "Shakespeare's Pastoral Metamorphoses." *Shakespearean Criticism* 96 (1982): 90-113

Ornstein, Robert. *Shakespeare's Comedies: From Roman Farce to Romantic Mystery.* Newark, NJ: University of Delaware Press, 1986.

Paster, Gail Kern and Skiles Howard, eds. *A Midsummer Night's Dream: Texts and Contexts.* Boston: Bedford/St. Martin's, 1999.

Quinn, Daniel. *Ishmael.* New York: Bantam, 1992.

Reid, Lindsay Ann. "Ovidian *Exempla* in *The Taming of the Shrew*" in *Ovidian Bibliofictions and the Tudor Book: Metamorphosing Classical Heroines in Late Medieval and Renaissance England.* London: Routledge, 2016.

Roberts, Jeanne Addison. *The Shakespearean Wild: Geography, Genus, and Gender.* Lincoln, NE: University of Nebraska Press, 1994.

Roe, John, ed. *New Cambridge Shakespeare: The Poems: Venus and Adonis, The Rape of Lucrece, The Phoenix and the Turtle, The Passionate Pilgrim, A Lover's Complaint, Updated Edition.* Cambridge: Cambridge University Press, 2014.

Root, Robert Kilburn. *Classical Mythology in Shakespeare.* New York: Gordian Press, 1965.

Shaughnessy, Robert. *The Routledge Guide to William Shakespeare.* Abingdon, UK: Taylor & Francis Group, 2011.

Shaw, John. "Fortune and Nature in *As You Like It.*" *Shakespeare Quarterly* Vol. 6, No. 1 (1955) 45-50.

Starhawk. *The Spiral Dance: A Rebirth of the Ancient Religion of the Great Goddess.* New York: Harper & Row Publishers, 1989.

Starks-Estes, Lisa S. *Violence, Trauma, and Virtus in Shakespeare's Roman Poems and Plays: Transforming Ovid.* New York: Palgrave Macmillan, 2014.

Steadman, John M. "Falstaff as Actaeon: A Dramatic Emblem." *Shakespeare Quarterly* 14, no. 3 (Summer 1963): 231-244.

Steffes, Michael. "The Ancient Greek Wild in *The Winter's Tale.*" *Renaissance and Reformation* 27, no. 4 (Fall 2003): 31-51.

Swann, Marjorie. "The Politics of Fairylore in Early Modern English Literature." *Renaissance Quarterly* 53, no. 2 (Summer, 2000): 449-473.

Taylor, A.B., ed. *Shakespeare's Ovid: The Metamorphosis in the Plays and Poems.* Cambridge: Cambridge University Press, 2000.

Taylor, A.B. "Ovid's Myths and the Unsmooth Course of Love in *A Midsummer Night's Dream*," in *Shakespeare and the Classics*. Cambridge: Cambridge University Press, 2004.

Truax, Elizabeth. *Metamorphosis in Shakespeare's Plays: A Pageant of Heroes, Gods, Maids and Monsters*. Lewiston: The Edwin Mellen Press, 1992.

Valls-Russell, Janice. "Erotic Perspectives: When Pyramus and Thisbe Meet Hero and Leander in *Romeo and Juliet*," in *Shakespeare's Erotic Mythology and Ovidian Renaissance Culture*. London: Routledge, 2013.

Vaughan, Virginia Mason. *Shakespeare and the Gods*. London: Arden Shakespeare, 2020.

Wagner, Matt. *Batman/Superman/Wonder Woman: Trinity*. New York: DC Comics, 2004.

Wood, James O. "Intimations of Actaeon in *Julius Caesar*." *Shakespeare Quarterly* 24 (1973): 85-88.

Woodbridge, Linda and Edward Berry, eds. *True Rites and Maimed Rites: Ritual and Anti-Ritual in Shakespeare and His Age*. Urbana, IL: University of Illinois Press, 1992.

Woodbridge, Linda. *The Scythe of Saturn: Shakespeare and Magical Thinking*. Urbana, IL: University of Illinois Press, 1994.

Character Concordance

Index

Deities of Greece and Rome are listed under their Roman names
because this is how Shakespeare referred to them.

Other Books by

j. SNODGRASS

Supernatural Shakespeare: Magic and Ritual in Merry Old England (2022)

Jolly Holidays (2022)

Sun Dance: Plains Life in Balance (2022)

Not I: A Backstage Travesty in Verse (2021)

Murder & Miss Conception -or- The Piety Contest Killings (2021)

Welcome to Tragedy: A Beginner's Guide to Greek Drama (2020)

Thirteenth Moon: A Star*Lite Fantasy (2019)

Chaos, Chaos (2018)

Natives Discover America: An Anthropological Study of the "White Man" (2018)

Romancing the Minotaur: Sex and Sacrifice and Some Greek Mythology (2015)

Libel: Sex and Sexuality in the Bible (2014)

Chaos (2013)

Turning the Tables: Farming and Feeding in the Gospels (2012)

Words (Between the Lines of Age): Empire, Satire and Revival in the Bible (2012)

Genesis and the Rise of Civilization (2011)

About the Author

j. Snodgrass has always been full of
questions. Every year he chooses some
topic about which he is curious and
launches into a research project.
He reads thousands of pages of
scholarship, writes tiny notes
in the margins, types and
organizes them into chapter
outlines, and assembles a book.
This helps him remember
interesting things he's learned
(or at least know where to look
for them) and often turns into a
book that he wanted to read but
could not find. The day after he finishes
one project, he starts on the next.

Snodgrass teaches college courses, usually Native American Studies and
Comparative Religion, but he has also taught courses on Shakespeare,
civic engagement, critical thinking, and other topics. He lives in Buffalo,
New York with Elizabeth and their four children, two of whom are
suddenly teenagers.

Available at
www.CityofLightPublishing.com
and wherever books are sold.

Become a citizen of the City of Light!
Follow @CityofLightPublishing